THE DEVELOPMENT OF THE
SECONDARY CURRICULUM

The Development of the Secondary Curriculum

Edited by Michael H. Price

CROOM HELM
London • Sydney • Dover, New Hampshire

© 1986 Michael H. Price
Croom Helm Ltd, Provident House, Burrell Row,
Beckenham, Kent BR3 1AT
Croom Helm Australia Pty Ltd, Suite 4, 6th Floor,
64-76 Kippax Street, Surry Hills, NSW 2010, Australia

British Library Cataloguing in Publication Data

The Development of the secondary curriculum
   1. Education, Secondary — England —
   Curricula — History — 19th century
   2. Education, Secondary — England —
   Curricula — History — 20th century
   I. Price, Michael H.
   373.19'0942   LB1629.5.G7

ISBN 0-7099-4006-8

Croom Helm, 51 Washington Street, Dover,
New Hampshire 03820, USA

Library of Congress Cataloging-in-Publication Data

The Development of the secondary curriculum.

   Includes bibliographies and index.
   1. Education, Secondary—Great Britain—Curricula
History—20th century. 2. Education, Secondary—Great
Britain—Curricula—History—19th century.
I. Price, Michael H.
LA634.D48   1986   373.19'0941   86-4155
ISBN 0-7099-4006-8

Printed and bound in Great Britain
by Billing & Sons Limited, Worcester.

CONTENTS

Acknowledgements

1. INTRODUCTION: CURRICULUM HISTORY AND ENGLISH
    SECONDARY SCHOOLS, 1870-1940
                            Michael Price   1
    Notes and References   7

2. CULTURE OR DISCIPLINE? THE REDEFINITION OF
    CLASSICAL EDUCATION
                            Christopher Stray

    Introduction: 'The Ambiguous Name of the
        Classics'   10
    Complacency and Threat: The New
        Equilibrium, 1870-1900   14
    An Orderly Retreat: The Early Years of the
        Classical Association, 1900-22   20
    Thoroughness and Unreality: The Triumph of
        Discipline, 1923-40   39
    Conclusion: Discipline and Its Discontents   41
    Notes and References   43

3. ENGLISH TEACHING: CLASSICS IN THE VERNACULAR
                            Eleanor Wright

    Introduction   49
    The Arguments for English   51
    The Status of English   52
    The Development of Practice   54
    Analysis of Textbooks   56
    Influences on Practice   67
    Notes and References   72

4. MODERN LANGUAGES: THE RETREAT FROM REFORM
                            William Rowlinson

    Introduction   77
    Language as Discipline   78
    Effects of Expansion   79
    The Alternative Tradition: Language as
        Communication   81
    French: A Pillar of the Curriculum   84
    1912 and 1918: The Board's Concern   85
    Languages for Girls   90
    The Examination Constraint   90
    Methods and Textbooks   92
    Relative Realism: Palmer and Hadow   94
    The Spens Report: Changing Ends,
        Stagnating Means   96
    Notes and References   98

Contents

5. THE PERRY MOVEMENT IN SCHOOL MATHEMATICS
                                    Michael Price

    Introduction   103
    Mathematics for Engineers   104
    Pedagogical Developments   109
    Pressure for Reform   114
    Examination Reform   121
    Textbooks and Teaching Aids   124
    Progress and Reaction   130
    The Movement's Achievements   137
    Conclusion   141
    Notes and References   143

6. SCIENCE FOR PROFESSIONALS: SCIENTIFIC METHOD
    AND SECONDARY EDUCATION
                                    Edgar Jenkins

    Introduction   156
    The British Association and the Schooling
        of Science   157
    Examinations, Resources and Methods   160
    H.E. Armstrong and Training in Scientific
        Method   165
    From Process to Content? General Science
        and Biology   171
    Conclusion   175
    Notes and References   177

7. THE ROYAL GEOGRAPHICAL SOCIETY AND GEOGRAPHY
    IN SECONDARY EDUCATION
                                    William Marsden

    Introduction   182
    Contexts: Exploration, Imperial Expansion,
        the RGS and Geographical Education   183
    The Discipline: The RGS, New Paradigms of
        Geography and Geographical Education   187
    Pedagogy: From 'Capes and Bays' to the
        'Higher Units'   191
    Direct Involvement: The RGS and
        Geographical Education   197
    Conclusion   203
    Notes and References   205

8. FROM A TEST OF MEMORY TO A TRAINING FOR LIFE:
    THE TEACHING OF HISTORY
                                    Gordon Batho

    History the Characteristic Activity of the
        Nineteenth Century?   214

Contents

    The Professionalisation of History
       Teaching, 1870-1914   219
    The Coming of Age of History Teaching,
       1914-40   229
    Notes and References   238

9.   CONCLUSION
                        Michael Price   244
    Notes and References   250

Contributors   251
Index   252

(In all Notes and References place of publication
is London unless otherwise stated)

ACKNOWLEDGEMENTS

I would like to thank a number of people for their encouragement and support in the production of this book. Specifically, Peter Sowden of Croom Helm, my Leicester colleague Bill Brock and Professor David Layton all lent early support to the idea of a collaborative curriculum history. I am grateful for the co-operation of all the contributors and particularly Professor Gordon Batho and Bill Marsden, for their general advice and help, and Christopher Stray for helping forward my own thinking in this field.

My Leicester colleague Margaret Mathieson and my brother Peter Price have assisted greatly with the editing and provided much encouragement and stimulus throughout the various stages of production. In addition, I would like to thank my brother for compiling the index.

Finally, my wife Jackie Price also helped me considerably by typing some of the draft material and the final copy owes much to the exemplary commitment and word-processing skills of Vivienne Paul.

Chapter One

INTRODUCTION: CURRICULUM HISTORY AND ENGLISH
SECONDARY SCHOOLS, 1870-1940

MICHAEL PRICE

Both in this country and America interest in the
field of curriculum history has developed considerably since the mid-1970s and now attracts the diverse attentions of historians of education, sociologists and ethnographers of school knowledge, general curriculum theorists and school subject specialists. Although, as Marsden has shown,(1) and as
the list of theses and dissertations provided by the
History of Education Society exemplifies,(2) curriculum history has its own history and literature
extending back over many decades, much of this early
work is unpublished or the product of isolated individual initiatives in the field. What is striking
about the developments in recent years is the growth
of collaborative and more ambitious approaches to
the history of the curriculum in general, and the
growing specialisation and refinement in the historical study of particular curricular areas. School
subjects such as science, mathematics and geography
now possess bibliographical and methodological overviews of aspects of their histories, though such
work may not be well known outside the respective
specialist subject communities. However, such specialist interest is international in scope.(3) More
generally, some notable collaborative work in curriculum history has recently been stimulated by Ivor
Goodson and the 'Sussex School', and the published
output to date is already impressive.(4) By comparison, the work of Gordon and Lawton, for example,
though useful in basic contextual terms, now appears
somewhat limited.(5)
    Perhaps surprisingly, historians of education
have typically tended to pay little attention to the
details and complexities of curriculum history. As
Whitbread has noted, in the context of the early
twentieth century, 'Educational historiography ...

1

has focused on administrative, sociological and political issues largely to the exclusion of the curriculum' with the attention on 'form to the neglect
of content'.(6) And yet this was a particularly rich
period in curricular as well as administrative
terms, as Whitbread argues and the chapters of this
book will clearly demonstrate. It should be added
that the publications of the History of Education
Society have not entirely neglected the curriculum
field and a Curriculum Study Group of the Society
has been in existence for some ten years. Furthermore, the fact that a recent editorial in the Society's Bulletin was devoted to curriculum history
('this fruitful area of study'), and recent developments in the field, may signify a growing interest
among historians of education at the present time.(7)
    By contrast, some general curriculum theorists
and sociologists have enthusiastically adopted historical perspectives on the curriculum as a natural
development of interests in the sociology of knowledge. Typical socio-historical foci of concern are
the conflicts among school subjects regarding status
and resources, the relationships between alternative
paradigms within a school subject, explanations for
major change at both instrumental and deeper struc-
tural levels, and the interests of and interactions
among individuals and identifiable groups which im-
pinge on curricula.(8) Such preoccupations and a desire to relate sometimes limited historical evidence
to general theoretical frameworks may yield histori-
ographical distortion. There is, of course, a fundamental and long-standing tension here between historical and social-scientific methodology. The historian Marwick has put the matter simply:

> it remains true that the social scientist far
> more regularly uses models and theoretical con-
> structs than does the historian, and that the
> constructs are nearly always of a more abstract
> character than the historian would be prepared to
> accept.(9)

He goes on to point out: 'the historian must always
accommodate the unique and the contingent, the social scientist is essentially orientated towards the
universal, towards the recurrent pattern'.(10) The
general conflict will not be pursued here, but in
relation to curriculum history the range of perspectives which are currently being applied has undoubtedly enriched the field. What then are the predispo-
sitions of the contributors to the present book and

what is the character of its distinctive contribution at the present time?

Each of the seven contributors to this book is a school subject specialist with contemporary interests in his or her subject as well as a particular concern for the historical dimension, not only on account of the distinctive questions and methodological challenges involved, but also because of the potential light which such study can shed on contemporary issues and priorities in the curriculum. Of particular interest here are the processes and instruments of change and resistance to change in the curriculum and the relationships between the rhetoric and pedagogical thinking on the one hand and the reality of curricular life in schools on the other. Goodson has fairly judged that 'The elucidation of the relationship between "rhetoric" and "reality" remains one of the most profound challenges to future curriculum historians.'(11) Where the focus is on school subjects the particular strength of specialist contributors lies in their capacity to understand and interpret internal subject developments. But, in addition, particular studies will also illuminate inter-subject relationships and probe the interface between the curriculum and the wider administrative, ideological, social and political contexts of the educational system. Perhaps it should be added that the focus on traditional school subjects in curriculum history is not a necessary but a natural one and has been adopted for this book.(12) Although it can be argued that subject categories are themselves problematic their dominance in the history of school curricular theory and practice is unquestionable. Thus the choice was an obvious one for a collaborative venture of the present kind. The basis for this collaboration warrants some further explanation, to place the subsequent chapters within a common context.

Hitherto much of the work in school subject history has been independently produced and not widely disseminated across and outside the subject boundaries involved. Thus, collaboration among school subject specialists, working within some common framework in curriculum history, raises some new and potentially exciting possibilities. Geographical location, time period and institutional context are three major variables in relation to curricula and the focus for this book is England and its secondary schools for boys and girls in the period 1870-1940. In these terms the general educational context for the various subject studies is fixed and comparative

studies crossing national boundaries are deliberate-
ly excluded. As will become clear, the category
'secondary' was itself problematic, both ideologically and administratively, in the period under
consideration. However, the principal concern is
with schools of the 'academic' secondary type as opposed to infant, elementary and technical schools,
technical colleges, teacher training institutions
and the universities, though institutional boundaries will be crossed where relationships are judged
to be significant for the subject under consideration. Also, the major though not exclusive focus is
upon public and secondary 'grammar' as opposed to
secondary 'modern' schools, which grew out of the
arrangements for 'senior' elementary pupils and developed after 1944 under the tripartite system, before the comprehensive era.

The period 1870-1940 was not intended to be
either rigidly applied or exhaustively treated in
its extent by each contributor, but it does provide
broad time limits within which the various subject
studies are principally located. The choice of this
period was based on a belief that in relation to
English conditions and secondary education in particular, it is potentially very rich in curricular
terms, and particularly the sub-period 1890-1920.
These three decades have been well explored in relation to various major developments in the political
and administrative context of English secondary education: the wide-ranging investigations of the Bryce
Commission in the 1890s; the establishment of a
single central authority for English education, the
Board of Education from 1899; the Education Act of
1902 and the involvement of the new LEAs in the provision of secondary schooling; the development of
grant-aided secondary schools under the various annual Regulations of the Board of Education from 1904
and the scrutiny of a new Secondary Branch of HMI;
and the protracted struggle to establish a co-
ordinated secondary examination system, culminating
in the School Certificate arrangements from 1917.
But, in parallel with these developments, there was
much specifically curriculum-orientated activity.
Such activity includes some of the work of the Consultative Committees of the Board of Education, and
their reports;(13) some of the published Circulars
and Pamphlets of the Board of Education and Special
Reports of its Office of Special Inquiries and Reports; the Reports of the Prime Minister's Committees on education and modern languages (1918), natural science (1918), and classics (1921), and of the

Departmental Committee of the Board on the teaching
of English (1921); growing specialisation and refinement in teachers' professional organisation and
the educational literature;(14) and the establishment of school subject associations for modern languages (1892), geography (1893), mathematics (1897),
science (1901), classics (1903), history (1906) and
English (1907) in particular.(15) As Lawson and Silver have concluded, the professional concern for
teaching and learning specifically developed on many
fronts from the late nineteenth century:

> A range of new departures was becoming evident
> in English education in the 1890s. There were
> new schools and new interests in child study
> and child development ... The constraints im-
> posed by payment by results were being removed
> from the elementary schools, and new approaches
> in the infant school were beginning to have an
> influence on the higher classes. Technical sub-
> jects and science were not only finding a place
> in school, but were also the focus of new
> thinking about methods and objectives in teach-
> ing. For most of the nineteenth century the
> major changes in education had been in terms of
> supply and structure. Under new pressures,
> changes in the final decades also began to fo-
> cus on content and method, and on children. The
> search for a new understanding of children and
> of educational processes was closely related to
> the wider changes of emphasis in discussions of
> the individual, society and social policy.(16)

By around 1920, it had become appropriate to refer
in the pedagogical literature not just to the 'new
education'(17) but to the 'new teaching'(18) of the
'modern teacher'.(19) Exploring the penetration of
this developing educational 'climate' and its effects within specific school subjects will be a major feature of the chapters which follow. However,
not all the subjects of the secondary curriculum are
here included; the restriction is to 'academic'
school subjects.

The Bryce Commission's categories for the
analysis of secondary school timetables in the 1890s
are of some interest. Under 'English Subjects' are
grouped religious instruction, English, history,
geography and arithmetic: these might well be termed
'basic subjects', given also their close association
with elementary education; under 'Languages' are
grouped Greek, Latin, French and German; under

'Sciences' we find mathematics and physical science; 'Art Subjects' include drawing, manual instruction, music and singing; 'Commercial Subjects' comprise book-keeping and shorthand; and, finally, physical exercises and an 'others' category are included.(20) The subjects chosen for this book are located within the first three of Bryce's categories i.e. they are broadly 'academic' as opposed to 'practical'. These subjects are the ones which featured prominently in the examinations for the School Certificate after the First World War. In 1926, in decreasing order of popularity, measured by the number of entries, the following subjects head the list: English, French, mathematics, history, geography, art, Latin and chemistry. In 1937 the only difference in the above order is the interchange of art and Latin.(21)

Thus, the seven subjects of this book, classics, English, modern languages, mathematics, science, geography and history are those which have dominated the academic secondary school curriculum from the late nineteenth century and, with the exception of classics, they still hold a strong place within comprehensive schools.(22) The label 'academic' here implies an important association with the universities, in terms of study of the subject at this level, teacher supply and education, and the provision of school examinations in the subject; also, this link was strengthened and refined in the two decades around 1900, by the development of academic subject associations with a major concern for secondary education in each case. Thus the studies which follow are located within a broadly uniform educational and ideational framework, thereby facilitating the investigation of relationships among the subjects, and comparative analysis and evaluation in curriculum history. But this does not imply a uniformity in the character of the developments considered nor in the manner of their treatment by the subject contributors.

Each school subject history has its own distinctive features and selected major aspects of growth and change will be brought to prominence in the studies of this book. Some degree of selection is involved both in the themes and time scale for emphasis and in the methodology and style of curriculum historiography. For example, the studies of modern languages by William Rowlinson, science by Edgar Jenkins and history by Gordon Batho are wide-ranging throughout the period 1870-1940, but with a strong emphasis on one major developmental theme in each case. More sharply, the treatment of

mathematics by the editor is centred on a single
movement associated with one individual, but with
roots and consequences extending throughout the period. By contrast, particular sub-periods are emphasised in the chapters on geography by William
Marsden and English by Eleanor Wright. Marsden's focus is upon a single society and certain key individuals involved in his subject's development,
largely in the nineteenth century. Wright's major
concern is the rhetoric and pedagogy in relation to
practices as embodied in textbooks, largely in the
interwar period.

Finally, it is appropriate that classics is
subjected to an ambitious but penetrating treatment
by Christopher Stray. He considers not only the subject's internal struggles, but also places these
within a much wider context of political, administrative, cultural and social change. Classical education formed the backbone of English secondary
schooling for much of the nineteenth century and its
ideals and relationships with other subjects are of
major importance for the present book. It is fitting
therefore that we commence with Stray's study of
classics in English secondary education.

NOTES AND REFERENCES

1.   W.E. Marsden, 'Historical Approaches to
Curriculum Study' in History of Education Society,
Post-War Curriculum Development: An Historical Appraisal (Leicester, 1979), pp. 77-101.
2.   History of Education Society, Theses and
Dissertations on the History of Education, Presented
at British and Irish Universities between 1900 and
1976 (Lancaster, 1979).
3.   See, for example, E.W. Jenkins, 'Some
Sources for the History of Science Education in the
Twentieth Century, with Particular Reference to Secondary Schools', Studies in Science Education, vol.7
(1980), pp. 27-86; M.H. Price, 'Historical Perspectives on English School Mathematics, 1850-1950',
Zentralblatt für Didaktik der Mathematik, no.1
(1985), pp. 1-6; W.E. Marsden (ed.), Historical Perspectives on Geographical Education (International
Geographical Union, 1980).
4.   See, for example, I.F. Goodson and S.J.
Ball (eds.), Defining the Curriculum: Histories and
Ethnographies (Falmer Press, Lewes, 1984) and the
ambitious series, Studies in Curriculum History,
beginning with I.F. Goodson (ed.), Social Histories

of the Secondary Curriculum: Subjects for Study
(Falmer Press, Lewes, 1985).

5.   P. Gordon and D. Lawton, Curriculum Change
in the Nineteenth and Twentieth Centuries (Hodder
and Stoughton, 1978).

6.   N. Whitbread, 'The Early Twentieth-Century
Secondary Curriculum Debate in England', History of
Education, vol.13, no.3 (1984), pp. 221-33 (p. 221).

7.   'Editorial: Curriculum History', History
of Education Society Bulletin, no.33, Spring (1984),
p. 1.

8.   See, for example, I.F. Goodson, School
Subjects and Curriculum Change: Case Studies in the
Social History of Curriculum (Croom Helm, 1983) and
the Studies in Curriculum History series.

9.   A. Marwick, The Nature of History (Macmillan, 1970), p. 106.

10.   Ibid., p. 106.

11.   I.F. Goodson, 'Subjects for Study: Case
Studies in Curriculum History' in I.F. Goodson (ed.),
Social Histories, pp. 9-17 (p. 11).

12.   I.F. Goodson (ed.), Social Histories includes studies with other curricular foci such as
the sixth form and technical schools.

13.   Whitbread, 'The Early Twentieth-Century
Secondary School Curriculum Debate in England' emphasises some of the Board's curricular concerns.

14.   For a valuable list of official and other
publications bearing on secondary curricula up to
the early 1920s see Board of Education, Report of
the Consultative Committee on Differentiation of the
Curriculum for Boys and Girls Respectively in Secondary Schools (HMSO, 1923), pp. 148-55. On the
growth of educational periodicals see A. Tropp,
'Some Sources for the History of Educational Periodicals in England', British Journal of Educational
Studies, vol.6, no.2 (1958), pp. 151-63. On teachers' professional organisation see S. Webb, 'English
Teachers and Their Professional Organisation', New
Statesman, vol.5, nos.129-30 (1915), additional pp.
1-22 and 1-24.

15.   Exceptionally, the Mathematical Association grew out of the earlier Association for the Improvement of Geometrical Teaching, established in
1871.

16.   J. Lawson and H. Silver, A Social History
of Education in England (Methuen, 1973), pp. 356-7.

17.   For a good analysis of various components
of the 'new education', a common phrase from around
1890, see R.J.W. Selleck, The New Education 1870-
1914 (Pitman, 1968).

18.   Adams, J. (ed.), The New Teaching (Hodder and Stoughton, 1918).

19.   A. Watson Bain (ed.), The Modern Teacher (Methuen, 1921).

20.   Royal Commission on Secondary Education, (Bryce Report) Vol.9 (HMSO, 1895), pp. 404-21.

21.   Board of Education, Report of the Consultative Committee on Secondary Education with Special Reference to Grammar Schools and Technical High Schools (HMSO, 1938), p. 99. The popularity of art probably relates to the fact that drawing was a prescribed subject in the Board's Regulations for Secondary Schools from 1904 following the encouragement given to it by the earlier grants of the Department of Science and Art. A study of art education is beyond the scope of this book but see, for example, G. Sutton, Artisan or Artist?: A History of the Teaching of Art and Crafts in English Schools (Pergamon, 1967).

22.   The religious dimension in relation to the history of the secondary curriculum warrants a major study, which goes beyond the scope of this book. For postwar syllabus developments see A. Bell, 'Agreed Syllabuses of Religious Education since 1944' in Goodson (ed.), Social Histories, pp. 177-201.

Chapter Two

CULTURE OR DISCIPLINE? THE REDEFINITION OF
CLASSICAL EDUCATION

CHRISTOPHER STRAY

INTRODUCTION: 'THE AMBIGUOUS NAME OF THE CLASSICS'

To ask 'What is classics?' is to invite the reply
'The study of Graeco-Roman civilisation': not a very
enlightened answer, but as much as the question de-
serves. If we ask instead 'What have the classics
been?' we may hope to capture some sense both of the
subject's internal plurality and of the variety of
its historical forms. In other words, 'Graeco-Roman
civilisation' refers to a repertoire from which a
multitude of versions has been assembled since it
first became 'classical'. It is worth remembering
that, for example, classical Greek was not 'classical' to the Greeks of the classical period. To them,
Greek was what civilised people spoke; the rest of
humanity spoke gibberish, 'bar bar', and hence were
generically referred to as 'barbarians'. What made
Greek classical was its adoption as a standard non-
vernacular language in the empire ruled by Alexander's
successors. And it is surely more than a coincidence
that just when, in the third century BC, non-Greeks
were being taught Greek for the first time on any
scale, grammatical rules began to be formulated, and
grammar itself emerged as a separate intellectual
category.(1)
    The relationship between Greek and Roman civi-
lisation, as variously defined by ideologists of
curriculum, constitutes the major theme of this
chapter: the tension between Greek culture and Roman
discipline. The Roman aristocrats who incorporated
Greece into their Mediterranean empire despised the
Greeks' lack of political discipline, but admired
their culture. It became normal for the male members, at least, of senatorial families to be fluent
in what were called simply 'both languages' - Greek
and Latin. Since the end of the ancient world,

10

classical civilisation has often been drawn on in
the construction of ideological self-images by social elites, concerned to signal their exclusiveness
and to render their domination legitimate. In most
cases, however, a close inspection reveals that
either Greek or Latin is especially emphasised. It
is this division which is stressed in the manifesto
offered by J.W. Mackail to the first general meeting
of the Classical Association in May 1904. In his address 'On the place of Greek and Latin in human
life', Mackail argued that:

> It is not undesirable, when this Association is
> being inaugurated, to emphasise the difference
> between the two spheres which classical studies
> include, and to realise fully that they repre-
> sent forces in the education and control of
> life which are complementary, or even opposed,
> to one another. Under the ambiguous name of the
> classics we include much to which the name
> classical can only be applied in different
> senses, and by far-stretched analogies. The
> distinction, no less than the likeness, between
> the two spheres of classical study is of impor-
> tance not only towards clear thought, but to-
> wards the pressing and practical question of
> the place which each holds separately and which
> both hold jointly in education, in culture, in
> our whole view and handling of human life.(2)

Later on in his speech, Mackail specified the distinction between the 'two spheres', in terms which
would have been congenial to a majority of his audience:

> The place of Rome, of the Latin temper and
> civilisation, the Latin achievement in the con-
> quest of life, is definite and assured. It rep-
> resents all the constructive and conservative
> forces which make life into an organic struc-
> ture. Law, order, reverence for authority, the
> whole framework of political and social estab-
> lishment, are the creation of Latin will and
> intelligence ... This Latin genius impressed
> itself most strongly on their grammar and their
> literature. And just as Latin grammar is an un-
> equalled instrument for training of the mind in
> accurate thought, Latin literature is an in-
> strument as unequalled for discipline of the
> practical reason.

> While Rome stands for the constructive and
> conservative side of life, Greece represents
> the dissolving influence of analysis and the
> creative force of pure intelligence. The return
> to Greece, it has been said, is the return to
> nature ... The return to Rome need never be
> made, because we have never quitted her. Rome
> we know ... Greece is in contrast something
> which we are so far from knowing that we hardly
> have a name for it ... While Rome has laid down
> for us a realised standard of human conduct,
> Greece rears aloft, wavering and glittering
> before us, an unrealisable ideal of superhuman
> intelligence.(3)

However rhetorical the style, Mackail's analysis has a firm basis in historical fact. The division of the Roman Empire into a Latin West and a
Greek East, and the subsequent collapse of the West,
led to the almost complete ignorance of Greek in
Western Europe until the fifteenth century. Latin,
on the other hand, became the language of the
Church, and hence of Europe. Throughout the Middle
Ages, it was made:

> the ground-work of education ... because it
> was the language of educated men throughout
> Western Europe, employed for public business,
> literature, philosophy and science, above all,
> in God's providence, essential to the unity,
> and therefore enforced by the authority, of
> the Western Church.(4)

Learning Latin was thus the route to all learning,
and to spoken and written communication. By the end
of the seventeenth century, however, this monopoly
had been successfully challenged by the growth of
vernacular printing; and as the learning to which it
had led was separated from Latin, the process of
learning Latin was defended as a 'discipline', something valuable quite apart from any knowledge to
which it might give access. 'Discipline' was further
defined as a superior alternative to the mere 'furniture' of the mind: as strengthening mental powers,
rather than simply filling the mind with facts.
    In nineteenth-century England, the mental dis-
cipline provided by Latin grammar, and the moral
discipline given by Roman literature, formed the
foundation of a gentleman's education. The crown of
such an education, however, was contributed by Greek
culture. Throughout the century, the prestige of

Greek was higher than that of Latin. The 'Greek revival' of the late eighteenth century, most visibly
evident in neoclassical architecture, had been reinforced by the influence of the German romantic
movement. Reacting against the Latinate culture of
their French-speaking princely courts, the politically powerless German upper bourgeoisie of the late
eighteenth century constructed a vision of ancient
Greece which might inspire the building of a German
nation. Against the 'Zivilisation' of France, they
counterposed the mystic radiance of 'Kultur'.(5)
This romantic movement fed into the specifics of
secondary school teaching through the appointment of
von Humboldt as Prussian Minister of Education in
1809. Under his influence, Latin was dethroned by
Greek as the most prestigious subject taught in the
gymnasia. After his death, Latin was reinstated; and
the subsequent polarisation of educational opinion
in Germany between the two languages is worth noting
because of its class overtones, which were commented
on by a perceptive American visitor in the 1890s:

> The place of the ancient languages in the cur-
> riculum of the German schools during the great-
> er part of this century has been determined by
> the shifting of opinion between these two ex-
> tremes - between that view which makes the
> study of the classics purely a formal disci-
> pline, and that other view which bases the
> worth of such study on the acquisition of hu-
> manistic culture, on contact with 'the best
> thoughts of the best men of antiquity'. In the
> one case it is considered of equal value as a
> means of preparation for all trades and profes-
> sions dependent on intellectual acumen; in the
> other case it is of worth only for those who
> can practically apply the technical knowledge
> thereby acquired, or who may have sufficient
> leisure to enjoy its aesthetic qualities. It is
> a question of making the ancient literature a
> means to an end or an end in itself.(6)

This correlation of classics and class - Latin
discipline for the commercial classes, (Greek) culture 'for its own sake' for their superiors - can
also be seen in England. Here the Greek revival of
the late eighteenth and nineteenth centuries coincided with the industrial revolution and the growth
of a class society. During the first generation after industrial take-off, between the two extensions
of the franchise in 1832 and 1867, the old noble

elite and the upper layers of the new bourgeoisie
merged to form a new, assimilated social elite; and
at the heart of this process lay the classical curriculum of the reformed public schools. Within their
secluded rural settings, nationally accessible
through the expanded railway network of the 1840s,
financial capital was transmuted into cultural capital.(7) 'Godliness and good learning' inculcated the
style and manners of a gentleman; and this learning
was almost entirely classical. The Clarendon Commission, set up in 1861 to investigate the nine leading
public schools, commented in its report that 'The
two classical languages, with a little ancient history and geography, held ... until a short time ago,
not only a decided predominance, but absolute and
exclusive possession of the whole course of study.'(8)
Secondary schools of a lower status (second-grade or
'middle-class' schools) would normally offer Latin,
but not Greek; third-grade schools provided neither.
Since leaving ages rose with the status of the
school (third-grade 14, second-grade 16, first-grade
18), the passage through a pupil's career replicated
mobility through the class structure, the distinc-
tions between grades of school, as the Taunton Commission remarked in 1868, corresponding 'roughly,
but by no means exactly, to the gradations of society'.(9) The argument, in this introduction, has
been that this system of social and educational
stratification was under-pinned by an ideological
hierarchy: furniture, discipline and culture.

COMPLACENCY AND THREAT: THE NEW EQUILIBRIUM,
1870-1900

The 1860s witnessed controversy and dissension, both
social and intellectual. This was the period:
(1) when Darwin's theories were furiously attacked
and defended; (2) when Arnold produced Culture and
Anarchy and debated with Huxley the relative merits
of science and the humanities; and (3) when the
question, 'What knowledge is of most worth?' engaged
widespread attention.(10) These debates, however,
appear to have issued not in resolution, but in a
reaction against controversy; the next thirty years
are marked by a general concern for compromise, fair
play and 'begging to differ'.(11) The social basis
of this orientation lay in the reconstitution of an
early-Victorian social equilibrium. By the end of
the 1860s, the radical potential of Chartism had
been exhausted and the franchise extended. A new

generation of 'respectable' union leaders had appeared, whose motto was 'Defence not Defiance'.(12)
The new assimilated elite was firmly established:
its progress had been marked by the abolition of
purchase, privilege and religious restriction, from
the Northcote-Trevelyan report of 1853 to the Test
Act of 1871.(13) It now reproduced itself through
the system of 'open competition' for entry to public
schools, universities and the Civil Service. This
competition, however, was based on examinations
which continued to be dominated by classics. It was
thus 'open' only to those whose fathers could afford the necessary preliminary education.(14)

The entrenchment of the new elite was reflected
in the consolidation of the influence of the public
schools. The Taunton Commissioners had recommended
the setting up of county education authorities, co-
ordinated by a department of central government. The
public schools joined in the successful opposition
to these interventionist proposals, and organised a
standing conference, the Headmasters' Conference,
which met for the first time in 1869.(15) The continuing domination of the public school curriculum
by classics was reflected in the headmasters' pre-
occupation with the pronunciation of Latin. This was
the subject of the first discussion held by the HMC
at its first meeting, after matters of constitution
and organisation had been settled, and was debated
at length and with vigour at several subsequent annual conferences.(16) These debates are of considerable interest, because of what they tell us about
the content and teaching of public-school classics.

The pronunciation of Latin in late-nineteenth-
century public schools was governed by three principles which were not only open to interpretation,
but often contradicted one another. These were:
(1) Latin should be pronounced as if it was English, (2) it should be pronounced as was the Roman
practice, and (3) pronunciation should follow the
tradition of the school. Between 1870 and 1930, the
second of these principles became dominant, but the
battle was lengthy and hard-fought. The main argument against (3) was that when boys from different
schools reached university, they were unable to
understand the Latin recited and quoted by each other, and by their tutors and lecturers. This might
seem an overriding argument, but in practice it
proved very difficult to detach schools from the
strange 'dialects' of Latin which functioned as
symbols of their independence. One headmaster remembered that at the 1906 Conference, Dr James of Rugby

'with characteristic incisiveness commanded us all
to use the new pronunciation, and with equal independence added, "But I'm not going to use it myself" '.(17) The new (otherwise the 'reformed' or
'Roman') pronunciation was based on principle (2).
An authoritative scheme had been drawn up at the request of the Conference by the Professors of Latin
at Oxford and Cambridge in the early 1870s, but made
little headway. To many heads and assistant masters,
scholarly accuracy was less important than pedagogic
possibility: and its opponents claimed that the reformed pronunciation could not be practised by 'stu-
pid boys', who made up the majority of their classes.
For such boys, classics meant discipline: 'gerund-
grinding' and repetition. Even if they reached university, many never progressed beyond 'the mere
grind of language' to the 'beauty, harmony, proportion and fitness' of literature,(18) but were content to struggle through 'Smalls' or 'Little-Go' and
scrape a pass degree.(19)

What did the 'grind' consist of? It began with
the rote learning of Latin grammar and syntax, the
explanations themselves being in Latin; this typically took place at a preparatory school at the age
of eight or nine. Next came 'daily construing and
occasional translation into English, repetition of
passages learnt by heart ... composition in verse
and prose. In the upper forms, the chief things are
construing, repetition and composition.'(20) The
boredom and suffering involved were commonly admitted, but regarded as an essential part of the process: its function, in fact, was to turn boys into
scholars if possible, but at least - and perhaps
more importantly - into men. A Headmaster of Eton,
defending the dominance of classics in the school,
explained to the Clarendon Commission that Latin and
Greek 'are in themselves distasteful to boys, and
only with great difficulty, and after much laborious
perseverance ... gain a hold upon them'.(21) Nor
should it be forgotten that this period saw the
spread of 'muscular Christianity' and the spread of
Social Darwinism. If these can be linked to the contemporary public-school passion for athleticism,
then by extension they can be seen as the context of
ideological justification in which the 'grind'
flourished.(22)

After discipline, in theory, came culture.
Greek was usually begun at twelve: its grammar and
syntax being similar to that of Latin, it was regarded as more quickly assimilable, though its
greater subtlety and irregularity made it less

suitable for 'grind'. In most of the public schools, classical work after this stage was directed primarily to producing facility in composition; verse composition being more highly regarded than prose, and Greek than Latin. In the more conservative schools, a Georgian notion of elegant taste persisted, exemplified by the Eton master of the 1840s who complained:

> If you do not take more pains, how can you ever expect to write good longs and shorts? If you do not write good longs and shorts, how can you ever be a man of taste? If you are not a man of taste, how can you ever be of use in the world?(23)

Even at the two ancient universities, where the old-style clerical don was being ousted by the professional scholar, the tradition of scholarship as manifested supremely in composition remained strong. The prizes and medals for composition in Latin and especially Greek constituted the pinnacles of achievement, their conquerors regarded with awe. This attitude is apparent in the eulogy delivered by Jex-Blake of Rugby during an HMC discussion on verse composition in 1876:

> I must say that there seems to be a finish and perhaps a beauty of mind in the few men whom one has known intimately and who have been Senior Classics at Cambridge or Chancellor's Medallist, or held one of the university scholarships at either university. There seems to be a finish and elegance and beauty in those men's minds that no other type of men I ever met possess. I only regret I was not one of them. It seems to be that you can trace in the fibre of the minds of those men, even at forty or fifty, the threads of the old versification.(24)

By 1900, the public schools were at the height of their influence. Organised for defence, if not for change, they were solidly established as the elite stratum of secondary education. The endowed grammar schools which had been surveyed by the Taunton Commission in the 1860s were in a much less comfortable position. Many of them had been founded to teach Latin and Greek, but the Commissioners discovered that nearly half taught neither, about a quarter Latin; only the remaining quarter taught both languages.(25) Some of these schools, freed from the terms of their endowments by the Endowed Schools

Act, modelled themselves on the reformed public
schools, and became boarding schools. Many of them,
however, became in effect commercial and technical
schools, and found it difficult to make ends meet.
The grants offered in support of science teaching by
the Department of Science and Art, based at South
Kensington, were thus taken up with alacrity. As
this trend accelerated in the 1890s, it was commented on with some alarm by the Bryce Commission on
Secondary Education, appointed in 1894. Its report
remarked that many grammar schools had abandoned
their 'tradition of literary education', and warned
that:

> we may run some risk of a lop-sided develop-
> ment in education, in which the teaching of
> science ... may so predominate as to entail
> comparative neglect of studies which are of
> less obvious and immediate utility, though not
> of less moment for the formation of mind and
> character.(26)

'Immediate utility', however, could not be dis-
missed so lightly in the 1890s as it might have been
thirty years earlier. The Clarendon Report had recommended the continued use of classics as the staple
of public-school education because it was there: it
was tried, it had a tradition, it had trained per-
sonnel.(27) In 1895, there were alternatives. In
particular, science teaching had expanded in non-
public schools and in the new civic universities.
More than this, the world had changed, and a series
of internal and external pressures toward state
intervention in education had built up, of which the
appointment and report of the Bryce Commission was a
symptom. Externally, the growth of commercial competition from the USA, France and especially from Germany brought demands for educational reform which
would encourage scientific and technical training.
Internally, this was exacerbated by the agricultural
depression of the 1880s and 1890s, and the tailing-
off of industrial output in the same period. 'National efficiency' became a popular slogan which reflected a widespread concern for Britain's survival; and not just commercially, since the growth of
German militarism gave evidence of an even more
serious threat.(28) 'Efficiency' offered a middle
course between the 'English ideology' of individual
freedom and toleration, which discouraged state
intervention, and the necessity to ensure England's
survival. The Bryce Report had followed this middle

course in recommending a 'systematic organisation of
Secondary Education':

> We mean by 'system' neither uniformity nor the
> control of a Central Department of government.
> Freedom, variety, elasticity are, and have
> been, the merits ... in English education, and
> they must at all hazards be preserved.(29)

Such preservation, however, would necessarily require a reassessment of curricular priorities. In
Bryce's discussion of the claims of different areas
of curriculum, those of classics - 'tradition, imagination and philosophy' - must have sounded feeble
in comparison with the apparent inevitability of
scientific advance - 'fresh from its recent tri-
umphs' - and with the sheer necessity of technical
education - 'needed for these days of stern competition'.(30)

The social pressures towards intervention and
reform in education were also mounting in the 1890s.
The period covered by this chapter saw the rise of
the 'representative/interventionist state'; the major steps in both state intervention and the extension of the franchise fall within it. At the turn of
the century, conservative alarm at the prospect of
mob rule and the collapse of social stability was
fuelled by a variety of events and trends: the rise
of caucus politics, the disasters of the Boer War,
the Khaki Election and the riotous street celebra-
tions after the relief of Mafeking. These fears gave
rise, among other things, to a 'new social psychology' which analysed - and emphasised - the irration-
al forces governing human behaviour. It is in this
climate of opinion that Mackail's address to the
Classical Association was delivered in 1904; and
this climate which gives additional resonance to his
insistence, in the earlier quoted passage that 'Rome
... represents all the constructive and conservative forces ... Law, order, reverence for authority', and that 'just as Latin grammar is an unequalled instrument for training of the mind in accurate thought, Latin literature is an instrument as
unequalled for discipline of the practical reason'.
What gives added point to this linking of moral discipline with Latin is that when he gave this speech,
Mackail was a senior official in the Secondary
Branch of the Board of Education. The Board's involvement in the defence and redefinition of classics will be considered in the next section; but it
is apposite here, bearing in mind Mackail's status,

to quote from another part of his 1904 address:

> If [the classics] suffer temporary eclipses of
> fashion, we may await the revolution of the
> wheel with confidence ... Signs of a reaction
> in their favour are already visible. The State
> is beginning at last to take the problem of
> higher education seriously in hand. In any
> scheme aided and supervised by the State, lin-
> guistic and literary training will henceforth
> have its part, will neither be ignored nor
> squeezed out.(31)

AN ORDERLY RETREAT: THE EARLY YEARS OF THE CLASSICAL
ASSOCIATION, 1900-22

The foundation of the Classical Association (hereinafter CA) was prompted by the passage through Parliament of the 1902 Education Bill. In November of
that year, there appeared in the Fortnightly Review
an article entitled 'Are the Classics to go?', written by J.P. Postgate, Fellow of Trinity College,
Cambridge, and Professor of Comparative Philology at
University College, London.(32) In the forthright
manner typical of him, Postgate came straight to the
point:

> At a time when we appear to be on the eve of
> extensive reconstruction in the higher educa-
> tional system of the country, the first duty of
> those who believe that a due recognition of the
> claims of Greek and Latin is vital to our in-
> tellectual welfare is to know what they want.
> It is clear that the Classics will not be al-
> lowed the lion's share which has been theirs in
> the past, and the question is, how much we must
> struggle to retain.

Postgate was diplomatic enough to phrase his decla-
ration in purely quantitative terms, as if classics
was a homogeneous whole from which a part might be
cut off to preserve the rest. It soon became apparent, however - and this was the point of Mackail's
address at the CA's first general meeting - that
classics was composed of different parts, some of
which would have to be sacrificed. The extreme opponents of classics, men like Ray Lankester and H.G.
Wells, identified particular aspects of classics
teaching as especially deserving of censure; and if
the CA's task was, as Gilbert Murray put it, to

'conduct ... a retreat ... in order and without pan-
ic', it was necessary to decide what must be 'thrown
to the wolves'.(33) But in the first instance at
least, what was discussed within the CA was the jet-
tisoning not of areas of classics, but of aspects of
classics teaching. Here, in conformity with the pre-
vailing notion of 'efficiency', it was hoped that a
streamlined version of the existing provision might
ensure its survival.

The Lion's Share: 'Classics and the Average Boy'
The problems involved in identifying aspects of
classics and its teaching which might be jettisoned
did not only spring from the relationship between
the CA and extreme anti-classical propagandists. As
will be seen, opinion was divided within the Association on several topics: the value of composition,
especially in verse; the pronunciation of Latin;
traditional versus 'direct' methods; and above all,
the 'compulsory Greek' question. The founders of the
CA wanted discussion and decision, but not dissension, and this has to be remembered in interpreting
the formulation of their pronouncements. At the second general meeting (1905), for example, T.E. Page
of Charterhouse, a celebrated scholar and teacher
known for his vigorous eloquence, moved that:

> Having regard to the smaller amount of time
> which can now be devoted in schools to classi-
> cal work, the Association ought to consider
> what part of the study of Greek and Latin is of
> lesser importance in order that attention may
> be more concentrated on what is essential.(34)

The debate on this motion led to the appointment of
a Curricula Committee whose brief was predictably
more blandly phrased: 'to consider in what respect
the present School Curriculum in Latin and Greek can
be lightened and the means of instruction improved'.
    What this committee actually concentrated on,
and what the CA was most sensitive about at the secondary level, was the 'grind': the great bulk of
classics teaching in the lower and middle forms of
public schools. The sensitivity of this issue is
clear from its inclusion in the introductory address
given by Sir Richard Collins, Master of the Rolls,
at the foundation meeting held in December 1903:

> they were perhaps not concerned to deny that
> some of those students who passed through our

public schools and had received a classical
training had not quite reached the standard of
senior classics when they came away from
school. (Laughter) The case was not proved
against classical studies by reason of the fact
that a considerable percentage of persons
passed through our public schools without at-
taining any very high degree of scholarship
while they were there.(35)

Both the speaker's phraseology and his audience's
laughter betray an over-hearty confidence with a
distinct undercurrent of nervousness; and this was
understandable, given the statistics of Oxford Responsions and the Cambridge Previous Examination.
Contemporary accounts vary, but the failure rate in
the Greek questions seems to have been between 35
and 50 per cent.
    The 'grind' of public-school classics was an
embarrassment to the CA for two reasons. First, it
was in theory a discipline from which emerged,
butterfly-like, the fluent versifiers whose 'finish
and beauty' of mind Jex-Blake had eulogised in 1876.
But very few butterflies actually emerged: certainly
not enough to justify the stultifying boredom in-
flicted on thousands of public schoolboys. As
Mackail's Board of Education colleague J.W. Headlam
said at the 1904 meeting:

    The great weakness of the classical system ...
    was the predominance of the tendency towards
    perfection of style, analysis of language,
    grammar, and stylistic criticism, [which]
    caused the weariness with which a large number
    of pupils regarded their classical training.(36)

This 'weariness' constituted the second reason for
the CA's nervousness: the 'grind' was difficult to
defend in its own right, as well as being ineffi-
cient in the production of elegant scholars.
    The Curricula Committee sent a questionnaire to
all HMC schools and to 'the Head Mistresses of certain Girls' Schools'. The returns showed that in the
classical sides of large boys' public schools, classical teaching made up just under half of the total
curriculum for 12-13 year olds; a proportion which
rose to just over a half for 16-17 year olds.
Smaller boys' schools devoted less time to classics
- about a third of the total timetable for 12-13
year olds - and girls' boarding schools showed a
similar picture. Girls' day schools, on the other

The Redefinition of Classical Education

hand, gave only between one and four hours a week to
Latin. The rarity of Greek in girls' schools, and
also the small time-allowance given to Latin, were
explained by the Committee as the result of pressure
from 'female subjects' (some girls' day schools, in
any case, only held formal lessons in the morning).(37
The Committee's verdict on classical teaching in
boys' public schools echoed Headlam's indictment:
'it seems to be directed towards the ultimate production of a certain number of finished scholars
both in Latin and in Greek, educated for the most
part on what may be called linguistic lines, i.e.,
with special attention to Grammar and Composition'.
They recommended that for 'the average boy, with
whom in this Report we are mainly concerned', the
load of grammar learning should be reduced, and concentrated in Latin; Greek being taught 'only with
a view to the intelligent reading of the Greek
authors'.(38)
        If the Committee's report had a main thrust, it
was against the imposition of composition, especially in verse, on the 'average boys' who would never
be scholars. Grammatical training, especially in
Latin, was to be streamlined, but remained a central
feature of middle-school teaching. It was the continued imposition of grammar on 'average boys' which
was the subject of a lengthy attack in the Times
Educational Supplement in January 1912. The writer
pointed out that since most Oxbridge scholarships
were tied to classics, parents forced their sons to
stay with the 'grind': 'four out of five boys are
sacrificed to formula-grinding in their [parents']
hope that theirs will be the fifth, and will obtain
scholarships'. He further alleged that the Empire
was suffering from the results of this 'bribery by
endowment': the public schoolboy's 'plasticity has
been killed and his mind stunted by formal discipline and mental gymnastics which involve a loss of
self-reliance'. The article provoked an enormous
correspondence which spilled over into the columns
of The Times; a selection of letters was later published under the title of the original article,
Classics and the Average Boy, a Question for the
Nation.(39)
        The problem of supplying resourceful and adapt-
able administrators for the Empire, on the model
perhaps of Sanders of the River, was likely to be
felt largely in the public schools. But as has already been suggested, while culture tended to con-
note exclusion and elite status, discipline, as
exemplified by Latin, was a paradigm of

23

incorporation. As Mackail had emphasised, Latin literature disciplined the 'practical reason', in other words, turned out responsible citizens. In the education of the potential 'new voters' who attended the maintained schools of the 1900s, classics might therefore have a vital part to play. However, as a semi-official article in the Assistant Masters' Association's <u>Circular</u> insisted in 1915:

> No one can dispute that the general public thoroughly disbelieves in classical education. 'General public' includes a good number of those who sit on governing bodies and places where they decide on curriculum, and who have got to be persuaded that Latin is not a waste of time, that it is not merely ornamental, and that it improves the breed of citizen.(40)

The LEA Schools and the Board of Education: Defence by Regulation

The CA Curricula Committee's final report, which appeared in 1907, was largely devoted to the teaching of Latin in public schools. A brief final section was, however, included on Latin teaching in 'schools with a leaving age of about sixteen', in other words, the LEA schools. The Committee stress that 'the complete and systematic study of Latin, both linguistically and as literature ... will be quite out of the question in schools of this type.' They point out that:

> The study of Latin in such schools has, in the past, met with the opposition of many parents, largely because on the older system of teaching the average boy rarely gained any real knowledge of the language in the time allowed ... We therefore recommend that in these schools Latin should be taught with a view to the intelligent reading of the easier Latin authors, and to supplying that discipline in clear and accurate thought which is not so readily obtained from the study of a modern language.(41)

Here the concern for popularity and the influence of the 'efficiency' doctrine coincide. One of the consequences is an ideological shift, characteristic of this period, from the conception of 'grind' as a necessarily laborious accumulation of facts aimed at strengthening the memory, to a more rationalist idea

of 'formal training' leading to clear thinking. This
shift is reflected in the report's warning that 'it
is specially important to ignore all that is uncom-
mon in grammar, and to ensure a thorough knowledge
of the grammatical forms and constructions commonly
occurring in the authors read ...' (42) The successive revisions of Kennedy's Public School Latin
Primer, by this time forty years old, follow something of the same pattern. In this case, however,
the revisions became entangled with issues of public-
school independence and the relations between heads
and assistant masters: a standardised public-school
Latin grammar was a symbol of excellence, not just a
teaching aid.(43)

Something of the same trend was also discern-
ible in the teaching of Greek. An Oxford don described to the CA general meeting in 1905 how he had
been asked to give an opinion of the Greek 'grammar
which was then mostly used in this country', and had
found that by

> going through it and drawing a pencil through
> all the forms which did not exist at all   ...
> Out of a quite moderate number of pages I found
> five or six whole pages which could be saved by
> this simple process ... and you might leave out
> a good many forms that are very seldom used.(44)

The teaching of Greek, however, did not bulk large
in the grant-aided schools. The results of a survey
carried out by the Board of Education, and published
in its report for 1910-11, showed that about 2,000
boys and 300 girls were learning Greek in these
schools. Of these totals, however, only 15 per cent
were provided by the municipal and county schools,
as opposed to grammar and other endowed schools. The
Board drew particular attention to the

> striking variation ... in the amount of Greek
> taught, even where the towns are broadly speak-
> ing of the same ... type. This ... difference
> appears to depend very much on the character
> and tradition of the existing schools; that is
> to say ... it is not so much the demand which
> creates the supply as the supply which governs
> the demand.(45)

The Board itself had by this time begun to influence the nature of this 'supply'. As the report
makes clear, the normal practice in drawing up grant
schemes was now to have Greek included, where a

school provided it, in the ordinary curriculum, instead of its being, as previously, an 'extra subject' for which additional fees were charged to parents.(46) This somewhat belated support for Greek is
in marked contrast to the Board's consistent support
for Latin. The Secondary Regulations of 1904, which
laid down the curricular pattern for schools in re-
ceipt of grant, specified that where two languages
other than English were taught, one of these must be
Latin, unless the Board could be convinced that this
was undesirable. This rule was retained when the
Regulations were amended in 1907.

Mackail was thus right to emphasise, in his address to the CA in 1904, that 'In any scheme aided
and supervised by the State, linguistic and literary training will henceforth have its part, will
neither be ignored nor squeezed out.'(47) And for a
very good reason: he had been appointed Assistant
Secretary in charge of the Secondary Branch of the
Board at the end of the previous year, and as such
must have been involved in the drafting of the Secondary Regulations. The issue of the Regulations, in
fact, formed part of a plan of Morant's to replace
the previous system of separate grants, at varying
rates, from a variety of sources, with a single
scheme of grant support for the whole curriculum. At
the same time, this enabled Morant to correct the
'lop-sided development' in favour of science teaching which had followed the accelerated take-up of
Science and Art grants in the 1890s.(48) Morant had
prepared the ground for the 1904 Regulations by arranging for Mackail's junior colleague J.W. Headlam
to survey the literature and humanities teaching in
several dozen municipal schools. Headlam had concluded:

> In the majority of the schools ... the nature
> of the literary education ... requires the most
> serious attention. In many of the schools ...
> no attempt is now made to give a classical
> education ... It is becoming increasingly dif-
> ficult for a professional man who cannot afford
> to send his son to an expensive boarding school
> to procure in the grammar school of his dis-
> trict an education which will prepare him for a
> professional career.(49)

Both Mackail and Headlam appear in the memoirs
of their contemporaries as the 'champions of the
Classics'; and with good reason. But it needs to be
emphasised that the climate of opinion among the

senior staff of the Board was also strongly in favour of literary and humanistic education. In 1910,
it consisted of 92 officials, of whom 58 had been at
Oxford and 23 at Cambridge. Of the former, about 60
per cent had read Greats; of the latter, nearly 70
per cent had taken the Classical Tripos. Of the 92,
73 had been to HMC schools, 43 of these to the nine
'Clarendon' schools.(50) In addition, several factors combined to make the views of the Board's staff
much more influential in formulating departmental
policy than was the case in other government departments. The Board had taken over the old Education
Office staff after it was set up in 1899, as well as
the Science and Art staff; it managed to retain appointment by patronage for inspectors and examiners
until 1914, and for some senior staff until 1919;
and finally, its presidents, who were political ap-
pointees, rarely stayed in office long enough to influence policy.(51)

Gentlemen and Players: 'Discipline' Redefined

Mackail and Headlam had both addressed the CA's
first general meeting, and continued to collaborate
and advise behind the scenes. The CA also had powerful allies in public figures like Lords Cromer,
Curzon and Bryce. Its custom in appointing its annual presidents was to alternate such men with eminent scholars like Jebb, Butcher and Murray. This
procedure acknowledged the Association's dual con-
stituency. As the chairman of the 1904 meeting had
put it:

> not only those trained scholars whose daily
> function it was to push out the boundaries of
> classical knowledge, and to instruct the rising
> generation in the study of the classics, but
> also that larger body of persons who had not
> been able to make the classics the one and
> principal study of their lives, but would never
> forget the debt they owed to that knowledge of
> the classics which they acquired in earlier
> days, and still found in them a refreshment and
> a delight.(52)

The problem faced by the CA's founders was that
these segments of its membership often pulled in
different directions, thus making it difficult to
formulate policies while maintaining solidarity. Nor
were these segments free from internal conflict; and
this was especially true of classical scholarship.

27

The Greek revival had inspired scholarship, first in Germany and then in England; but even after the mid-nineteenth century, when it began to split into a number of specialist fields, Greek scholarship retained the sense of a broader cultural context as well as of professional discipline. Those classicists who gained a literary and public reputation outside their specialist field - men like Blackie, Jebb and Murray - were usually Greek, rather than Latin scholars. Latin scholarship, in fact, had become professionally introverted, and had gone through an 'ivory tower' period in the thirty years before the First World War.(53) To some extent, therefore, its professional 'discipline', concentrated largely on textual scholarship, reinforced the grammatical 'discipline' of school Latin. Greek scholars, on the other hand, had turned to art, archaeology and the anthropological analysis of ancient religion. They had founded a Society for the Promotion of Hellenic Studies in 1879, and in 1910 a similar society for Roman Studies was set up. The CA committee was, in private, firmly opposed to this later development, though they were forced to acquiesce in it. The prospect of a potentially competing alliance was alarming; yet the differences went deeper. The promoters of the Roman Society saw the challenge to the traditional 'grind' of the public schools as an opportunity to make classics the scientific, professional study of culture. This novel combination and redefinition of culture and discipline is summed up in the phrase used by Percy Gardner, the Oxford classical archaeologist: 'wider and more special'. Classics was to be extended beyond the traditional concentration on text and language, but to be the subject of specialist study by professionals.(54)

The foundation of the Roman Society represents, in part, the failure of Percy Gardner and his allies to convert the CA to their case. Gardner had greeted the CA's foundation meeting in 1903 with a mixture of congratulation and criticism. In a letter to The Times, he argued that the expansive redefinition of classics as the vehicle of a new Renaissance was the best way to stave off the encroachments of science and modern languages.(55) The other division within the CA which led to the foundation of a separate body also had to do with discipline and professionalism, but of a rather different sort. This arose from the advocacy of direct method teaching in Greek and Latin by W.H.D. Rouse and his followers. Here the professionalism was one of pedagogic method,

28

rather than of scholarship; and while the latter received at least lip-service from most CA members,
they felt themselves above the detailed discussion
of teaching methods. This was essentially a class
attitude: 'A schoolmaster should be a gentleman and
a scholar. Professionalism, methodology and teacher-
training were for the elementary school teachers,
who were neither.'(56)

Rouse is a complex and fascinating figure. He
belonged to the old-fashioned Cambridge school of
classical scholarship: a blend of precise linguistic
knowledge and compositional skill. He published
handbooks of composition in both Latin and Greek,
was the co-translator of a voluminous German handbook of comparative philology, and taught Sanskrit
for the Board of Indian Studies at Cambridge. He
translated Struwelpeter and English sea-shanties
into Latin, and the Lord Chancellor's patter-song
from Iolanthe into Greek. But in the 1890s, as he
moved through the career structure of the public
schools from assistant masterships (Bedford and
Cheltenham) to the post of sixth-form master at
Rugby (1895-1901), he became convinced that conventional classics teaching was stultifying, and that
the direct (or oral) method being popularised in
Germany for modern languages could be the salvation
of classics too. 'Salvation' is appropriate, for
Rouse was the son of a missionary, and saw himself
as one. His father, a Baptist missionary in India,
had translated the Bible into idiomatic Bengali.
Rouse himself promoted a vernacular; but it was not
English.

As a staunch Tory, a lover of the grandeurs of
Elizabethan English, and a vigorous supporter of the
Navy League who looked back with nostalgia to the
exploits of Drake and Hawkins, Rouse harked back to
the Renaissance. In that period, when Greek culture
was being rediscovered, Latin was still the international language of communication, and the upper-
class language of composition. Rouse was a reactionary radical; his vision was essentially one of a return, an escape from the brutalities of modernism,
science and progress. In 1902 he became Headmaster
of the Perse School, Cambridge, and stayed there
until he retired in 1928. While he was Headmaster,
no external examinations were taken in the school.
The Board of Education's bureaucrats were inveighed
against, and its forms filled in and returned late
and inaccurately. What enabled Rouse to do this was
not just the independence of any headmaster. It was
the success and the reputation of his reforms, not

only of classical teaching but also of the curriculum as a whole; and by the time of the War these had made him possibly the best-known headmaster in the country.

Rouse believed that the classical languages should be treated as vernaculars. He taught them without using English, except where absolutely necessary, and used gesture and dramatic performance to convey meaning. The Perse developed a strong dramatic tradition: this is also evident in the work of its English teacher H. Caldwell Cook, author of The Play Way, whose work also manifests the escapist longings felt by Rouse. The support Rouse attracted from educationists came from the resonance of his work with several current concerns. His commitment to Elizabethan England and the glories of English literature gave him common ground with Quiller-Couch, George Sampson and Robert Bridges. His claim that classics could be taught effectively and in less than the traditional time allowance attracted both classicists and the advocates of 'efficiency'. Finally, his concern to make Latin and Greek something living and enjoyable struck a responsive chord in both dissatisfied classicists and opponents of conventional classical teaching.

One way of expressing Rouse's message was that he believed in 'discipline' but redefined it. To use his own analogies, lifting stones or turning a treadmill will give discipline, but so will football or Morris dancing - and the latter also give life. The basic difficulty with the direct method in classics was that it required dedication, scholarship and dramatic ability: very nearly, it required one to be Rouse. Many of those who possessed the first two qualifications also had a stiff upper lip, and were unable to contemplate talking to pupils in Latin about the blackboard and the weather, and acting playlets with them. In the CA, as in the Headmasters' Conference, he became a somewhat isolated figure, always ready to deliver 'The Message'. Ironically, given his antipathy to the Board of Education, he gained powerful support from Robert Morant, to whom he wrote direct for help. Morant provided the Perse with an additional grant for extra staff for direct method teaching, and the results were reported in great detail in two pamphlets published by the Board.(57) But Rouse's attempts to gain converts in the CA failed, and in 1911 he organised a 'Summer School of Latin', including demonstration lessons, at Bangor. This was advertised through the Assistant Masters' Association (of which

he had been secretary while at Rugby), and was a
great success. Larger schools followed, and at Cambridge in 1913, the Association for the Reform of
Latin Teaching (ARLT) was founded, with Rouse himself as first president. It was an unfortunate time
to start a missionary body. The 1914 school, to
which several German educationists were to have
come, had to be cancelled. Several of Rouse's potential successors were killed in the War. Less dramatic, but perhaps even more telling, was the relationship of the new body with the CA.

After the successful 1913 summer school, Rouse
and his colleagues approached the CA to arrange a
joint discussion on direct method, and this was held
at the 1914 CA meeting. The secretary of the ARLT
introduced a session on 'The new movement towards
oral method in teaching classics'.(58) The discussion was inconclusive, in part because many of the
participants had not experienced what they were
talking about. The ARLT representatives were careful
to defer to the CA as the repository of scholarly
authority, but backed away from a proposal that the
Association should set up a committee to report on
the direct method: conversion, rather than assessment, was for them the only acceptable public outcome. Relations between the two bodies were there-
after distant at best, often strained, and at times
broken off. In November 1921, for example, the ARLT
wrote to the CA asking it to nominate members for a
committee the former had set up 'to draw up a [clas-
sical] curriculum for modern secondary schools'. In
reply, the CA pointed out that the existing committee members were also members of the CA, and that in
any case 'questions of method were for the moment
impossible for Council to consider, while its attention was necessarily concentrated on matters of educational policy'.(59) This double barb - inclusion
and exclusion - severed diplomatic relations for
over a year. More seriously, perhaps, it reinforced
the division of labour between the CA's annual discussions of high culture and the ARLT's concentration on technique - one technique. One of the results can be seen by looking at the flood of teaching manuals, encyclopedias and handbooks which appeared between 1900 and 1920. Almost without exception, their classical contributions are provided by
Rouse or one of his disciples. Teachers who looked
for advice on method would find advice on one particular method; those who turned to the CA would
find very little. Nevertheless, some teachers learnt
and practised 'oral', if not 'direct' method. In

other words, they acknowledged the importance of
spoken Latin and Greek, if they did not follow Rouse
in banning English from their teaching. But to use
the languages orally, they had to decide how to pronounce them; and this was one of the questions most
hotly debated in the early years of the CA.(60)

Scholarship, Pedagogy and Prejudice: The Pronunciation of Latin

The course of the HMC debates on this subject has
already been traced. By the 1900s, the arguments had
surfaced at Conference several times; the discussions usually led to three to one votes in favour of
the reformed pronunciation, but implementation was
left up to members. Hence the minority ignored the
decisions, and the debate reappeared a few years
later. The Headmaster of Shrewsbury, listening to
the arguments at Conference in 1906, declared that
he seemed to be reliving a past life: he had heard
the same discussion at another Conference, twenty-
five years before, with the same arguments on either
side.(61) By this time, however, the advent of the
CA had raised hopes that the whole matter could be
resolved by the production of an agreed and authoritative set of rules.

A committee was appointed by the Association in
1905 to recommend rules of pronunciation. In the
discussion which preceded the appointment, S.H.
Butcher pointed out that:

> You will find schools in England in which there
> are at least two and probably half a dozen dif-
> ferent pronunciations ... boys have to unlearn
> at the secondary school what they have learnt
> at the preparatory school ... Neither at Oxford
> nor at Cambridge, perhaps not within a single
> college, does any uniform system prevail - not
> even a consistently incorrect system.(62)

Butcher went on to say that reform could be argued
for on grounds of 'scientific precision', but he
preferred to press for it as a matter of 'urgent
practical convenience', and stressed that it must
not make teaching 'more irksome or vexatious'. Here
he was steering a diplomatic course between con-
flicting views within and without the Association.
The 'scholarly' view, emanating largely from Cambridge (Postgate was a fervent reformer), was concerned with accuracy: Latin should be pronounced as
the Romans had pronounced it, and scholarship could

reconstruct this. Many public schoolmasters, on the
other hand, wanted something simple and easy to
teach to 'average boys'. This requirement meant that
they favoured a variant of the 'traditional' or
'English' pronunciation, in which Latin was spoken
as if it were English. Thus one compromise put forward by some schoolmasters was that the 'English
pronunciation' should be used up to the top of the
middle school, when the 'reformed' version could be
introduced to prepare boys for its use at university. Other more individual suggestions were also
made, which attracted little support, such as the
use of the traditional scheme for reading Latin
prose, and the new scheme for poetry. On the whole,
though, most schoolmasters were prepared to acknowledge the demands of 'accuracy'. It did not follow,
however, that they were happy to be instructed in it
by dons.

'In plain truth ... education is being much in-
jured by professors ... they live in a world of
theory, and from it, hold out a guiding hand to men
in hourly contact with hard facts.' Thus fulminated
T.E. Page in the course of his battle with Percy
Gardner in the correspondence columns of The Times.(63)
For many public schoolmasters, this feeling was combined with a suspicion of the new-style classics
don, who seemed to be a trainer of professionals,
rather than the source of a liberal education. This
feeling was further reinforced by a chauvinistic
hostility to the Germanic classical scholarship
which stood as the paradigm of the new style. It is
worth bearing in mind the wider context of these attitudes. Since 1870, while German efficiency and
economic performance had been admired in England,
her regimented education system and her military ambitions had been viewed with alarm. Germany was successful but un-British. The problem, as many in England saw it, was to match her achievements without
becoming 'Prussianised'. The fact that Germany was
the 'land of professors' did nothing to reconcile
supporters of the English pronunciation of Latin to
the scholarly accuracy of its reformed alternative.
Thus among the more conservative schoolmasters and
classically educated country gentlemen in the CA,
the English pronunciation symbolised national pride,
rather like Chesterton's 'rolling English road': it
might be wrong, but by God! it was English.(64)

In 1906, the CA committee's report on the pronunciation of Latin was approved by the Association,
supported by the HMC, and, in February 1907, endorsed by the Board of Education.(65) When the Board

reissued its Circular on the subject in March 1909,
it stated that the CA's scheme had been generally
adopted in the maintained schools.(66) In the independent sector, the trend was less definite. By
1913, several public and preparatory schools had re-
verted to the old pronunciation, each group accusing
the other of leading the retreat from the CA's recommendations. Of 300 preparatory schools circular-
ised by the HMC for information, about two-thirds
had adopted the new rules, but by 1912 this had
dropped to 165. The CA set up a committee to investigate the position, and was told in 1913 that of 39
schools supplying information, 24 followed the rules
completely, twelve partially, and three rejected
them.(67) Later in the same year, this report was
debated by the HMC, which then voted by 31 to 17 in
favour of the new rules - a smaller majority than in
1906. Nevertheless, the public schools slowly came
into line. Although a speaker at the 1926 Conference
managed to raise the matter by proposing that the
new pronunciation should be rejected, he was told by
the chairman that there was now no chance of regain-
ing uniformity on the basis of the old pronunciation, and his motion was defeated by 39 votes to
9.(68)

'A Certain Phrase': Reconstruction and the Decline
of Greek
In his address to the CA's 1904 meeting, to which
reference has several times been made, J.W. Mackail
declared his reluctance to

> aggravate the controversy, already sufficient-
> ly heated, as to the necessity of Greek and
> Latin at certain stages and in certain places
> of education ... The President of Magdalen,
> with tears in his voice, implored me not to
> utter even in a whisper a certain phrase which
> at present distracts this University.(69)

The phrase which was distracting Oxford, and would
continue to distract it until 1920, was 'compulsory
Greek'. Until the relevant regulations were changed
at Oxford in 1920, and at Cambridge in 1919, almost
all undergraduates at the two universities were
forced to pass an intermediate examination which included questions on Greek. Since this had first been
attacked in the 1870s, it had been the subject of
constant battles at Oxford and Cambridge. It is an
accurate indication of the relative strength of

support for the two languages that the major bone of
contention with Latin was its pronunciation, with
Greek its retention or abolition. The issue dragged
on through the first two decades of the century because 'compulsory Greek' became a symbol, for many
conservatives, of a humanistic education under
threat from the promoters of 'modern, useful and
scientific education'. At Oxford and Cambridge, it
also symbolised the universities' right to control
their own affairs without interference from the
State.(70) Within the CA, the issue was rarely discussed, for fear that debate would split the Association. The seriousness of this particular issue is
to be measured by its comparative absence from the
CA's Proceedings.
     The issue of compulsory Greek began to be
forced in 1916, when a group of radically pro-
science propagandists sent an open letter on 'The
Neglect of Science' to The Times.(71) This led to
the setting up of a Prime Minister's Committee on
science in education later the same year. It also
provoked a humanist 'counterblast' which, warning
that the War was being fought for more than material
and technical ends, urged that 'too narrow a regard
for practical efficiency' brought with it 'a risk
that we may ignore elements in education vital to
the formation and maintenance of national character'.(72) The most vociferous propagandists for science (notably H.G. Wells and Ray Lankester) were
contained by the scientific establishment, who found
them something of an embarrassment. Under the diplomatic chairmanship of a 'scientific classicist' (Sir
Frederic Kenyon, Director of the British Museum), a
'Conjoint Board of Scientific Societies' and a
'Council for Humanistic Studies' managed to agree on
statements which acknowledged each others' claims.(73)
It was clear, however, that educational reconstruction would be a priority when the War ended, and
that classics as a whole would suffer unless the
Greek issue could be settled.
     Negotiations between the CA and the Board of
Education began in 1917, after the Association's annual meeting. Mackail attended the meeting, and reported to his immediate superior at the Board, W.N.
Bruce, that it was of particular importance because
of Lord Bryce's presence, and because of what he had
said there. Bryce, who was at that time probably the
most influential public spokesman for humanistic
education in England, declared that it was the duty
of classicists 'to adopt a combatant and aggressive
policy'. Mackail commented that:

> The position of compulsory Greek at Oxford is
> critical and even dangerous ... If abolition
> were thrown out, the effect on public opinion
> would be disastrous ... the great mass of pub-
> lic opinion is all against Greek. The scientif-
> ic extremists always concentrate on Greek; if
> they claim this point, they will be willing to
> leave Latin alone.(74)

By this time Herbert Fisher, the new President of
the Board, had agreed to receive a deputation from
the CA. The published accounts of the deputation's
speeches and of Fisher's reply suggest that he was
largely sympathetic to their cause,(75) and this is
confirmed by the evidence in the Board's files and
by Sherington's recent analysis of Fisher's policies.(76) In a letter to his close friend Gilbert
Murray, Regius Professor of Greek at Oxford and
recruited by Fisher to work half-time in the Board's
University Branch, Fisher declared that:

> The disappearance of Greek from our system of
> humane studies would be so great a catastrophe,
> that we must do all we can here to help procure
> ... a free and easy access to them. I am par-
> ticularly anxious that the funds expended in
> Oxford and Cambridge on Classical scholarships
> should not be diminished. Indeed, it was mainly
> to this end that I planned the new State schol-
> arships.(77)

By this time, all except the most reactionary supporters of Greek at Oxford had realised that the
battle would be lost after the War. In a memorandum
sent to Mackail in January 1917, Headlam reported
that 'Sir Richard Livingstone and his co-workers' at
Oxford were now ready to accept the abolition of
compulsory Greek, but felt that in return they
should be given some guarantee by the Board of the
protection of Greek in schools.(78)
    As in the case of the containment of 'the sci-
entific extremists', we are witnessing a humanistic
establishment at work, discreetly arranging for the
protection of what it holds dear. As Sherington remarks:

> In public Fisher was a man of compromise,
> seeking to strike a balance between ancient
> and modern studies ... Behind the scenes he
> was more alarmist. His policy aimed at pre-
> serving classics from what he saw as a

dangerous threat ... (79)

Fisher was bound to both Murray and Mackail by
friendship. All three belonged to that 'compact
group of late-Victorian literati', as John Gross
calls them, whose 'shared outlook' made them the
'earnest custodians of tradition'.(80) In public,
they responded to each other's speeches; in private,
they might well have planned both speech and reply.
Compulsory Greek was finally abolished by Cambridge in January 1919, and by Oxford in March 1920.
The Cambridge decision prompted Selby-Bigge, the
Board's Permanent Secretary, to ask his HMIs whether
a classics committee was needed, on the same lines
as the Committees on Science and on Modern Studies
set up in 1916. They replied that:

> the position of Classics in secondary education
> was more precarious and ill-defined than that
> of any other subject in the recognised second-
> ary school curriculum ... Nobody knows how many
> pupils study Greek or Latin ... but things have
> gone further than was probably suspected ... (81)

Thus the appointment of a committee was recommended.
The Prime Minister's Committee on Classics was set
up in November 1919 and reported in 1921. Its conclusions express a cautious optimism about the future of Latin, a rather less cautious pessimism
about the future of Greek:

> Latin so far occupies a fairly secure position.
> It is taught in all Preparatory Schools and in
> the middle and lower forms of most Secondary
> and Public Schools. Its position in the Univer-
> sities is not seriously impaired, and in some
> at any rate of the new Universities it is
> studied to a high Honour standard, in partial
> or complete dissociation from the study of
> Greek ... The position of Greek is much less
> favourable and is indeed critical. Its hold on
> the Preparatory Schools is ... precarious; it
> is not taught to an increasing proportion of
> boys in Public Schools. In the Secondary
> Schools and in Girls' Schools it can generally
> be begun, if at all, only at a late age ...
> while in many schools and in some areas there
> are no facilities for teaching it at all.(82)

The abolition of 'compulsory Greek' marked the
end of an era; the Prime Minister's Committee wrote

its epitaph. The Victorian certainties of class and
classics, questioned by the liberals of the Edward-
ian era, had been shattered by the War. That classics survived to the extent that it did can be ascribed to several factors. First, the continued control of decision-making in education by members of a
late-Victorian humanistic establishment for whom
classics was the foundation and the crown of education, the source of discipline and culture. Second,
the strategic turn, during the War, from conservative defence to an aggressive liberalism. This involved the invocation of the ideology of 'fair
play', discussed earlier in this chapter, in defence
of classical education. The adoption of this strategy dates from 1916, when responses to the 'Neglect
of Science' manifesto were being planned by Murray,
Livingstone and Kenyon. The principle of mutual toleration is the basis on which the agreed statements
of the 'scientific' and 'humane' societies were issued under Kenyon's chairmanship.(83) The same
strategy appears in Kenyon's address to Fisher as a
member of the CA deputation in April 1917:

> We are not asking ... for any privileged posi-
> tion on behalf of the classics ... We are not
> asking that classics should be made compulsory
> upon anyone; we are asking that ignorance of
> the classics should not be compulsory upon any-
> one.(84)

Compulsion had, in any case, been distasteful to
liberal classicists - men like Murray, Livingstone
and Zimmern at Oxford - who while convinced of the
supreme cultural value of Greek, felt unhappy about
the compulsory imposition on students of a subject
which symbolised intellectual freedom. Now that
Greek was out on the open market, it remained to be
seen how many takers it would attract. In the opinion of Cyril Norwood, then Master of Marlborough,
it would have to shake off the odium created by the
tactics of its defenders:

> at the present moment [1918] we are in a rather
> bad tactical position ... due to the continued
> maintenance of compulsory Greek ... The policy
> of the Universities hitherto has seemed to me a
> policy of trench warfare. They have erected
> compulsory Greek into a sort of Hindenburg Line
> on the future of which depend the humanities
> and most that makes life worth living.(85)

THOROUGHNESS AND UNREALITY: THE TRIUMPH OF DISCIPLINE, 1923-40

The dominant mood among CA members in the 1920s was one of qualified optimism. The battle seemed over, and the victory, at least for Latin, to have been won. The Association, moreover, could pride itself on being the prime mover in a successful campaign. The Prime Minister's Committee had commended its work and urged all classics teachers to join it.(86) For the ARLT, the prospects were bleaker. The Committee had sent representatives to see Rouse's teaching, but the section on direct method in their report was distinctly lukewarm. As the editor of the ARLT journal put it, 'the committee appears to praise with faint damns'.(87) This rebuff, from a committee whose members included several CA stalwarts, was followed by another from the CA itself which has already been described. A final attempt to secure a favourable verdict from the CA on direct method, at the CA's 1923 meeting, also failed. The editor of <u>Latin Teaching</u> reported that:

> Papers ... were of the lofty and scholarly character expected of the C.A. ... this very fact seems to emphasise the value of our own smaller body. It might be said that the C.A. provides for the higher inspiration of classical teachers, for which we are grateful, but on the whole does not give them much solid help for their daily needs.(88)

This deployment of a division of labour between high culture and pedagogic expertise was, of course, undertaken for defence and justification. But while hardening divisions, it did not create them. The Prime Minister's Committee had pointed out that:

> Classical teachers too often plough a lonely furrow, and they have at present no professional organisation which quite corresponds to those established for other subjects.(89)

By 1930, both associations had suffered, the CA from success, the ARLT from failure. The <u>Proceedings</u> of the former become very desultory in the late 1920s. The stirring issues of the Association's early years had been resolved. Its membership, which had begun at 450 and reached 1,000 at the beginning of the War, was now well over 2,000.(90) But since 1923, it had not taken any active interest in

classics teaching in schools. The complacency engendered by success, and the division of labour with
the ARLT, together go to explain why 'the Association should ... have withdrawn from the field at a
time when the crusading vigour of other Associations
was growing stronger and stronger'.(91) The ARLT's
membership had reached 300 by the mid-1920s, but its
struggle to maintain its status in relation to the
CA was not helped by a predominantly female recruitment. About two-thirds of its members were women,
and at some of its annual summer schools, the male
to female ratio of new recruits reached one to
eight. The 1930 summer school was attended by four
men and over forty women; and while 'some half of
the women were newcomers, this was not true of any
of the men'.(92)

Recruitment to classics in secondary schools
showed a slight increase through the 1920s. Greek
numbers remained low (about two per cent of the total School Certificate entry), and a large proportion was accounted for by the public schools. Latin,
on the other hand, averaged about 38 per cent of the
entry, and seemed permanently established, buttress-
ed as it was by the universities' entrance requirements.(93)

In the new universities, separate honours
schools in Latin and Greek, rather than in classics,
were typical. This trend, and the shift to Latin,
can be seen in the statistics of classics recruitment at Manchester, Liverpool, Leeds, Newcastle and
Sheffield. The numbers graduating from them in classics between 1914 and 1928 rose from 31 to 50, while
graduations in Latin over the same period rose from
10 to 61.(94) At sixth-form level, the Board of Education's attempt to encourage the 'organic unity' of
classics by offering grants for advanced courses in
Latin, Greek and Ancient History had had little impact, since few schools were able to provide adequate staffing.(95) In the lower and middle school,
Latin was widely supported as a discipline of mind,
and as giving a firm grammatical foundation for
other languages. It thus became a benchmark against
which pupils were judged, a series of hurdles which
many failed to clear. By the second half of the
1930s, the CA's educational subcommittee could warn
that:

> The place of Latin in the curriculum is gravely
> jeopardised when it can be pointed out that a
> very large proportion of those who start Latin
> in the Secondary School do not continue it to

the Certificate stage, and of those who do continue it ·not a large proportion achieve the
credit mark.(96)

To most classical teachers, however, even a
little Latin might promote clearer thinking and mental discipline; and these were virtues which came to
be highly prized in the 1930s.(97) Such attitudes
were laid bare, most noticeably, when a shortage of
time forced teachers to select what they taught and
could hope to achieve. The HMI who wrote the Board's
1929 Memorandum on Latin and Greek quotes from a report by a teacher who had only three years to reach
School Certificate:

> The work is primarily linguistic and very lit-
> tle attempt is made to graft upon it growths of
> general culture. Such an excellent result in
> thoroughness and accuracy is now being achieved
> that it would be a pity to spoil it for any
> doubtful embellishments.(98)

The 1929 Memorandum was written by the then Staff
Inspector for Classics at the Board, D.A. Macnaughton. A decade later, his successor R.H. Barrow wrote
a pamphlet for the Board entitled 'Suggestions for
the Teaching of Classics', in which he remarked that
'The strength of Latin teaching in some quarters has
been its "thoroughness", but thoroughness has been
combined with unreality.'(99)

CONCLUSION: DISCIPLINE AND ITS DISCONTENTS

In the 1860s, the Taunton Commission

> were impressed by the failure of the tradition-
> al classical education to meet the needs of the
> country as a whole, and at the same time by the
> general belief of the schoolmasters of the day
> in the virtues of Latin, particularly Latin
> grammar. Latin was the only subject taught
> thoroughly ... they regarded Greek as unneces-
> sary except for first-grade schools ... the at-
> titude to Greek and Latin shown by the Commis-
> sioners has been to some extent reflected in
> educational practice since their day, in the
> divergence between the school with a classical
> sixth form, where Greek is on a level with La-
> tin, and the school where of the two languages
> only Latin is effectively taught. In the latter

> case Latin becomes not what it was in the major
> classical schools of the nineteenth century,
> one of the constituents, perhaps the less im-
> portant one, in the study of the ancient world,
> but something valued mainly as a linguistic
> discipline, teaching accuracy of thought and
> expression and contributing to the understand-
> ing of modern languages, but doing little to
> enlarge and stimulate the mind.(100)

This sums up very well the passage from the cultural
elitism of the nineteenth century to the disciplined
thoroughness of the twentieth which has been described in this chapter. To the Victorians, Latin
was certainty and order, the solid foundation of
high culture, a necessary but not sufficient condition for its acquisition. Latin grammar became an
exemplar of sure knowledge. In his diaries, Harold
Nicolson noted a conversation he had in May 1933
with Lord Eustace Percy, formerly President of the
Board of Education:

> Is economics a science or an art? We agree that
> the Victorians regarded it as pat as Latin
> grammar. Now there is the something unknown.
> That has rendered economics more dynamic and
> far less respectable.(101)

Respectability: that is part of the key to the
understanding of the transition from culture to discipline. Culture had been a class badge. Discipline
incorporated what Lowe had called 'our future masters' into a respectable middle class. Between the
wars, the scholarly voices heard by the public were
largely those of Hellenists like Murray, Livingstone
and Dickinson. Latinists tended, rather, to talk to
one another, following the stern tenets of scholarly
professionalism laid down by Housman.(102) Bourgeois
respectability, self-discipline, professionalism: it
was this influential complex of ideology and social
groupings with which Latin became involved in the
1930s. For those parents who lived through, or later
remembered, the Depression, especially in the working class, it was 'the academic subject', a symbol
of the certification which led out of their class
and into the security and status of middle-class
careers.(103) It was the strength of this involvement, and the illusion of permanence it engendered,
which rigidified the teaching of Latin and intensi-
fied the postwar crisis it suffered with the rise of
the comprehensive school.(104)

The Redefinition of Classical Education

NOTES AND REFERENCES

1. R. Harris, The Language Makers (Duckworth, 1980), ch. 5.
2. Proceedings of the Classical Association
(hereinafter CAP), 1904, p. 12.
3. CAP, 1904, pp. 14-17.
4. C.S. Parker, 'On the Theory of Classical
Education' in F.W. Farrar (ed.), Essays on a Liberal Education (Macmillan, 1867), p. 7.
5. On 'Kultur', see N. Elias, The Civilising
Process, Vol.1: The History of Manners (Basil Blackwell, Oxford, 1978), pp. 3-34; on the romantic movement, E.M. Butler, The Tyranny of Greece over Germany (Cambridge University Press, 1935); on its influence on classical scholarship, R. Pfeiffer, History of Classical Scholarship from 1300 to 1850
(Clarendon Press, Oxford, 1976), pp. 167-90.
6. J.E. Russell, German Higher Schools: The
History, Organisation and Methods of Secondary Education in Germany (Longmans, Green and Co., New
York, 1899), p. 246.
7. On the Greek revival, see F.M. Turner, The
Greek Heritage in Victorian Britain (Yale University
Press, 1981); R. Jenkyns, The Victorians and Ancient
Greece (Basil Blackwell, Oxford, 1980). On the reformed public schools, see J.R. de S. Honey, Tom
Brown's Universe (Millington, 1977). An excellent
comparative analysis of classics and class in the
nineteenth century is provided in J.A. Armstrong,
The European Administrative Elite (Princeton University Press, 1973).
8. Report of Her Majesty's Commissioners Appointed to Inquire into the Revenues and Management
of Certain Colleges and Schools, and the Studies
Provided and Instruction Given Therein (Clarendon
Report), Vol.1 (HMSO, 1864), p. 13.
9. Schools Inquiry Commission, (Taunton Report) Vol.1 (HMSO, 1868), p. 16.
10. A.M. Kazamias, '"What Knowledge Is of Most
Worth?" An Historical Conception and a Modern Se-
quel', Educational Review, vol.30 (1960), pp. 309-30.
11. See W.E. Houghton, The Victorian Frame of
Mind (Yale University Press, 1957), pp. 176 ff.;
A.C. MacIntyre, Secularisation and Moral Change
(Oxford University Press, 1967).
12. R.T. Shannon, The Crisis of Imperialism
1865-1915 (Paladin, 1976), ch.1.
13. N. Annan, 'The Intellectual Aristocracy'
in J.H. Plumb (ed.), Studies in Social History
(Longmans, 1955), pp. 243-87.

43

14.   Armstrong, The European Administrative
Elite, ch.7; J.P.C. Roach, 'Victorian Universities
and the National Intelligentsia', Victorian Studies,
vol.3 (1959-60), pp. 131-50.
15.   A.C. Percival, The Origins of the Headmasters' Conference (John Murray, 1969); J.W. Roche,
'The First Half-Century of the Headmasters' Conference 1869-1919', unpublished PhD thesis, University
of Sheffield, 1972.
16.   See HMC, Bulletins for 1869, 1870, 1872,
1873 and 1876.
17.   HMC, Bulletin, 1913, p. 62.
18.   Edward Thring, in his defence of verse
composition, which he claimed acted as a bridge between the two states: HMC, Bulletin, 1876, p. 72.
19.   'Smalls' (Responsions) and 'Little-Go'
(The Previous Examination) were compulsory intermediate examinations at Oxford and Cambridge respectively; they included questions on Greek and Latin.
The failure rate in these questions in the 1890s was
variously estimated at between one third and one
half.
20.   Clarendon Report, Vol.1, p. 13. 'Construing' is a mechanical technique for translation,
each word in a text being followed by an English
equivalent.
21.   Clarendon Report, Vol.3, p. 114, answer
no. 3,537.
22.   For Social Darwinism and games, see J.A.
Mangan, 'Social Darwinism, Sport and English Upper-
Class Education' in Aspects of the Social History
of Sport (School of Physical Education, University
of Liverpool, 1982), pp. 121-43.
23.   Quoted by M.L. Clarke, Classical Education
in Britain 500-1900 (Cambridge University Press,
1959), p. 56. 'Longs and shorts' are the alternate
hexameters and pentameters of the elegiac couplet,
as every schoolboy knows!
24.   HMC, Bulletin, 1876, p. 80. The 'senior
classic' was the top first at Cambridge in the Classical Tripos; cp. the 'senior wrangler' in mathematics
25.   Taunton Report, Vol.1, p. 131.
26.   Royal Commission on Secondary Education,
(Bryce Report) Vol.1 (HMSO, 1895), p. 48.
27.   Clarendon Report, Vol.1, p. 12.
28.   G.R. Searle, The Quest for National Efficiency (Basic Blackwell, Oxford, 1971).
29.   Bryce Report, Vol.1, p. 326.
30.   Ibid., p. 284.
31.   CAP, 1904, pp. 21-2. On the climate of
opinion, see R.N. Soffer, Ethics and Society in

England (California University Press, 1978), ch.10; on the social pressures, S. Hall, 'The Rise of the Representative/Interventionist State' in G. McLennan et al. (eds.), State and Society in Contemporary Britain (Polity Press, 1984), pp. 7-49.

32. Fortnightly Review, new series, vol.72 (November 1902), pp. 866-80.

33. Gilbert Murray, speech at the Imperial Conference of Teachers' Associations, 15 July 1912. See The Times, 16 July 1912. The 'wolves' was used within the CA to refer to pro-science extremists like Wells and Lankester.

34. CAP, 1905, p. 53. On Page, see N. Rudd, T.E. Page: Schoolmaster Extraordinary (Bristol Classical Press, 1981).

35. CAP, 1925, pp. 94-5. For 'senior classics', see n. 24.

36. CAP, 1904, pp. 37-8.

37. CAP, 1906, pp. 40-75 (discussion); pp. 85-96 (interim report).

38. Ibid.

39. The original article appeared in the Times Educational Supplement on 2 January 1912, column 7c. See also The Times, Classics and the Average Boy, 1912.

40. AMA, Circular, May 1915, p. 73.

41. CAP, 1907, pp. 107-8.

42. Ibid., p. 108.

43. For the lengthy and embarrassed wrangles within HMC over the Primer, see J.W. Roche, 'The Great Latin Primer Question', British Journal of Educational Studies, vol.17 (1969), pp. 281-5.

44. D.B. Monro in CAP, 1905, p. 69.

45. Board of Education, Report of the Board of Education for the Year 1910-1911 (HMSO, 1912), pp. 45-7.

46. Ibid., p. 47.

47. See n. 31.

48. ' ... if I remember rightly, we got the Headlam report in order to support the changes we were anyhow going to make': Morant to Gill, March 1909, quoted by E. Eaglesham, 'Implementing the 1902 Education Act', British Journal of Educational Studies, vol.10 (1962), pp. 153-74.

49. J.W. Headlam, Report on the Teaching of Literary Subjects in Some Secondary Schools for Boys (HMSO, 1903): British Sessional Papers, (Commons), 1903, vol.21, pp. 61-6. See n. 48. Headlam had been one of Bryce's assistant commissioners, and Professor of Greek and Ancient History at Queen's College, London (1894-1900). He and two other inspectors were

appointed by the Board in 1903 specifically to deal
with literary subjects.

50.   P.H.J.H. Gosden, The Development of Educational Administration in England and Wales (Basil
Blackwell, Oxford, 1966), pp. 106-7.
51.   G. Sutherland, 'Administrators in Education after 1870' in G. Sutherland (ed.), Studies in
the Growth of 19th Century Government (Routledge,
1972), pp. 263 ff.
52.   CAP, 1904, p. 6.
53.   R.R. Bolgar, 'A Century of Interpretation'
in Fondation Hardt, Les Etudes Classiques aux XIXe
et XXe Siecles (Vandoeuvres, Geneva, 1980), pp. 91-117
54.   Gardner belonged to the 'Museum vote' at
Oxford: see A. Engel, From Clergyman to Don (Oxford
University Press, 1983).
55.   The Times, 24 December 1903, 6c. He was
answered by T.E. Page on 26 December, 8f. See also
29 December, 10e (Gardner) and 2 January 1904, 10d
(Page). Gardner had previously tried to persuade the
HMC to encourage the teaching of classical archaeology in schools: HMC, Bulletin, 1900, pp. 56 ff.
56.   J.E. Sharwood Smith, On the Teaching of
Classics (Routledge, 1977), p. 33.
57.   Board of Education, The Teaching of Latin
at the Perse School Cambridge, Educational Pamphlet
No.20 (HMSO, 1910); Board of Education, The Teaching
of Greek at the Perse School Cambridge, Educational
Pamphlet No.28 (HMSO, 1914).
58.   CAP, 1914, pp. 38-47.
59.   CAP, Council Minutes, 26 November 1921.
60.   The above paragraphs draw on unpublished
material which I hope to incorporate in a forthcoming memoir on W.H.D. Rouse.
61.   Dr Moss in HMC, Bulletin, 1906, pp. 27-46.
62.   CAP, 1905, p. 7.
63.   The Times, 2 January 1904, 10d (cp. n. 55).
64.   For those who might sympathise with Protestant Germany, the similarity of the new pronunciation to modern Italian could nevertheless arouse re-
sentment. And 'Roman' sometimes suggested 'Romanism'.
For an example, see J.P. Postgate, How to Pronounce
Latin (Bell, 1907), p. 2.
65.   HMC, Bulletin, 1906, pp. 31-46. The voting
was 32 to 11 in favour. Board of Education, The Pronunciation of Latin, Circular 555 (HMSO, 1907).
66.   Circular 555, reissued in 1909 as Circular
707 under the same title.
67.   CAP, 1913, pp. 123-8.
68.   HMC, Bulletin, 1926.
69.   CAP, 1904, p. 19.

70. See further, for Oxford, Engel, _From Clergyman to Don_; for Cambridge, S. Rothblatt, _The Revolution of the Dons_ (Faber, 1968).

71. _The Times_, 2 February 1916.

72. _The Times_, 4 May 1916.

73. F.G. Kenyon (ed.), _Education: Scientific and Humane_ (John Murray, 1917).

74. Mackail to Bruce, 18 May 1917: PRO, Ed. 12/221, S. 763.

75. _CAP_, 1918, pp. 5-33.

76. G.E. Sherington, _English Education, Social Change and the War, 1911-20_ (Manchester University Press, 1981), pp. 138-42.

77. Fisher to Murray, 21 July 1921, quoted in Sherington, _English Education_, p. 139.

78. PRO, Ed. 12/221, S. 763, memorandum from J.W. Headlam, 24 January 1917.

79. Sherington, _English Education_, p. 140.

80. J. Gross, _The Rise and Fall of the Man of Letters_ (Weidenfeld and Nicholson, 1969), pp. 163-4.

81. PRO, Ed. 24/1188, HMIs' meeting, 24 January 1919.

82. _The Classics in Education: Report of the Committee Appointed by the Prime Minister to Inquire into the Position of Classics in the Educational System of the United Kingdom_ (HMSO, 1921), pp. 57-8.

83. See n. 73.

84. _CAP_, 1918, pp. 10-11.

85. _CAP_, 1918, pp. 110-11.

86. _The Classics in Education_, pp. 299-301.

87. Ibid., pp. 144-7; _Latin Teaching_, vol.4, no.3 (1921).

88. _Latin Teaching_, vol.6, no.2 (1923).

89. _The Classics in Education_, pp. 137-8.

90. _CAP_, 1925, p. 11.

91. CA Education Subcommittee, _Report to C.A. Council on the Position of Classics in the Schools_ (April 1937), p. 5. The English Association had the same problems of complacency: see Nowell Smith, _The Origin and History of the Association_ (English Association, 1942), p. 9.

92. _Latin Teaching_, vol.7, no.3 (1924); vol.13, no.3 (1930).

93. See Board of Education, _Memorandum on the Present Position of Latin and Greek in the Grant-Aided Secondary Schools of England_ (HMSO, 1929).

94. Ibid., p. 44.

95. See, for a detailed discussion, C.A. Stray, 'From Monopoly to Marginality: Classics in English Education since 1800' in I.F. Goodson (ed.), _Social Histories of the Secondary Curriculum_ (Falmer Press,

Lewes, 1985), pp. 19-51; C.A. Stray, 'Classics in Crisis', unpublished MSc thesis, University of Wales, 1977.

96. CA, The Position of Classics in the Schools, p. 7.

97. For an attempt to relate 'discipline' to the wider social and cultural context of the 1930s, see the works cited in n. 95.

98. Memorandum on Latin and Greek, p. 28.

99. Board of Education, Suggestions for the Teaching of Classics (HMSO, 1939). 'Some quarters' may refer to the preparatory schools, of whose Latin teaching Barrow had earlier used the same phrase: PRO, Ed. 12/283, HMI report of 13 January 1932.

100. Clarke, Classical Education, pp. 95-6.

101. H. Nicolson, Diaries and Letters 1930-64 (revised ed. by S. Olson, Collins, 1980), p. 55.

102. See the remarks of R.R. Bolgar and K.J. Dover in Fondation Hardt, Les Etudes Classiques, pp. 107-26.

103. For a detailed analysis, see Stray, 'Classics in Crisis', chs. 3 and 4.

104. This chapter is based on preliminary work for a forthcoming major study of classics in English education. I should like to offer apologies to the reader for any incoherencies which may have arisen from the attempt to conceptualise the subject-matter at an early stage; thanks to Michael Price for helpful discussion, which has reduced such incoherencies if not removed them; and gratitude to the officers of the Classical Association and the Association for the Reform of Latin Teaching, who have allowed me to consult their archives and in general given me every assistance.

Chapter Three

ENGLISH TEACHING: CLASSICS IN THE VERNACULAR

ELEANOR WRIGHT

In the 1980s, there is little doubt about the prima
facie case for English as a main subject on the
school curriculum and no one would have any trouble
in producing a list of reasons for its inclusion in
any description of core subjects. 'English is a key
subject in the school curriculum' is the opening
sentence of a statement from the Secretary of State
for Education and Science accompanying a recently
proposed set of curriculum objectives.(1) It would
be hard to imagine nowadays having to make the following plea which was made in 1919:

> The English Association desires to urge upon
> all responsible authorities the importance of
> the matter, and the need for ensuring that,
> whatever other subjects appear in the curricula
> of the schools, the national language shall
> have a place of honour as a subject in itself
> of the highest educational value; as the means
> of instruction and as the medium of social
> intercourse.(2)

A measure of the seriousness with which English
is taken now is the degree to which it can be seen
clearly as a focus for competing theories on the
educational role of the school; in particular, the
extent to which it has for example a vocational or
aesthetic or political function; and the competing
claims made for example by the DES, by university-
based examination boards and by teachers, for control over classroom practice. This was not the case
in the early part of the century, particularly at
secondary school level, and it is interesting in
this respect to compare two documents produced by
the governmental bodies responsible for education,
English from 5 to 16, issued by the Department of

Education and Science in 1984, and <u>The Teaching of English in England</u> (The Newbolt Report), issued by the Board of Education in 1921. The former takes the importance of English for granted in fostering the intellectual and social development of the child, with an assured place on the school timetable and specialist departments in the secondary school staffed mainly by specialist teachers. None of this is taken for granted in the latter report, which traces the history of English within educational institutions and its struggles for survival, never mind status, in the face of indifference and hostility, and which has to take every opportunity to argue the case for locating English teaching in the forefront of the curriculum in all schools and establishing it as a major field of study in the universities.

The decades immediately after the First World War were important in the development of English teaching. Mathieson characterises the interwar period by referring to 'the national sense of inferiority to Europe in education, the rising demand for secondary school places and the general feeling that reform was necessary'.(3) Within such an atmosphere of flux, English became the subject of a major Board of Education enquiry. The results of that enquiry, the Newbolt Report, as will be discussed later, included recommendations about far-reaching changes in the nature of the subject and the extent of its penetration into the curricula of all educational institutions. Multiplying numbers of candidates taking School Certificate English attest to the growth in its serious study at secondary schools: Shayer quotes figures showing a threefold increase between 1918 and 1931.(4) To meet the demands of change and growth, a mass of teaching materials was produced, a process highlighted by the English panel of the Association of Assistant Mistresses in Secondary Schools in a complaint against:

> the tendency of successful English teachers to publish manuals of their own methods so that the market is flooded with textbooks covering more or less the same ground, no single one of which commends itself altogether to any other teacher, causes perplexity, and may perhaps give a bias to those who have not yet reached a clear conception of aims and method.(5)

The period, consequently, was something of a turning-point in the acceptance of the subject at all levels

of schooling and will therefore be examined in this
chapter, to discover in what form English was being
established in the schools and its relationship with
the older-established teaching of classics.

THE ARGUMENTS FOR ENGLISH

The Newbolt Committee was set up in 1919 by the
Board of Education 'to inquire into the position occupied by English (Language and Literature) in the
educational system of England, and to advise how its
study may best be promoted in schools of all
types'.(6) Its Report, published in 1921, ranged
widely to include the nature of a liberal education,
the history of English teaching, its position in
schools, colleges and universities and its immense
potential. Shayer's judgement that 'it would be
wrong to assume that the 1921 Report was necessarily
in the forefront of current method thinking'(7) is
certainly sound, as other views, such as those of
the English Association,(8) and other accounts of
practice, such as those of Tomkinson,(9) O'Grady,(10)
Greening Lamborn (11) and Finch (12), make plain.
However, as Shayer goes on to suggest, its importance lay in its unequivocal espousal of the cen-
trality of English within a complete and coherent
liberal education for all, the unitary nature of
English studies and the particular importance of the
English teacher.(13)
    The Newbolt Report represented a consolidation
of the view, expressed by many of those giving evidence to the Committee, that English could succeed
where the classics could not. English was described,
in quasi-biblical terms, as the 'keystone' of an entirely rebuilt education system, of a liberal education which, in Sampson's words, would be 'A preparation for life, not merely a livelihood, for living,
not for a living. Its aim is to make men and women,
not "hands".'(14)
    Sampson also asserted that, although education
in the classics had produced some fine scholars:

> No attempt has ever yet been made to give the
> whole English people a humane, creative educa-
> tion in and through the treasures of their own
> language and literature. The great educational
> reform now needed is to begin that universal
> education. English, in the large sense here
> used, is the one subject that will cover all
> three aspects of education - intellectual,

moral and emotional ... (15)

The Report argued strongly that the language problems presented by the study of Latin and Greek effectively prevented classics from being the core of a liberal education for more than a very few people. In practice, most time was spent on painstaking and often ineffective language study. Furthermore, where a classical education was socially divisive, the study of English - the language and literature - had potential for unification within a common cultural inheritance. Also English as a language was far from being the debased vulgar tongue portrayed by classics scholars. It displayed new qualities such as flexibility, efficiency and subtlety according to evidence supplied by Professor Jespersen,(16) and its literature exhibited qualities of thought and expression second to none.

The Committee had also taken account of the arguments of proponents of progressive education such as P.J. Hartog, Caldwell Cook and Greening Lamborn. In her chapter on progressive theorists in relation to English teaching, Mathieson emphasises their belief that the classical curriculum and traditional teaching methods were personally destructive, remote from pupils' experience and needs, and dehumanising.(17) They perceived the capacity of English for fostering personal and intellectual growth through creativity and appreciation of literature in the mother tongue - a medium uniquely suited to this purpose. In addition, they were highly critical of the use of traditional grammatical methods in the teaching of English.

Other arguments propounded by the Report were related less centrally to the subject's role in the curriculum than to the subject itself. It drew attention to the claimed disparity in attitude to both spoken and written language in England and in France, pointing out the pride which the French nation took in its language and literature. It also argued that the language itself would benefit from being taken seriously, by being defended against the trivialisation and secularisation particularly of the mass media and popular literature.

THE STATUS OF ENGLISH

By the time of the Newbolt Report, English had had a place on the elementary school curriculum for some time, albeit not always in a form endorsed by the

Committee. They claimed that:

> teachers have not really envisaged the right
> dimensions of English in the Elementary
> Schools, and they are expending their very ad-
> mirable enthusiasm and skill upon it as a spe-
> cific and limited subject, or worse, as a col-
> lection of detached subjects.(18)

However, its mere existence became more problematic the further one advanced in the education
system. Within state secondary schools, whereas
girls were very likely to have studied English literature, the boys' curriculum was dominated by classics and science.(19) Public schools hesitated to
provide for English within school hours, for fear of
ruining a pleasurable spare-time activity, and in any
case it did not correspond to their idea of what a
school subject should be: it was associated with
utilitarian and functional rather than cultural
values.(20)

Recommendations made within the Newbolt Report
suggest that the minimum conditions for establishing
the subject on a school-wide basis were still not
universal and that other subjects were held higher
in priority. For example, it recommended that at
least one period a day should be spent on English up
to the age of twelve, that between the ages of 14
and 16 English should not be subordinate to other
languages or science, that English should be encouraged as a main study at Higher level and that the
senior teacher of English should have equivalent
powers to the senior mathematics, science and modern
languages teachers.(21) In this, it followed many of
the proposals previously made by the English Association.

At the universities, particularly the ancient
ones, the study of English was even more precarious-
ly situated. In the late nineteenth century, its
value at Oxford was in providing suitable courses
for weaker candidates such as women and 'the second-
and third-rate men who were to become schoolmasters',(22) and it was its development as a study
of philology which ensured its respectability after
the First World War.(23) More progress had been made
at Cambridge in establishing the critical study of
English literature as an independent discipline
(despite the mockery enshrined in its nickname 'the
novel-reading Tripos'), not least to provide a suitable background for prospective school teachers,(24)
which formed a basis for the crusading work of F.R.

Leavis in the 1930s. Nonetheless, the Newbolt Committee felt constrained to take time to dispatch the view that English was a soft option at university level.(25) Its recommendations show that, at university level also, English did not enjoy a status equivalent to the traditionally established disciplines such as classics, history, science and mathematics. It asked that English students should enjoy equal access to entrance scholarships, that postgraduate work in English should be endowed, that English should be compulsory for matriculation, that Schools of English should be equal in status to other Arts Schools and 'that the endowment of an English Chair should be at least equal to that of any other humanistic Chair in the same university'.(26) The evidence which it had received indicated that none of these provisions existed at that time. In effect, the Newbolt Committee was claiming that such advantages, which were also indicators of status and value, should now be granted to English.

THE DEVELOPMENT OF PRACTICE

Between the wars the thrust of educational and method theory was conceptualising the subject in a different way from the way it was perceived in most schools and universities. That this had implications for practice was not lost on the Newbolt Committee, which outlined what it believed to be the important principles. A basic premiss was the emphasis on experience and use of language and literature rather than on knowledge. The Committee warned against treating literature as a knowledge subject rather than a source of enjoyment and was particularly critical of using works of literature as quarries for grammar and style exercises, such as analysis, parsing and paraphrasing. It was insistent on the importance of oral work, including what it called 'conversational methods', as a way of promoting reflective thought and as the foundation for written expression.(27) On writing itself, the Report stressed the importance of its derivation from experience generated by personal interests and circumstances, reading or other stimuli, and was hostile to methods which required children to write on abstract themes for set periods of time. It argued for less emphasis on grammar and that any grammar taught should be what it called 'pure grammar', that is to say the grammar of function, concerned with modes of thought, rather than form.(28) Here the Report

54

looked forward to a time when notions such as case,
declension and conjugation in English would be little known. In all these respects, the new approach
to English teaching would be quite different from
the methods of the past and from the influential
methods then used in the teaching of classics. What
its proponents believed was that English had all the
advantages of classics as a basis for a humane education and few of its linguistic disadvantages, in
that it was a language of which children already had
experience, with a more approachable structure, and
through which they lived their lives. The time which
had had to be spent on the minutiae of grammar in
learning classics could now be deployed more profit-
ably in the enrichment and exploration of experience
through oral and written expression and through literature.

A major question remained regarding the implementation of the ideals and practices so eloquently
argued. The title of Mathieson's study, The Preachers of Culture, suggests one answer: what was required was educators in whom were combined missionary endeavour and cultivated taste. In fact, the
Newbolt Report believed that English teachers should
be specially gifted people whose enthusiasm, interest, sympathy and knowledge were more important than
training or formal study of English.(29) However the
reality of the situation, as the Committee itself
recognised, was that only a minority of students
emerging from training colleges were considered sufficiently competent.(30) Their social background and
previous academic experiences provided little basis
for the professional confidence necessary to inno-
vate on the scale envisaged. In terms of classroom
practice they were more likely to be familiar with
techniques of drill and practice routines, grammatical grind and construing literary texts, derived
from the methodology of classics teaching, than, for
example, imaginative and creative writing and promotion of reading for pleasure, which were central to
the new conception of English.(31)

A resource which teachers could turn to was
textbooks and Shayer's history of English teaching
clearly indicates their importance throughout this
century.(32) In this key period, textbooks were
likely to be particularly influential in developing
the pedagogy of the subject, guiding and supporting
teachers, and to some extent compensating for the
poverty of their educational experience and the lack
of tradition at this stage in the history of English
teaching. The books provided models of practice:

many of them were written by teachers, based on
their own successful experience, and designed to be
practical and to meet practical concerns, often suggesting in fairly precise terms how they could be
used on a week-by-week basis. In addition, therefore, to their value for teachers at the time, their
content also provides a clear indication of what
English teachers were implementing in their class-
rooms.

ANALYSIS OF TEXTBOOKS

The expanding secondary school sector presented a
major area of development for English teaching; this
was previously a sector where English was neglected
but one which provided a route to higher education.
Such circumstances would be likely to present the
clearest demonstration of how practitioners were reacting to new thinking in terms of their own priorities. The following analysis is of textbooks for
use in secondary schools which were published in the
1920s and 1930s, or which were published earlier
than that and were recommended for use by the Incorporated Association of Assistant Masters in a memorandum in 1927.(33) The focus is on textbooks whose
emphasis is on the language side of English teaching
and does not include school editions of literary
texts. At the time the practices enshrined in these
school editions were the target of a great deal of
criticism because of the obsessive annotation of
texts following up every nuance of meaning, every
literary allusion and every historical or mytholog-
ical reference. However, given the importance attached to effective use of language, books which
covered such topics as the study of language, the
development of skill in writing - including précis,
paraphrasing and essays - and the analysis of literary style are concentrated on. These include general
course books and books on specific aspects of English teaching. What seems to emerge from this analysis is that although the mother tongue was now at
the core of the humanities curriculum instead of the
classics, far from breaking away from traditional
teaching methods the pedagogy of the subject was
very much the same as before, and English in many
important respects was 'classics in the vernacular'.
Several major discontinuities are apparent between
the theory and the practices of the classroom, call-
ing into question whether English was indeed the
core of a liberal education for all.

In the majority of cases, the tone adopted by the books was authoritative, didactic and formal. The writers' authority was derived from extensive classroom experience and their role was that of a transmitter not only of what was culturally important but also of the principles by which learners could be taught to discriminate between what was worthy and what was worthless: the writers saw themselves as both makers and guardians of good English. Specific directives were commonplace, for example: 'in general, young writers should not write long paragraphs'.(34) But it was not only on matters of linguistic correctness that assertions were made; aesthetic judgements were voiced equally strongly, for example: 'Failure to appreciate the essay is a sign of imperfect education.'(35)

These opinions often carried strikingly moral overtones including the imputation of personality characteristics. Low and Briggs included 'sincerity', 'moderation' and 'industry' amongst the characteristics of great writers.(36) The moral element was evident also in advice to pupils on their own linguistic behaviour, which was described as if it were a variety of good breeding. Pupils were urged to show humility, suitability, restraint, frankness and pleasantness and to avoid excess, disagreeableness and unsuitability. 'Simple terms do not draw undue attention to themselves' was how one book summarised its teaching about choice of words,(37) and 'an essay is an orderly collection of sentences suitably grouped into paragraphs' prefaced a chapter on sentence construction.(38) Particular criticism was reserved for those who publicly breached the standards of well-formed prose, specifically journalists and writers of 'cheap' fiction.

Changes in three specific aspects of English teaching were fundamental to the new theories and these will be considered in turn.

Grammar

H. Caldwell Cook in a prefatory essay to a collection of suggestions for and examples of pupils' writing was clear in his views of the value of grammar:

> To labour in the early stages for precision in punctuation and spelling, in sentence construction and the arrangement of matter, and to draft one's syllabus on a hierarchy of these things is beyond all doubt to begin at the

> wrong end of the stick ... As regards grammar,
> whether it should be taught or not and to what
> extent hardly enters the discussion of English
> composition, for it should not be necessary for
> me to point out that English is not written
> correctly only because the writer has been
> through a course of grammar.(39)

However, almost invariably grammar was the starting
point for most English courses.

In 1916, E.A. Sonnenschein had produced, in
three volumes, A New English Grammar based on the
recommendations of the Joint Committee on Grammatical Terminology, which had reported in 1911 on ways
of simplifying and unifying the terminologies and
classifications used in the grammars of different
languages; Sonnenschein produced grammars of Latin
and of French as well. His aim was to make 'English
grammar both more intelligible in itself and more
useful in the process of acquiring other languages'.(40) He had made the startling discovery
that Browning's poem The Pied Piper of Hamelin contained examples of most English forms and constructions; consequently he used the poem extensively,
among other literary sources, to illustrate his
grammar, which he insisted was a grammar of function
rather than form. Many of the textbook writers acknowledged their debt to him and their books showed
similar features to his, particularly the use of
literary sources for illustrative examples (Kenny,
for example, used Milton's sonnet On His Blindness
as an exercise in punctuation),(41) the order in and
routine by which material was presented for learning, the complexity of the classifications and the
explanations, the importance of knowledge of grammatical theory and the use of grammar for learning
other languages.

Approaches to grammar teaching followed a similar pattern, starting with simple parts of speech,
paying meticulous attention to the variety of functions which each might have and how the form might
change with each function, and progressing to types
of sentence, the structure of sentences and of
clauses and more complex parts of speech. Full use
was made of such concepts as case, tense, voice and
mood, and such techniques as parsing, sentence
analysis and correction of erroneously constructed
forms. The method usually proceeded from definition
and explanation to examples to copious exercises.
Explanations were often complex, laden with technical terms. In a book recommended in 1927 by the

Association of Assistant Masters, Bate explained the
subjunctive in this way:

> The tenses of the Subjunctive require great
> care in use, because their time significance is
> not always the same as that of the correspond-
> ing tenses of the Indicative. Thus the Present
> may refer to the Future, and the Past to the
> Present. Again there are alternative forms,
> which, however, are not used to express the
> same notions.(42)

And he went on to explain the forms taken by the
subjunctive in conditional and final sentences,
touching on jussive and optative uses. Treble and
Vallins, in a book for twelve to thirteen year olds,
explained, 'In the first passive sentence, the indirect object of the active sentence has become accu-
sative after a preposition in a case-phrase.'(43)

The books make use of elaborate systems of
classification: Hammond, for instance, gives the
principal parts of over 150 verbs, and uses the verb
'to see' to demonstrate the form that the verb takes
according to its voice (active and passive), mood
(indicative, imperative or subjunctive) and tense
(e.g. the active indicative had eight tenses), not
forgetting the verb adjective and four types of verb
noun.(44) Also, they laid emphasis on grammatical
knowledge, especially a familiarity with terminology. This was demonstrated in exercises such as asking pupils to write two sentences containing a nomi-
native absolute phrase,(45) or one which asks 'What
are attributive and predicative adjectives?'(46)

That grammar should be taught as a basis for
learning other languages, especially Latin, was a
principle enunciated by a number of writers, and
some explicitly drew parallels between English grammar and that of Latin or French. But its value as a
training in logical and disciplined thought lay at
the basis of the continued support for its inclusion
in English.

The Incorporated Association of Assistant Masters expressed the belief that training in formal
grammar was necessary and desirable: 'Without it, it
is hardly possible to promote clear thought about
the purpose and structure of language, or to expect
clear expression.'(47) It was an essential component
in the improvement of writing and they urged 'concentration on the vital and essential points of
grammar, those common to all languages and without
which neither the structure of sentences nor the

functions of words can be apprehended'.(48)
     Many textbooks, in their content and organisa-
tion, appear to have taken such ideas very much to
heart, treating grammar as a complex, disciplined
study and as an essential preliminary training before embarking on composition and literary appreciation.

Writing

In many courses, learning to express oneself in
writing was an incremental process beginning with
the word and building up through the sentence and
the paragraph to the composition. The ultimate des-
tination was the essay. Oliphant put it in this way
in his introduction to the second section of his
book:

> In the first part of the book we have dealt
> with all these subjects ... that lead up to the
> writing of the whole composition, and it now
> remains for us to devote some attention to this
> final stage of our work.(49)

By that he meant that, having mastered the main
rules of grammar, syntax and vocabulary, the structure and analysis of sentences (including clause
analysis of literary texts such as a Shakespeare
sonnet), parsing, punctuation and the paragraph, pupils were then able to proceed to the essay, letter-
writing, paraphrasing and literary appreciation. The
view of writing which was put over was of an enor-
mously difficult activity, requiring elaborate
preparation and redolent of danger at all levels:
most books devoted long chapters to 'Common Errors'
or 'Common Confusions', which could apply to errors
in vocabulary, accidence, syntax and paragraph
structure. In this respect, very little had changed
from the beginning of the century.(50)
     English Composition, by R.S. Bate, which was
recommended to teachers in the late 1920s, is a particularly striking example. Fourteen chapters were
devoted to words and sentences, and contained exposition, with examples and lengthy exercises, followed by supplementary information entitled 'Note' or
'Caution', for example: 'Caution - Remember that
Cherubim and Seraphim are not singular; and that
Cyclops is not plural; the plural is Cyclopes.'(51)
     The chapter on common errors in speech listed
over 140 solecisms of one kind or another including
violations of grammatical propriety, of idiom and of

sense, vulgarisms, misuse of words, use of non-
literary expressions and hybrids, and invoking
phrases such as 'habits of inaccuracy', 'sloppy
thought' and 'disfigurements of speech' to condemn
such use of language. After working on words and
sentences the book then moved on to 'the paragraph',
first of all providing content for the writing of 35
separate paragraphs and then listing a hundred additional topics, such as 'Bagpipes' and 'Street
noises', for original composition.

The first chapter on the essay itself was devoted to warnings against 'blunders' such as Ambiguity, Pedantry and Mechanical Humour (the use of
capital letters personifying them like the Deadly
Sins), advice on the construction of essays emphasising the difficulties involved and the need to remember the preceding chapters, and more exercises on
sentence and paragraph construction. It was not until the second chapter on the subject that the writing of essays was attempted, but only after having
studied examples of poor and good efforts by young
writers, received more hints and cautions, memorised
sample essays, and read good models of both essay
plans and essays themselves. Sixty plans and 275
titles were given as the basis for pupils' essay
writing.

If Bate's book was conspicuously laborious in
its treatment of the subject, it was by no means un-
usual in its content or method. Learning to write
was a question of mastering and adhering to principles. To do this a number of techniques were used.
Firstly, the principles were enunciated along with
examples of good and bad practice; secondly, the
skills arising from the principles were practised in
isolation and at length - for more complex tasks,
the focus of effort on the skills themselves was
often made clearer by providing the content or an
outline of material to be used, or by using trivial
subjects such as 'Eggcups' or 'Gates'; thirdly, model passages, usually drawn from literature, were
analysed, imitated and reproduced. The principles
themselves were concerned not only with grammatical
structures and correct vocabulary, although much effort was expended on that, but also with organisational qualities of writing such as unity, precision
and balance, and with quasi-moral qualities such as
sincerity, restraint and purity. It was important to
have an explicit knowledge of the principles, rules
or laws which were specifically tested throughout
the exercises, as the following example shows:

State with regard to each of the following
paragraphs on what principle it is constructed.
State also its main theme, and show how the
sentences are related to one another:-
a) A House of Commons was a necessary part of
the new policy. In constituting this body, the
Protector showed a wisdom and a public spirit
which were not duly appreciated by his contemporaries ... (52)

Even personal letters were bound by rules -
Moon and McKay, for example, list eight. On the
whole, these rules were informed by notions of good
behaviour as much as linguistic norms. Anything
which smacked of undue haste, such as the use of
postscripts and showing emphasis by underlining
words rather than choosing more forceful vocabulary
or structures, was forbidden; anything which suggested more interest in oneself than in the recipi-
ent, such as overuse of 'I', was frowned on. The
desirable qualities in an informal letter were spon-
taneity, intimacy, vivacity, abundance of interesting details, homeliness, candour, sincerity, and a
lively concern about the affairs of the person addressed.(53) Clearly, the private letter was seen as
an art form and reference was often made to published letters such as those of William Cowper, Charles
Lamb and Fanny Burney, as models of what could be
achieved. In fact, it was a subset of the essay and
bore many of its characteristics.
    For many of the textbook writers of this peri-
od, it is in the essay that all the principles of
writing came to their finest fruition. Cruse, quoting Dean Church, described it as a 'combination of
perfect ease and unassuming frankness with severity
of plan and the most artistic polish',(54) and later
on claimed that 'The essay ... is a form of writing
which belongs to an advanced stage of civilisation.'(55) Admiration for the great writers of the
past, such as Bacon, Addison, Lamb, Goldsmith,
Hazlitt and Macaulay, led to their being set up as
models of both manner and content. Pupils were required variously to study them, memorise or summa-
rise or reproduce selected examples, and observe
their wit, sincerity, clarity, balance and vigour.
In preparing for their own original work, pupils
were urged to read omnivorously in order to acquire
suitable knowledge, to cultivate appropriate interests, to collect a range of subjects for essays and
to keep a commonplace book of words and quotations
which could be used. 'Suitable' subjects were

historical, geographical, literary, whimsical, moral
and so forth, as the following sample of titles will
indicate:

> A wasp with a sense of humour.(56)
> A dialogue between G.K. Chesterton and John
> Milton on the Freedom of Women.(57)
> The Suez Canal or The Panama Canal.(58)
> The Chivalric Ideal.(59)
> The Sea in Literature.(60)
> 'Sweet are the uses of Adversity.'(61)
> Canada and Australia - a contrast.(62)

Although the majority of textbooks were using
this approach, there was a growing minority which
based the content of pupils' writing more directly
on experience. In 1916 E.A. Greening Lamborn had
written:

> Abstract subjects like 'Honesty' or 'A stitch
> in time saves nine', 'Salt' or 'Railways',
> though very popular with teachers are not suit-
> able for children; they involve word-spinning
> without interest, whereas we need above all
> things, to awaken the zest for self-expression,
> and the sense of delight that comes with power
> over words.(63)

He later repeated the point by stressing that 'the
true purpose of composition is to help [a boy] not
to your own [i.e. the teacher's] ideas, but to a
clear and fine expression of his own',(64) and that
'[The average child] writes because he has to say
something, and not because he has something to say
 ... '(65)
　　　Caldwell Cook used pupils' activity - drama,
discussion, research - as the springboard for writing;(66) Lewis built a long unit of work round the
research for a class novel loosely based on Steven-
son's Treasure Island;(67) a number of textbook
writers used prose extracts or poems, not as models
but to suggest content,(68) and subjects from within
pupils' own experience, such as accounts of events
which they had attended, descriptions of known
places, or more theoretical subjects which could be
informed by personal knowledge, e.g. 'Men's manners
are better than women's.'(69) Nonetheless, the cultivation of the cultured essay, as a form of literary accomplishment polished in style and subject,
was still a strong force to be reckoned with.

Literature

The material under consideration in this section is that which is found in course books, dealing with literary appreciation as a distinct part of the English syllabus. Of course, there was a great deal more produced in other forms including poetry anthologies such as John Drinkwater's The Way of Poetry, J.C. Smith's Book of Verse for Boys and Girls and the English Association's collections of contemporary poetry and prose. These tended to be less directive in their approach, although that could be 'remedied' by the teacher, and emphasised emotional response and enjoyment. 'Appreciation' is a more appropriate word to describe what the textbook writers were fostering, enjoyment being buried under a mass of information.

Writers were not averse to expressing strong opinions, couching their value judgements in the language of fact. Kenny stated that 'The poets of England are her glory, and four names stand out preeminently: they are Chaucer, Spenser, Shakespeare and Milton.'(70) Mais 'only mention[s] the greatest names' in his chapter on the history of English literature and claimed that 'Before the age of Shakespeare there is very little that need detain you.'(71) Pocock asserted that 'James Boswell, in spite of being silly and vain and thick-skinned, was a very great genius.'(72)

There can be no doubt that this strength of feeling for literary values led textbook writers into two courses of action. One was to attempt to induct pupils into the principles of literary appreciation and the other was to base all English work, including language work, on literature, thus surrounding pupils with good writing. Pritchard outlined a strategy for the cultivation of literary taste:

> The first step is to see that the formation of literary judgement is no light matter. Many questions have to be answered before a book ... can be given its due place. We have to consider its form; why it was written; and whether it was primarily intended for reading aloud, for private reading, or for acting upon the stage. We must have some idea of the date so as to get the right perspective, and not judge a sixteenth century book according to twentieth century notions. We shall take care to grasp the main idea and note how it is developed, nor shall we neglect to notice any qualities of

64

harmony, rhythm, and style that the work may
have, and to see how all these help in the general effect.(73)

However well-intentioned Pritchard himself was,
in practice this meant, firstly, that emphasis was
laid on rules, labels and classifications, following
a similar pattern to that adopted in the teaching of
grammar. Definitions, characteristics and examples
were provided on at least thirty figures of speech
(in one book, a distinction was made between figures
of speech, figures of rhetoric and other aids to effect),(74) prosody (covering every conceivable feature of metre, rhyme, rhythm, and stanza form) and
types of style (Oliphant lists ten main kinds including Terse, Graceful, Metaphysical and Sub-
lime).(75) An extreme, comprehensive system of classification is found in Ogilvie and Albert who assigned literary forms into two groups: Forms Suitable for School Composition and Higher Literary
Forms.(76) There were three Higher Literary Forms:
prose, prose/verse and poetry. Poetry was further
divided into narrative and lyrical, which themselves
were subdivided. Thus the subgroup narrative was
divided into idyll, ballad and epic. Under the head-
ing 'epic', there were five areas to be considered:
epical nature, plot, characters, setting and style,
and each of these was characterised briefly. For
example, the plot should have unity, simplicity and
sublimity. In this way every piece of literature
could be assigned its appropriate place on the 'tree
diagram' of literary forms. No other book went to
such elaborate lengths but many subscribed to a
similar approach. And many subscribed to Ogilvie and
Albert's book - it had been reprinted nine times by
1926.(77)
Secondly, emphasis was laid also on acquiring
wide literary knowledge, such as knowledge of writers and their works, of literary tradition, of classical literature and of a literary language, as
these questions typify:

What evidence of the influence of Milton can
you detect in the work of Gray, Wordsworth and
Tennyson?(78)

In a single sentence, endeavour to give the
main idea of the following literary works:
Milton's Paradise Lost, Dickens' Pickwick
Papers, Shelley's Adonais, Walton's Compleat
Angler, Boswell's Life of Johnson, Tennyson's

Lotus Eaters and Scott's Kenilworth.(79)

Kenny asked pupils to identify a list of sixty characters drawn from over twenty different Shakespear-
ian plays.(80) Exercises to develop vocabulary related to classical writing were common, such as deriving adjectives from Cicero, Plato, Arcady and
Styx.

The second course of action was to use poetry
or prose extracts as the core for all work.
Pritchard described the method thus:

> [an] extract studied intensively is made to
> yield material for all the English practice
> that is needed during the week ... The extracts
> have been chosen from a wide field, so as to
> make a collection that shall have a value of
> its own and at the same time be fairly repre-
> sentative of all the forms and periods of mod-
> ern English literature.(81)

Pritchard was describing the 'direct method' in
English teaching, i.e. using real literature rather
than invented passages. However, many other writers
who followed his example made heavy weather of the
method, sometimes introducing teaching about grammar
alongside the extract and linking the two aspects in
the questions. Oliphant's Progressive English Course
used this method, organising the week's work around
a poem or extract and a specified point of language
instruction, such as the arrangement of words in a
sentence, and including reference work, written and
spoken exercises, literary appreciation and exercises in thinking.(82) The extracts or poems served
several purposes: they were a quarry for words and
phrases whose meaning had to be discovered; they
were a springboard for finding information about the
subject matter, the author, places mentioned in the
poem and so on; they provided examples of the forms
of language being taught that week; they provided
the basis for questions on literary style, history
and form; and they provided an inspiration for writing. For example, the extract from Lockhart's Life
of Scott, which describes Scott's death, was paired
with a study of complement/object, transitive and
intransitive verbs, and direct and indirect objects.
Pupils were asked about Scott's writing, Lockhart's
life, the style of the passage and the impression it
made on them. That was after questions on word meanings, word opposites, punctuation, sentence comple-
tion and deriving adjectives from nouns - all using

material from the passage. They also had to write an
account of Charles II's death, modelled on the passage.(83) In sum, in this book and the many others
like it, the personal reaction of the pupils was
prefaced by a mass of linguistic and literary questions demanding the deployment of skills and knowledge. Sometimes, that was all that was asked and the
choice of extract or poem was based on its potential
for demonstrating appropriate forms or styles.

Despite Greening Lamborn's opinion that 'Paraphrasing itself as an exercise may be a good intellectual discipline like construing, but poetry cannot be translated without ceasing to exist',(84) the
art of paraphrasing passages from literature was
promoted in most textbooks, although not always for
the same reason. Walmsley called it 'Both a test of
understanding and a test of skill in clear composition ... the features of a good close translation
are mainly those of a good paraphrase.'(85) In
Treble and Vallins' minds it aimed at developing
'clear and natural language and expression',(86) but
for Pritchard it was the basis for 'true appreciation'.(87) It was indeed poetry that was most often
used as material, including Portia's speech to Shy-
lock 'The quality of mercy ... '(88) One cannot help
suspecting that the main aim of paraphrasing was not
to encourage literary appreciation but to practise
language that was clear, organised, plain and
straightforward, following Nesfield's advice to
'Cancel epithets that contribute nothing to the pur-
port of the sentence, but merely conduce to poetic
ornament, or merely suit the necessities of the metre or the rhyme.'(89)

INFLUENCES ON PRACTICE

When we turn to estimate the extent to which the
teaching materials provided in textbooks show potential for developing the aims which were discussed in
the Newbolt Report and other writings of the period,
it is clear that there are a number of apparent discontinuities. As the foundation on which to build a
liberal education, English had been seen to have two
distinct advantages over the classical languages:
one of them linguistic and the other social. Because
so much of the time available to classics teachers
had had to be devoted to acquiring the languages
themselves by learning their vocabulary and structures, insufficient attention could be paid to what
was thought to be the real value of classical

studies: appreciation of the philosophy, experience
and beauty finely expressed in these languages.
There would be no such problem for English, it was
thought, where the language was the mother tongue
and there would be little need for intensive grammatical work. However, the textbooks continued the
tradition that the classics had developed, promoting
in many cases elaborate systems of classification to
describe the structure and forms of English, which
were taught comprehensively through examples and
lengthy exercises which acted as a type of drill.
Work on grammar was accompanied by work on words and
idioms - vocabulary learning in effect - tested in a
similar way. Such teaching was usually a preliminary
to any continuous writing: clearly the language had
to be learned first and that language was rich in
complexities.

The second advantage proposed for English was
that it would not be socially divisive in the way
that Latin or Greek had been, the English language
and its literature forming a common cultural bond
for all groups. The type of social distinction con-
ferred on those who had studied the classics would
not be possible as all could participate within a
shared heritage. The fulfilment of this aim does not
seem very likely, given the approach of the textbooks, which were not drawing upon anything which
could be deemed to be some sort of common culture,
but were inducting pupils into what the Incorporated
Association of Assistant Masters called 'cultured
knowledge', that is to say, a specific range of content, both literary and non-literary, a specific way
of looking at knowledge and a specific type of language.(90) One can see this very clearly in the
teaching about writing - the selection of suitable
subjects and the desirability of certain features of
writing style - and the teaching of literature.

Another discontinuity between the aspirations
and the practice concerns the relationship between
experience and knowledge. It was believed that the
study of English would have a particular role to
play in the education of the emotions, as well as
the will and the intellect, because it would draw
on, enlarge and explore experience through oral expression, creativity and enjoyment of reading. An
urgent need was perceived to redress the over-
intellectual balance in education, and this could be
done because English was not a 'knowledge' subject
but an experiential one. However, most of the textbooks treated English largely as a knowledge subject. Every chapter had its definitions to be

learned and reproduced, on grammatical categories,
prosody, literary forms, figures of speech, points
of style and so on. Such a response to any literary
work could easily become a matter of detecting known
categories within that work rather than enjoyment
and empathy, and writing was a question of following
the rules of both grammar and style, and using approved material, rather than self-expression.

Another aspiration of which there is little
evidence in the practices proposed by textbooks is
emphasis on oral expression. Of course, it is difficult to assess this accurately from simply looking
at the books, but it seems unlikely that oral work
played a very important role in most courses. Where
it is suggested by the textbook writers, it is confined mainly to question and answer sessions on
grammatical or vocabulary matters. Given the amount
of writing to be accomplished, there simply would
not have been the time to devote to the type of reflective and creative oral work which had been envisaged.

The common feature of all the discontinuities
is that the practice of English teaching, as exemplified in textbooks, resembled much more closely
the rule-governed, knowledge-based approach of classics teaching than the experiential holistic approach one might have expected from the new method
theory. There appear to be five main reasons why
English continued to identify itself with this older
pedagogy.

In the first place, the tradition of English
teaching which already existed, and with which
teachers were more familiar, was indeed modelled on
that of classics. P.J. Hartog in 1907 wrote that
'our methods of teaching English are largely based
on the ancient methods of the schoolmaster devised
from the teaching of foreign languages'.(91) The
following year, in a lecture which was printed over
twenty years later, Fowler noted the tendency of
teachers to fall back on methods of the classical
curriculum.(92) The Newbolt Committee had been
critical of those teacher training establishments
which taught English literature in a manner resem-
bling the teaching of Latin and Greek classics in
public schools. Their fear was that English would be
treated as 'a pale reflection of the discipline of
classical studies'.(93)

Secondly, the perception that, for all sophisticated purposes, English was indeed as good as a
foreign language to most English people was embodied
within a wide spectrum of opinions. Sampson wrote,

'The English, as a nation, are inarticulate, almost illiterate, and contemptuously indifferent to art and beauty ... We have a language of incomparable beauty and we talk and write illiterate drivel.'(94) P.J. Hartog was perhaps the most clear in his belief that 'the average English boy cannot write English', contrasting this ineptitude with the much greater capability displayed by French boys in their native tongue.(95) Like Sampson, he did not recommend, however, that English teaching should be based on foreign language teaching and was of the view that one should 'Take care of the sense and the sentence will take care of itself.'(96) But there were many others, such as Hammond, who believed that mastery of the rules of grammar, vocabulary and style was a necessary prelude, to writing in particular.(97) Of course, they were not saying that children were inarticulate but that the language they used was limited and contaminated, and liable to degenerate into imprecision and disorganisation. The teacher's task was to counteract the bad habits of speech such as vulgarisms, journalese and foreign words, gleaned from the everyday world. In fact it was a two-way process. The children had to learn the language through all its rules of grammar, syntax, semantics, style and so on, and the language itself, by the reiteration and propagation of these rules, would be protected against debasement particularly by commerce, the media and popular fiction.

Thirdly, there was the question of the teacher's role. In classics teaching, teachers were the authorities, dispensing their knowledge through well-organised, preplanned content. If, however, emphasis was to be placed on the pupils' experience, imagination, creativity and oral expression, some of that control of content would have to pass into the pupils' hands. The basis of the teacher's authority would change from their possession of knowledge to their skill in managing a process of learning in which pupils would be treated as active primary contributors. This role not only would have been unfamiliar to many teachers but also would have presented difficulties because of the confidence and expertise demanded in sustaining it. Many teachers at that time did not have such professional confidence, for reasons discussed earlier, and in consequence were less likely to adopt a pedagogy which appeared to expose them to such a risky position in the classroom.

Fourthly, English was not envisaged simply as an addition to or expansion of the curriculum but as

the lynchpin of the whole nation's education. The
basis of a liberal education for all was to be English not classics, including not only intellectual
but also moral responsibilities: 'To English Studies, [the Newbolt Report and Sampson] transferred
the classics' and religion's traditional responsibilities for character development.'(98) There
were several consequences of this line of argument
which meant that classics teaching was still looked
upon to provide a model of what a subject of such
standing should be like. For example, the view that
training the mind and discipline were central aims
of the curriculum was still strongly held. The Association of Assistant Mistresses expressed the position cogently:

> Clarity in both thought and expression is the
> other crying need. We are conscious everywhere
> and continually of a lack of clear thinking,
> clear expression, accuracy and precision. Noth-
> ing has yet supplied the discipline given by
> Classical Studies to thought and speech togeth-
> er. The claim of the Panel is that for the ma-
> jority today, the study of English language and
> literature must meet this need; and they be-
> lieve that if the subject is given its due
> place in school life it can do so adequately ...
> We need cohesion, a strong foundation to give
> the steadiness essential to a true education
> which Classical Studies gave in the older sys-
> tem.(99)

Quite unequivocally, this located the subject within
the systematic rule-based pedagogy characteristic of
learning the classical languages.
    Also, English was not perceived as a real dis-
cipline in the traditional sense, particularly by
universities and public schools, an attitude which
had not entirely disappeared by as late as the
1960s.(100) Clearly it was important that the study
of English could demonstrate that it could make
tough intellectual demands on pupils and was as
worthy a language with as prestigious and complex a
literature as the classics. A way of doing that was
to imitate the pedagogy, displaying similar rigour,
content and style.
    Finally, and much more speculatively, one of
the products of classical studies was an academic
elite, familiar with a highly valued culture which
was out of the grasp of the majority of the population. In this respect, the idea of a common culture

for all presented a quite radical departure, imply-
ing a degree of democratisation which the education
system may not have been able to accommodate or even
endorse in principle. By making English courses into
a series of increasingly severe tests and by defining its appropriate linguistic and literary content
in exclusive ways, it would be possible to continue
to reproduce and protect the expertise of a cultured
elite.

For these reasons, therefore, the nineteenth-
century methodology of classics teaching influenced
the practice of English in its formative years more
strongly than did even the most passionately argued
cases for alternative approaches. It presented an
available and respected pedagogy for coping with
both the immediate tasks of the classroom teacher
and the broader concerns of the education system. As
Shayer points out, 'Advances in teaching tend to be
of the nature of modification and adaptation of
existing practices rather than being sweeping new
advances brought in overnight from scratch.'(101) To
that comment on the conservatism of teaching, one
could add that all subjects operate within a system
of educational ideas and hierarchies which cannot be
ignored, as they too have a role in creating each
subject's identity and pedagogy.

NOTES AND REFERENCES

1.   Sir Keith Joseph, English from 5 to 16
(HMSO, 1984) in an attached statement dated 2 October 1984.
2.   English Association, The Essentials of
English Teaching (Longmans, 1919), p. 3.
3.   M. Mathieson, The Preachers of Culture
(Allen and Unwin, 1975), p. 71.
4.   D. Shayer, The Teaching of English in
Schools 1900-1970 (Routledge and Kegan Paul, 1972),
p. 117.
5.   Association of Assistant Mistresses in
Secondary Schools, Memorandum on the Teaching of
English (University of London Press, 1932), p. 2.
6.   The Teaching of English in England (hereinafter Newbolt Report), (HMSO, 1921), p. 1.
7.   Shayer, The Teaching of English in Schools,
p. 68.
8.   English Association, The Essentials of
English Teaching.
9.   W.S. Tomkinson, The Teaching of English:
A New Approach (Clarendon Press, Oxford, 1921).

10. H. O'Grady, Matter, Form and Style (John Murray, 1912).

11. E.A. ·Greening Lamborn, The Rudiments of Criticism (Clarendon Press, Oxford, 1916) and Expression in Speech and Writing (Clarendon Press, Oxford, 1922).

12. R. Finch, How To Teach English Composition (Evans Brothers, 1919).

13. Shayer, The Teaching of English in Schools, pp. 71-4.

14. G. Sampson, English for the English - a Chapter on National Education (Cambridge University Press, 1921), p. 4.

15. Sampson, English for the English, p. 105.

16. Newbolt Report, pp. 286-9.

17. Mathieson, The Preachers of Culture, ch. 5.

18. Newbolt Report, p. 58.

19. Ibid., pp. 97-102.

20. Ibid., pp. 121-4.

21. Ibid., pp. 350-1.

22. Mathieson, The Preachers of Culture, p. 125.

23. Ibid., p. 125.

24. Ibid., p. 126.

25. Newbolt Report, pp. 202-4.

26. Ibid., pp. 354-7.

27. Ibid., p. 70.

28. Ibid., p. 290.

29. Ibid., pp. 125-7.

30. Ibid., p. 171.

31. Mathieson, The Preachers of Culture, pp. 179-80.

32. Shayer, The Teaching of English in Schools.

33. Incorporated Association of Assistant Masters in Secondary Schools, Memorandum on the Teaching of English, new ed. (Cambridge University Press, 1927), pp. 77-90.

34. E.W. Edmunds, Junior Course of English Composition, 3rd ed. (University Tutorial Press, 1933), p. 31.

35. A.R. Moon and G.H. McKay, A New English Course (Longmans, 1931), p. 315.

36. W.H. Low and J. Briggs, Matriculation English Course, 4th ed. (University Tutorial Press, 1926

37. G. Ogilvie and E. Albert, A Practical Course in Secondary English (Harrap, 1913), p. 10.

38. P. Leach and J.B.C. Barnard, English for Present-Day Examinations (Macdonald and Evans, 1934), p. 15.

39. The First Fruits of the Play Method in Prose, Perse Playbooks No. 4 (Heffer, Cambridge, 1912), p. 37.

40. E.A. Sonnenschein, A New English Grammar, 3 pts (Clarendon Press, Oxford, 1916), pt 1, p. 9.

41. E.J. Kenny, A New Course in English Composition (University of London Press, 1927), p. 102.

42. R.S. Bate, English Composition (Bell, 1914), p. 37.

43. H.A. Treble and G.H. Vallins, The Gateway to English, 4 pts (Oxford University Press, 1926), pt 2, p. 16.

44. C.E.L. Hammond, An Introduction to English Composition (Oxford University Press, 1925), ch. 2.

45. Treble and Vallins, The Gateway to English, pt 2, p. 73.

46. Low and Briggs, Matriculation English Course, p. 35.

47. Association of Assistant Masters, Memorandum on the Teaching of English, p. 5.

48. Ibid., p. 6.

49. L. Oliphant, A Matriculation and General English Course (Gregg Publishing Co., 1928), p. 191.

50. Shayer, The Teaching of English in Schools, p. 12.

51. Bate, English Composition, p. 12.

52. Low and Briggs, Matriculation English Course, p. 191.

53. Moon and McKay, A New English Course, pp. 126-8.

54. A. Cruse, English Composition, Based on the Study of Literary Models (Oxford University Press, 1913), p. 2.

55. Ibid., p. 16.

56. A.R. Moon, A Concise English Course (Longmans, 1937), p. 197.

57. Oliphant, A Matriculation and General English Course, p. 280.

58. Treble and Vallins, The Gateway to English, pt 4, p. 86.

59. Leach and Barnard, English for Present-Day Examinations, pp. 82-7.

60. Edmunds, Junior Course of English Composition, pp. 308-9.

61. Ibid., p. 298.

62. Low and Briggs, Matriculation English Course, pp. 308-9.

63. Greening Lamborn, The Rudiments of Criticism, p. 140.

64. Greening Lamborn, Expression in Speech and Writing, p. 28.

65. Ibid., p. 34.

66. Perse Playbooks, 5 nos. (Heffer, Cambridge, 1912-15).

67. R.T. Lewis, Composition through Story Writing - a Book for Adventurers (Harrap, 1927).

68. G.N. Pocock, The Master Pen, 3 bks (Dent, 1931).

69. J.W. Marriott, Matriculation English (Harrap, 1928), p. 63.

70. E.J. Kenny, An English Course for Secondary Schools (University of London Press, 1928), p. 118

71. S.P.B. Mais, An English Course for Schools (Grant Richards, 1919), p. 361.

72. Pocock, The Master Pen, bk 3, p. 99.

73. F.H. Pritchard, Training in Literary Appreciation - An Introduction to Criticism (Harrap, 1922), p. 13.

74. Bate, English Composition, ch. 20.

75. Oliphant, A Matriculation and General English Course, ch. 20.

76. Ogilvie and Albert, A Practical Course in Secondary English, pp. 287-340.

77. Shayer, The Teaching of English in Schools, p. 61.

78. Moon and McKay, A New English Course, p. 318.

79. F.H. Pritchard, Essentials of Modern English (Harrap, 1934), pp. 358-9.

80. Kenny, A New Course in English Composition, pp. 66-7.

81. F.H. Pritchard, Intermediate English Extracts and Exercises for Comparative Study and Training in Composition (Harrap, 1924), p. 5.

82. L. Oliphant, A Progressive English Course, 4 pts (Gregg Publishing Co., 1929).

83. Ibid., pt 1, pp. 105-9.

84. Greening Lamborn, The Rudiments of Criticism, p. 120.

85. A.M. Walmsley, A Modern English Course for Schools (University Tutorial Press, 1935), pp. 261-2.

86. Treble and Vallins, The Gateway to English, pt 3, p. 53.

87. Pritchard, Essentials of Modern English, p. 380.

88. Low and Briggs, Matriculation English Course, p. 325.

89. J.C. Nesfield, Matriculation English Course (Macmillan, 1914), p. 201.

90. Association of Assistant Masters, Memorandum on the Teaching of English, p. 19.

91. P.J. Hartog, The Writing of English, 2nd ed. (Clarendon Press, Oxford, 1908), p. 1.

92. J.H. Fowler, The Art of Teaching English (Macmillan, 1932), ch. 1.

93. Newbolt Report, pp. 44-5.

94. Sampson, English for the English, p. 104.

95. P.J. Hartog, The Writing of English, p. 1.

96. Ibid., p. 60.

97. Hammond, An Introduction to English Composition, pp. v-vi.

98. Mathieson, The Preachers of Culture, p. 79.

99. Association of Assistant Mistresses, Memorandum on the Teaching of English, p. 3.

100. Mathieson, The Preachers of Culture, pp. 135-6.

101. Shayer, The Teaching of English in Schools, p. 54.

Chapter Four

MODERN LANGUAGES: THE RETREAT FROM REFORM

WILLIAM ROWLINSON

1870 marks a watershed in Great Britain's relations
with the Continent of Europe. The Hanoverian monar-
chy, outward-looking to its continental relations,
was still securely on the throne, but the unification of the German states, the formation of a great
German empire under a thrusting, menacing chancellor
produced a change in the balance of power in Europe
that involved a gradual British withdrawal from its
German connections, culminating in the complete re-
nunciation of them at the First World War. The
entente cordiale, the alternative continental connection, was politically expedient but had no deep
emotional roots among the population at large. The
traumatic effect of the First World War at a personal level continued to motivate the drawing-back from
Europe through the twenties and early thirties. As
far as government was concerned, Great Britain may
have deplored American isolationism and supported
the League if only to continue to contain Germany;
at grass-roots level, with family breadwinners dead,
a generation decimated, swathes cut through the male
youth of village and town, there was a withdrawal
from Europe and a blinkered inward-lookingness. The
Second World War, when it came, was seen by many as
simple confirmation of the dangerous nature of the
foreigner.
    Or rather the European; for this was still the
Britain of the British Empire. Cracks there might be
in the structure, but for most this was where British greatness lay. A third of the world was red on
the map; it was to the Empire Britain turned for
supplies, troops, money in time of need: here in
contrast to Europe was where British responsibilities and commitment lay.(1)
    It is against this background that the lack of
progress, indeed perhaps a growing ineffectiveness,

in language teaching in our schools during the period we are dealing with needs to be seen: not caused
by it but interacting with it, the political disen-
gagement from Europe reinforcing the move away from
commitment to language learning for oral communication with the foreigner - who was in practice, in
secondary school terms, the Frenchman and the German.(2)

LANGUAGE AS DISCIPLINE

Foreign language learning as a 'respectable' discipline, with at the highest level a university chair
and concomitant research, and below that a central
role in the public or grammar school curriculum, was
a late developer. Though a Tripos in Medieval and
Modern Languages had been established at Cambridge
in 1886, this was very much medieval and philological rather than modern. No oral examination at all
was included until 1894, when an optional test of
pronunciation was offered. Only in 1909 was a test
of ability to converse in the foreign language made
part of the Tripos examination, and even this remained optional. Not until 1917 was there a move to
include civilisation and significant work within the
modern language in a reorganised Tripos. Oxford was
even slower off the mark: its Honours School in Modern Languages was only instituted in 1903, again
highly philological in content. In 1918 Cambridge,
Bristol and the four Scottish universities still had
no professor of French: Oliver Prior, Cambridge's
first French professor, was not appointed until the
early 1920s. Modern languages at this level desper-
ately needed to gain the respectability of a genuine
mental discipline. The model had to be the established teaching of the dead languages: language was
a sort of mental wrestling match that, successfully
completed, opened up a world of classical literature
and philosophy. Racine, Voltaire, Corneille,
Montesquieu were the ends, verb paradigms and subjunctive constructions the means. The university
view of language as a discipline triumphed with ease
over the radical view of language as communication.
The university-controlled School Certificate examinations set up in 1917 for the many, the prestigious
Open Scholarship papers of the Oxford and Cambridge
colleges for the few reflected a view of language
learning that was based on the study rather than the
market place.
    In this, however, it drew on a tradition with

respectable roots in the eighteenth century and much earlier. The great linguistic innovation of the eighteenth century was the search for generalis- ability of language structure. Language, like the rest of the natural world, must be susceptible to general rules. The study of grammar was the study of language structure, the determining of linguistic universals common to all languages. Translation was a central skill in language comparison, concerned as it was with these universals. The mentalist view of language learning, if not born at this time, was strongly reinforced then.(3) It should be traced back not simply to dusty nineteenth-century peda- gogues teaching form because they had no content to teach, but more importantly to the excitement of the scientific universalism of the Age of Reason. It is rooted in a far from dubious tradition, and drew strength from it.

EFFECTS OF EXPANSION

If, as we shall see, the period we are considering is characterised by stagnation or even decline in language-teaching effectiveness, judged by communi- cative standards, it is also a time of considerable expansion in the number of pupils receiving some sort of instruction in modern languages, which in 1870 were taught virtually entirely within the sphere of private education. It is important to re- member how small the whole secondary system was in the nineteenth century. The 1851 census estimated it at only 600,000 pupils, defined as those paying fees of 9d a week or more. Of these, a quarter were re- ceiving their education from private tutors or gov- ernesses; a further quarter were in public or gram- mar schools, and about half were in private schools of one kind or another.(4) The lack of foreign lan- guage teaching in such British secondary schools as existed was pointed out in Matthew Arnold's 1866 re- port to the Taunton Commission, on secondary educa- tion in France, Germany, Italy and Switzerland, which goes on largely and unequivocally to recommend that the 'elements' of 'the chief modern languages' be part of every boy's [sic] education.(5) The nine- teenth-century language-teaching norm was an uneasy reliance on earlier grammar-translation methods, leavened by expatriate teachers who offered some sort of value for money by presenting the native model and some approach to language for use. The revolutions of the nineteenth century, especially in

France, had provided the British secondary schools
with a steady supply of these indigent foreigners
happy to earn if not enthusiastic or competent to
teach. The better and more concerned of them formed
themselves into the Société nationale des professeurs de français en Angleterre, meeting annually
from 1882 on; the worst helped perpetuate the view
of the modern languages teacher as a comic incompetent. The tradition of the native language teacher
continued into the twentieth century, gradually
transformed into the foreign language assistant. As
early as 1908 grants were allowed under article 40
of the Secondary Regulations for 1907 to appoint
foreign language assistants to the staffs of secondary grammar schools; in 1909, 23 of them were approved under arrangements with France and Prussia.(6)
     But the foreign assistant and the vocational
use of a foreign language he or she represented were
by no means central to the teaching tradition. The
Report of the Royal Commission on Secondary Education (1895) says that 'the chief tongues of modern
Europe ought to be studied not only as instruments
of linguistic training, but as the keys to noble
literatures'.(7) Here is reflected the still common
view of modern languages at A-level as being about
grammatical exactitude, demonstrated by prose translation, together with literary appreciation shown
through essay writing in English. It is significant
that this report does not even consider that foreign
language as communication should be among the aims
of secondary education. Far from it indeed - it
stands firmly behind the Taunton Commission's report
of 27 years earlier which, whilst advocating the
teaching of French, or German, or both in secondary
schools, had gone out of its way to castigate teaching languages for communication and those (relatively few) schools it found doing that rather than
teaching sound grammar work in English: schools
where 'the French lesson is too frequently conducted
in the French language'. This report had recommended
more attention to grammar generally, for 'the sub-
tler parts of French grammar afford a very good discipline to the mind'.(8) It was to this tradition of
grammar and translation work in English, as we shall
see, that expanding twentieth-century modern language teaching turned to cope with its vastly increased numbers, both for its respectability - mental discipline plus the appreciation of a literature's classics - and its relative ease for teachers
with, themselves, only a limited grasp of the spoken
language.

THE ALTERNATIVE TRADITION: LANGUAGE AS COMMUNICATION

But it was not the only tradition. In Britain, as elsewhere in Europe, the growth of the direct method movement (more exactly, movements) was considerable at the end of the nineteenth century. As early as 1852 J.S. Blackie, Professor of Greek at Aberdeen and Edinburgh, was advocating - or rather, since these were basic pre-Cartesian methods, re-advocating - the avoidance of the mother tongue, the direct association of word with object and the relegation of grammar to a position of subordination. In the 1880s the distinguished French teacher, François Gouin, created a stir in Germany (where he was effectively Professor of French to the Berlin court) and later in England with his natural method.(9) He was translated into English in 1892. Gouin takes as his starting point the apparent speed and facility with which a child learns its own language and advocates in second-language learning a return to methods employed by the child in learning the mother tongue. Critics were quick to point out the fallacy of assuming that the adolescent or adult learning a foreign language has the same starting point as a child learning its mother tongue. More recently the sheer inefficiency of natural learning in terms of amount learned relative to actual exposure to the language has been emphasised. But Gouin made his impact because of a growing climate of opinion among aware modern language teachers and educators that applied grammar approaches were ineffective. In Germany, and for some time in England, the debate also centred on W. Viëtor's pamphlet <u>Der Sprachunterricht muss umkehren</u> with its stress on language for communication and the use of phonetics.(10) Phonetics generally, and the recently devised international phonetic alphabet, gave the movement under its various names (11) a scientific respectability whilst apparently providing a short-cut to speech by avoiding the time-consuming and often difficult learning and use of the written word. Otto Jespersen, Henry Sweet, the Bells and others had formed the International Phonetic Association in 1886, building on the work of Alexander Melville Bell and his son Alexander Graham Bell (he of the telephone) in establishing exact written correlatives to spoken sounds. It was A.M. Bell's <u>Visible Speech</u> (1867) that first showed the possibility of organising and recording the sound structure of a language in the way that the grammatical structure could already be analysed and recorded.

The period from 1870 onwards was, of course, as
may be seen elsewhere in this book, a period of
widespread dissatisfaction with the traditional curriculum, and although this tended to be reflected in
a growing demand for more natural science, influential academics like Professor Henry Sidgewick of
Cambridge were also advocating a greater stress on
the study of modern foreign languages.(12) The Taunton Report had also shown itself aware of the movement for a more vocational orientation towards modern languages and proposed, probably on the Prussian
model, that they should take a place in the curriculum of schools with a leaving age of 14 or 16.(13)
    It was against this background that a group of
modern language teachers in Britain concerned to
change the direction of language teaching came together in a national conference in 1890. Inspired by
Viëtor (who addressed the conference) they passed
resolutions supporting oral work, the direct method
and the use of phonetics, and with the impetus thus
generated founded two years later the Modern Languages Association. Influential teachers such as
MacGowan of Cheltenham, Widgery of University College School, Siepmann of Clifton found support from
dons of the calibre of Karl Breul of Cambridge
(whose dictionary remained indispensable for students of German until quite recent times) and the
Association, especially in its early years, did
something towards raising the status of modern languages, though the original stress on the utilitarian aspects of language teaching had to be diluted
in order to achieve this.
    But these teachers were swimming against the
stream in that the national consciousness was more
and more turning away from Europe. As Horn points
out, perhaps as a result of the Boer War and the
availability of cheap newspapers, it became increasingly popular from the last years of the century to
stress that children - even in the rural elementary
schools - were being trained for an imperial mission.(14) However, the reformist enthusiasts for the
teaching of European languages were buoyed by notable and influential publications in the burgeoning
field of applied linguistics. Henry Sweet's The
Practical Study of Languages was published in 1899
and was especially concerned to deny the 'universal
rule' ideas of Cartesian thought that ultimately
underlay the applied-grammar plus translation approach of the time. Precise listening is what is important to Sweet, the recording of what is heard now
being practical by means of the phonetic alphabet.

Only then comes imitation, and certainly not a formulation of language according to pre-learned rules.
The starting point is observed reality, not a mental
construct. Sweet, though Reader in Phonetics at Oxford, had only very limited success with his ideas
in Britain. This may have been, as Shaw points out
in his preface to Pygmalion, most of which concerns
Sweet, because of his uncompromising nature and personal irascibility. Certainly he was much better
known in Europe than in his own country.

Even more influential throughout Europe, and
also making a considerable impact on reformers in
Britain, was Otto Jespersen. Jespersen, Professor of
English at the University of Copenhagen, wrote many
books on language, the philosophy of grammar, phonetics and the teaching of English. He even invented
an artificial language, Novial. But he owed his pan-
European success to one book especially, Sprogunder-
visning.(15) Easy to read, full of common-sense observation, unpretentious, it helped spread the acceptance of the 'reform method' (one more name for
direct method) throughout Europe, leading to its
adoption as the sole method to be used in the
schools of France, Belgium and Germany. It assumes
communication as a principal end, looks to efficiency of means, above all points to the motivational
importance of reality of material (Jespersen has
great fun with sentences from a current textbook
like 'My aunt is my mother's friend', 'My dear
friend, you are speaking too rapidly', 'The boy has
drowned many dogs'). It suggests a range of highly
practical means to achieve its ends, most of them
quite acceptable to a modern secondary school teacher, who would in fact have not dissimilar aims. The
notable exception is Jespersen's uncritical view of
the possibilities opened up by the science of phonetics; this aside, his requirement of natural and
useful language material, his stress on careful listening as a first stage of the learning process, his
desire for direct association of word and object
where possible, his advocacy of the foreign language
as the principal classroom means of communication,
his view of grammar as descriptive of known language
rather than a set of prescriptive rules for language
construction - all these chime with a modern communicative view of language teaching. The reform movement had its broad effect in Europe: in England,
however, it coincided with the Morant expansion of
secondary education, a need for new language teachers and demands on existing teachers that frequently
could not be met. As modern languages moved towards

the centre of the secondary curriculum, ironically
its methods regressed to (or stagnated in) the easy
option, grammar-translation. Let us look at some of
the factors involved.

FRENCH: A PILLAR OF THE CURRICULUM

Modern languages as such were never at all central
to the secondary curriculum before the present century. Though French, the 'language of culture', and,
subsequently, of courts and diplomacy, had been
taught throughout Europe since the end of the thir-
teenth century as a foreign language, it was only in
the early seventeenth century that modern languages
became an acceptable part of the school curriculum,
and even then they were on its fringe. Fleury
(Traité du choix et de la méthode des études, Paris,
1686) nicely characterises classical languages as
études utiles, whereas modern languages are merely
études curieuses. The mother tongue is, of course,
an étude nécessaire.(16) The dominance of the classics, encouraged - indeed, demanded - by the ancient
universities, continued in the nineteenth century.
Sir Charles Lyell, speaking of a school he views as
typical to the Oxford University Commission of 1851,
points out that of the 80 boys in the school only
five are destined for Oxford. The head, an Oxford
graduate:

> models his plan of instruction for all the pu-
> pils in such a way as will tell best in prepar-
> ing these five favoured youths to cut a figure
> at the University ... The parents of the other
> 75 boys may wish for the introduction of the
> French and German languages ... but they must
> submit to being ruled by the standard set up at
> Oxford.(17)

The Reverend R.H. Quick, surveying the modern languages scene in 1875, finds even the more language-
conscious schools devoting at most only two hours
per week to modern language teaching.(18)
   But from the beginning of the twentieth century
the movement of foreign languages to the centre of
the curriculum gained impetus, in part from the
Board of Education. The Regulations for Secondary
Schools issued in 1904 as a result of the 1902 Act
define languages ('at least one language other than
English') as one of the four principal subject areas
of the secondary school curriculum (the others were

English plus history and geography, mathematics plus science and - surprisingly perhaps - drawing). A foreign language is to be compulsory with a minimum of three and a half hours teaching per week. If two languages are taught, six hours per week is allocated, though 'where two languages other than English are taken, and Latin is not one of them, the Board will require to be satisfied that the omission of Latin is for the advantage of the school'. The protection of the pre-eminent Latin has grown even stronger two years later:

> The Board attach so much importance to the inclusion of Latin where possible in the curricula of Secondary Schools that they have for some years past made it a rule that in all schools which take two languages other than English, Latin must be one of the two unless there is a clear educational advantage in its omission.(19)

Nonetheless, the other was generally French, and 'Languages' rather than 'Classics' was to be one of the four central pillars of the secondary curriculum. Below the secondary grammar school level the Board was prepared to concede even greater importance to modern languages. The higher elementary schools, regularised by a Board of Education Minute of 6 April 1900, and forerunners of the secondary modern schools, were required to include one foreign language in their curriculum - a daring and perhaps difficult innovation. It may have been because of the precise requirements for a broad curriculum with new subjects that so few higher elementary schools had been recognised (a mere 30 or so in England) by the time regulations governing them were withdrawn in 1919.

In this expansionist atmosphere the direct or reform method faced a numbers and resources problem. Teachers, many new to language teaching, themselves taught by grammar-translation methods and with small active vocabularies, poor accents, limited fluency, found teaching large classes in the foreign language beyond them.(20) The Board of Education investigated modern language teaching, and in Circular 797 of 1912 presented its not entirely complimentary opinion.(21)

1912 AND 1918: THE BOARD'S CONCERN

The Circular begins by pointing to the staffing

problems of the recent past:

> It had in fact in too many schools been common
> to assign a substantial part of the work to
> Masters who, quite apart from possible defects
> in their teaching methods, had not even a sat-
> isfactory knowledge of the language.(22)

The staffing problem was compounded by the fact that
in the past modern language masters often received a
lower salary than other members of staff. However,
the Circular goes on, 'the supply of properly trained and competent teachers, in Boys' Schools especially, is still seriously unequal to the demand'.(23)
Furthermore:

> Until the supply of well-qualified teachers is
> largely increased, much of the Modern Languages
> work, especially in Boys' Schools, will prob-
> ably continue to be taken by teachers who have
> not had the opportunity of acquiring any con-
> siderable degree of fluency in the foreign
> speech.(24)

The problem for these inadequate staff lay of course
in what the Circular calls 'the newer methods': 'In
many Schools which claim to have adopted the newer
methods, the staff is either unequal to the task or
insufficiently familiar with the conditions which
are essential to its effective performance.'(25)
Though it notes the success of a small but increasing number of teachers 'vivifying the whole study of
French and German' by their use of these new approaches it is less than entirely convinced of the
methods' efficacy. The Circular sees the aims of
modern language teaching in secondary schools as:
(a) understanding clearly enunciated French speech,
(b) using readily and correctly the spoken and written language, and (c) reading French prose and verse
and having a first-hand acquaintance with some of
the masterpieces of the literature. Within this
framework it criticises much direct method teaching
as 'too ready to condone grammatical inaccuracy',
'neglecting the literary aspect of Modern Language
work', involving a 'lamentable waste of time' in
refusing to use English explanation where French
proves incomprehensively difficult to the pupils,
'attempting to deal with more difficult foreign
texts without recourse to translation' and doing too
much for pupils and expecting too little from them.
What the Circular finds it difficult in practice to

reconcile within the limited curricular time available are the communicative and the literary aims it has set out. Whilst 'harm has been done by attempting to use in modern languages methods far more suitable for the classical authors', on the other hand, 'if the study of modern languages is to be placed in the same rank as that of the ancient languages, it must be based on the reading of authors comparable in importance, literary merit, and intrinsic interest' and 'something will have been lost if the pupils are not trained in the difficult art of rendering literary French and German into the best English that they can command'. Its recommended methodology consists of an oral start, with careful use of phonetics and systematic teaching of grammar, but 'after the necessary foundation has been laid, good literature should be the staple of class work' from the third year or in many cases earlier.(26) It was this attempt to reconcile the efficient teaching of the spoken language with the necessity to produce a 'respectable' literary course that presented an impossible task for all but the best pupils and the most effective teachers, and led to the compromise methods of the interwar years that frequently achieved no aim at all except the passing of the School Certificate examination.

The Board was not surprisingly equally concerned not to broaden (and thus dilute) modern language teaching still further by allowing it to move into the commercial field. Its Circular 826 of 1913, whilst accepting some vocational courses in secondary schools, specifically rules out work in modern languages principally concerned with their commercial use.(27) Five years later the 1918 Report on Modern Languages was to find 'business hampered by British ignorance of foreign languages' and castigated the 'abysmal' level of modern language competence in the armed services.(28)

The 1912 Circular may have fuelled concern with subject organisation and methods generally. From 1916 to 1919 the Board set up four committees to report on major subjects of the curriculum. The report of the Modern Languages Committee under Stanley Leathes was published in 1918.(29) It is worth considering this too in some detail, not least for the revealing picture of the status of modern languages in the secondary curriculum that it contains.

The modern sides of the public schools, it points out, were at the turn of the century viewed 'by both masters and boys as the refuge of the intellectually destitute'. 'Dealing with material [i.e. pupils] on the whole inferior, the [modern language] teachers were content with narrow ambitions.'(30) And of course this low status of modern languages was not recent. It had existed throughout the nineteenth century. The Clarendon Commission's Report of 1864 on the public schools quotes Harrow: 'the modern languages hold the lowest place in the estimation of masters' and Eton: 'it is a complete impossibility to teach French at Eton'.(31) Outside examinations continued to be based on the classics tradition - no orals, simply translation, composition and questions on grammar, together with literary questions answerable without the pupil ever having read the works in question. The low status and limited competence of the secondary teacher of languages had been somewhat improved in the last few years, the 1918 Report noted, but much remained to be done: the Committee looked with approval on the Scotch [sic] Education Department which since 1906 had required the modern language teachers in its secondary schools to have spent at least a year in the country whose language was being taught, in addition to having an honours degree in the subject. Sadly, the Committee saw no prospect of approaching this level in English secondary schools in the near future. At the university level the situation, in terms of qualified staff in post and subject status, was even worse. The Report speaks of a 'paralysing deficiency of university staff even in French and German', with many chairholders being professors in name only, paid at a lower rate than other professors.(32) Its enquiries found, in 1918, only fifteen professors of French, eleven of German and two of French plus German in all the British universities. In 1911-12 the colleges of Oxford and Cambridge had, out of a total of 440 scholarships, awarded just 8 in modern languages (the classical languages were awarded 205). In these circumstances the dearth of competent secondary school modern language teachers that the Report comments on is hardly surprising.(33) This lack of teaching expertise seems to lie at the heart of the growing failure of the direct method, where attempts had been made to put it into practice. 'The falling-off [in the linguistic standards of pupils applying to university] was attributed by our informants to misuse of the "Direct Method"; and this method misapplied or applied by incompetent teachers would lead to the results indicated.'(34)

The Committee remained nonetheless convinced of the efficacy of reform methods properly applied. It was firm in its championship of an oral approach:

'for the acquisition of sound knowledge of any foreign country a speaking knowledge of the language is
the first necessity',(35) gave a welcome, if cautious, to foreign trips and home-to-home exchanges,
stressed the importance of civilisation (the 'Modern
Studies' approach) and pointed to the current British ignorance of views, attitudes and way of life of
the French and the Germans (and still more of the
Italians and the Russians). It viewed with dismay
the inadequate dabbling in several languages it
found in many British secondary schools, looked to a
'thorough grounding' in one language as the norm for
most secondary pupils and firmly stated that where
pupils are to learn only one language, this should
be French.(36) Breathtakingly, it avers: 'French is
by far the most important language in the history of
modern civilisation.'(37) It is scarcely surprising
that, in 1918, German was not highly regarded
(though the Report did suggest that secondary German
should be maintained and indeed where possible extended); much more surprising is the firm anti-Latin
tone of the Report.(38) Latin and the classics generally were seen as squeezing modern languages from
the secondary curriculum, and providing with their
established example an unsuitable methodology for a
living language. The Report went so far as to recommend that Latin should no longer be compulsory for
university entrance, even for arts courses. It wished to see a serious study of one modern language as
a central part of the secondary curriculum, recommending a minimum of four hours per week for the
first two years of the language, together with two
or three hours of 'preparation' time. It wanted a
two-year gap between the start of the first and the
start of any second foreign language, and it was
willing to have the less linguistically gifted pupils in four-year secondary schools drop their language entirely after a trial period. Modern language
teachers should not have to cope with classes of
more than 20 to 25 pupils, nor should they teach
more than 20 hours a week. Like the other subject
reports, the Report on Modern Languages contains
more than a little special pleading for its subject.
    One of the effects of the four reports was to
move the curriculum away from general applicability
towards a choice of specialisms. In modern languages
this led the Board virtually to accept the Modern
Languages Report's recommendation with regard to
time allocation and to itself recommend five periods
of 45 minutes each per week as the norm for a single
foreign language.(39) The Hadow Report of 1926 and

the Spens Report of 1938 both went along with this allocation.(40)

LANGUAGES FOR GIRLS

Something of the continuing low status of modern languages was undoubtedly due to its still being seen as a girls' subject. French had been a central element in the limited curriculum of a 'good' girls' education since the eighteenth century, and though there was a move between 1850 and 1870 to assimilate the curriculum of girls' education more to that of boys, the curriculum of the girls' high schools at the end of the nineteenth century was distinctly arts-based. Manchester High School for Girls at this time typically had French, Latin and, for virtually all girls, German among its compulsory sixth-form subjects. The Board of Education Circular 826 of 1913 on the curriculum criticises the common inclusion of two foreign languages in girls' schools for girls whose secondary education may be limited to the years from 12 to 16, and the Consultative Committee's Report of 1923 on boys' and girls' curricula notes that more time in girls' schools is devoted to French, English and history and less to Latin, maths and natural sciences.(41) It finds, not surprisingly, that examination results reflect this.(42) This Report singles out modern languages as a girls' subject, suggesting that the girls' higher attainment, especially in oral work, is due partly to a tradition that requires women teachers to be specially qualified, partly to 'the better trained ear and greater mimetic ability which girls possess'.(43) At a time when girls' education was still seen as less important than boys', to be regarded primarily as a girls' option did not confer a high status on modern languages.

THE EXAMINATION CONSTRAINT

If subject status, together with expansion of teaching and staff, and attendant incompetencies, presented major problems, the establishment in 1917 of the new School Certificate and Higher School Certificate examinations created another. It was this that dominated the two interwar decades, affecting the scale of modern language teaching in the pre-School Certificate years of the secondary school and the content of what was taught at both this and,

especially, the higher level. The 1911 Report of the
Consultative Committee on Examinations in Secondary
Schools advocated the new examinations and the Report was one of a series of official expressions of
concern at the proliferation of external examinations that were coming to determine the school curriculum.(44) These originated with the London University Matriculation examination of 1838 and included the Oxford, Cambridge, Durham and NUJMB Local
examinations, the Royal Society of Arts examinations
and those of the City and Guilds of London Institute. Their variety inhibited any real reform across
the board: only a new, single, national examination
could initiate real changes, but the effects of this
new School Certificate examination were not entirely
foreseen. The Certificate demanded either Latin or a
modern language as one of its minimum pass requirements, and the interwar years saw a growth of French
especially, to the point where, by 1937, French had
become the second most popular subject in terms of
School Certificate entry numbers, with 73,367 entries, beaten only by English with 78,071. 92 per
cent of all entrants offered French. Only French
among the modern languages had made this headway:
German had a mere 12 per cent of entrants and ranked
twelfth in 'popularity'. The other languages were,
as usual, nowhere to be seen. The French growth had,
at this stage, been by no means entirely at the expense of Latin, which was still, in spite of the recommendations of the 1918 Report, a university entrance requirement. Latin continued to command 38
per cent of all entrants and came sixth in the popularity table.(45) By the outbreak of war in 1939
French (93 per cent) and German (13 per cent) had
made still more progress, Latin (35 per cent) had
slipped a little further.

In terms of syllabus content, the universities
were still dominant. The Certificates were their examinations, set with an eye both to their matriculation requirements and to the content of their
undergraduate courses. University modern languages
departments, fighting in a conservative milieu to
preserve (or, often, establish) their status vis à-
vis the classics, stressed the literary and mental-
discipline aspects of their subject. Prose translation, minute examination and exegesis of literature
were derived from the classics syllabus. Free written work in the foreign language was in a highly
abstract and philosophical register; the spoken word
still counted for next to nothing. All this was
reflected in what was examined in the Higher School

Certificate, and only to a somewhat lesser degree in
the School Certificate also.(46) And naturally
enough what was tested was taught, in French as in
many other subjects throughout the school, with a
constant eye on the examination. The Ritchie Committee's Report of 1928 found considerable and 'in the
main justified' teacher criticism of the School
Certificate: 'it reacts very strongly on the teaching of French in schools'.(47) The Hadow Report of
1926 had seen it as 'manifestly unsuited' to pupils
other than those in grammar schools and proposed a
new leaving examination 'of a character widely
divergent from that of the First School Examination'.(48) The Spens Report of 1938 was similarly
unequivocal in its condemnation of the examination:
'There can be little doubt that in many Secondary
schools the Certificate Examination is now the dominant factor in determining the curriculum for the
majority of pupils below the age of 16.'(49)

METHODS AND TEXTBOOKS

This combination of expansion and examination orientation confirmed the existing methodological conservatism of modern language teaching. This may not
be immediately clear from an examination of textbooks available: the interwar modern language textbook is a much more attractive work than its prewar
equivalent. The level from which it had improved,
however, was low. As far back as 1658 J.A. Comenius
had produced what was in effect an illustrated language workbook,(50) but by the mid-nineteenth century the average language textbook had become dull indeed. This was partly a result of publishing exigen-
cies. A single textbook in use throughout a class
(as opposed to each pupil having a different textbook, or none) only became general in the early
nineteenth century. It created a demand for multiple
copies of cheap editions; and the standard textbook
- any textbook - of course also favoured formal
grammatical methods rather than oral ones. The reformers were suspicious of all textbooks: 'Give your
pupils the books to read at home', counselled Lambert Sauveur, an American exponent of the direct
method, 'but forbid them to open it in class: their
ears alone must be occupied there.'(51) In the face
of available textbooks their hostility is entirely
understandable. Textbooks such as de Fivas's The New
Grammar of French Grammars (1840) or Ollendorf's
A New Method of Learning to Read, Write and Speak

the French Language in Six Months (1843) put lengthy
and abstruse grammar explanation first and followed
it with sentences for translation. Both these textbooks were still in print in the 1890s. Hugo's
German Simplified, a popular course at the end of
the nineteenth century, still follows this procedure, completing each lesson with 'Conversation
Practice' which consists merely of reading aloud
disjointed sentences.(52) Hossfield's New Practical
Method for Learning the German Language by Brenkmann, still in print in 1909, though apparently
first published some decades earlier, is even more
daunting. The opening section ('First Division, Elementary') begins with lists of hundreds of dis-
connected words for 'pronunciation practice', and
continues with page upon page of noun declensions
with interminable lists of exceptions. On reaching
'Conversation' we are offered translations of, among
other gems, 'Have you the aunt's watch?' and 'Yes,
(sir), I have the aunt's watch and fork.'(53)
     In comparison to this such interwar courses as
A.S. Macpherson's Deutsches Leben (1931) with its
integral line drawings and background illustrations,
H.F. Collins's A French Course for Schools (1929),
similarly illustrated and with a continuous French
presentation, or E. Saxelby's Cours de Français
(1936), strongly direct method in its approach, appear to represent tremendous progress. And it is
true that the average modern language teacher relied
heavily on the textbooks - what else was there? The
gramophone record, to a very limited extent: the use
of this as a classroom aid developed slowly after
the First World War,(54) and with more effectiveness
after the change to electric recording in 1926. But
it never became at all central to classroom teaching, and beyond the gramophone there was little -
perhaps the odd poster or flashcard,(55) a few real
objects, a blackboard. The textbook was central, but
even if he or she wished to, the textbook author
could not control the use made of it in the classroom. Textbooks between the wars might have phonetic
introductions or exercise instructions in French
(often incomprehensible to the pupil): the tacit assumption was that what occurred in the classroom after the first year's work was grammar teaching in
English plus exercise work largely based on translation.
     This is made very clear in the results of the
Inspectorate's enquiry, published in 1926, into
French teaching in 1,000 grant-aided secondary
schools.(56) The supply of teachers had improved

from the 'lamentably inadequate' position at the
start of the century, and French was 'no longer the
Cinderella of school subjects'. However, honours
graduates still only accounted for half the teachers
who were predominantly teaching modern languages,
and in some schools, 'including some of the largest
and most important grant-aided schools for boys,
progress is still seriously hampered by the inadequate proportion of teachers who possess any special qualifications in the language'.(57) The Memorandum is clear that it is lack of teacher competence that causes the common resort to old-fashioned
methods. 87 per cent of the schools surveyed had a
'mainly oral and direct' approach in their first
year; this, however, rapidly ceased 'in favour of
translational methods, sometimes associated with,
but often sharply dissociated from, a residual provision for oral work'.(58) That this was essential
because of the need to prepare for the School Certificate examination was not entirely accepted by
the Inspectors: the dropping of oral methods was
'often due to the fact that particular teachers of
middle Forms have relatively little mastery of the
spoken language'.(59) The clear implication is that
many teachers were not competent to continue to
teach in French beyond an elementary level: 'it
would be long indeed before the French staffs of the
majority of schools could be exclusively composed of
teachers possessing the very high qualifications
indisputably essential to its effective application'.(60) This methodological conservatism was undoubtedly reinforced by the trauma of the 1914-18
war in a generation of schoolchildren and their
teachers - a teaching force weakened at any rate on
the male side by the slaughter of the war years, and
working in a social climate that was inward-looking
and anti-European. Foreign language teaching during
this time only too easily turned for the content of
its subject to language as abstract logic.

RELATIVE REALISM: PALMER AND HADOW

As always, though, there were to be heard representatives of the view that language is communication. One of the most influential of these during
this period was Harold Palmer. Palmer, essentially a
teacher of English (most of his experience was in
the Far East), himself differentiated his own 'oral
method' from the direct method - 'The Direct Method
may be based on oral teaching (in which case the

course will probably be successful) or it may be
based on book-work and writing, with a minimum of
oral work (in which case it will probably yield poor
results).'(61) - but in fact for most people this
was a practical classroom version of the direct
method that attempted to systematise oral teaching.
In The Scientific Study and Teaching of Languages
(1917), The Principles of Language Study (1921) and
its pendant, The Oral Method of Teaching Languages
(1921), Palmer suggests strategies for teaching efficient oral communication whilst at the same time
attempting to formulate underlying principles rigorous enough to justify this as an overriding aim. He
was practical, consciously eclectic (he called this
'the multiple line of approach'), suspicious of
panaceas but with his eye firmly on the students'
needs rather than a philosophy of language learning.
'A programme of study depends on the aim or aims of
the students. All we can say in advance is that we
must endeavour to utilise the most appropriate means
to attain the desired end.'(62) Palmer believed
firmly in some things though: heavy exposure to the
language (he had his own students listen to the target language for three months before he would allow
them to use it);(63) the pattern drill, which,
though he did not invent it,(64) he systematised
into a whole way of teaching; the development of the
skill of silent reading; an organised movement within the language teaching strategy from (his terms)
'conventional conversation' to 'normal conversation'. All of these principles were variously adopted by the 'behaviourist' and 'mentalist' schools of
reaction to grammar-translation methods that flourished after the Second World War and many audio-
visual course compilers and textbook writers of the
postwar period acknowledged their debt to Palmer.
But in the interwar years he had only limited impact in encouraging teachers to, as he put it, 'venture off the beaten track of grammar, translation
and reading'.

The Hadow Report of 1926 endorses enthusiastically such a move off the beaten track. It proposes
a foreign language 'for all those who could benefit
from it', a single foreign language which, like history, geography and elementary mathematics 'should
be "practical" in the broadest sense, and directly
and obviously brought into relation with the facts
of everyday experience'.(65) It sets speaking and
understanding as the first objectives of modern language teaching, followed by reading, writing and the
exploration of literature; it suggests that

preliminary training should be mainly oral and rec-
ommends the use of songs and games, maps, advertise-
ments, periodicals, together with gramophone records
and lantern-slide lectures on aspects of everyday
life. 'French should be spoken during the lesson as
a rule, if not exclusively, by both teacher and pupil.'(66) We have come a long way from the Taunton
Commission's indictment of the use of the foreign
language in the classroom. But it should be remembered that Hadow was concerned with a new concept of
secondary education, secondary education for all,
and with the curriculum and methods suitable for its
proposed 'modern' schools rather than those in use
in the existing secondary grammar schools.

Hadow was acted on with more enthusiasm than
competence. His Majesty's Inspectors, reviewing the
position of French in modern schools in 1929,(67)
comment on 'the rapidity with which foreign languages are spreading in these schools: out of the
512 schools [teaching a foreign language] 128 had
begun the teaching of a foreign language since
1926',(68) but with very varying amounts of time
spent on the language and with 'work that varied
from very good indeed to very bad ... in a disap-
pointingly large number of the schools the teaching
of French was of such poor quality that it would
have been wiser to devote the time to some other
subject'.(69) The Inspectors castigate external examinations as having a harmful influence on the
teaching, especially in their stress on the written
word, but above all are concerned at the lack of
teacher competence, at schools attempting French 'in
which the first essential of success was lacking - a
teacher with the necessary knowledge of the French
language and of sound methods of language teaching'.(70)

THE SPENS REPORT: CHANGING ENDS, STAGNATING MEANS

It is not surprising, then, that in 1938 when Will
Spens and his committee considered modern languages
in the context of the existing secondary curriculum
they were not over-impressed. Nodding towards a
'quickened realisation of the way words express
thought', the Spens Report sees the most important
cultural values of modern language learning as 'the
enlargement of sympathy and interest' and goes on:
'in an age dominated by the spoken and written word
and a world in which distance is ceasing to count,
these qualities are of outstanding importance'. With

some understatement it adds:

> These cultural values may be obscured by bad
> methods of teaching or by the necessity of
> bringing pupils with little linguistic ability
> up to the standard of composition [i.e. written
> translation into the foreign language] required
> in the School Certificate Examination. But many
> boys and girls who will never write a prose in
> a modern foreign language can learn to read a
> book or newspaper in that language intelligent-
> ly and to understand and speak on simple top-
> ics, and may acquire some understanding of the
> people who use that language and of their con-
> tribution to civilisation.(71)

There is some fudging here, in that starting from
'an age dominated by the spoken and written word',
oral communication has slipped by the end of the
paragraph to the second of the three aims; however,
in 1938, with talkies only a decade old,(72) in the
early days of sound broadcasting and with television
unknown, Spens's committee was living in a world
much more dominated by the written word than that of
today. It is indeed surprising that they felt able
to go so far in the other direction. As Kandel wrote
in an appendix to the Report:

> In the case of modern languages opportunities
> for travel, the development of the wireless and
> the interchange of foreign films give new mean-
> ing to the desirability of training in ability
> to speak one or more of them, but for the ma-
> jority it still remains true that reading abil-
> ity should receive the first emphasis.(73)

Throughout the period we have been considering, the
written word was indeed the dominant means of serious communication, in the field of information and
in that of aesthetics. The relative ease with which
a change of emphasis in language teaching was accepted after the Second World War paralleled the
move away from the hegemony of the printed word in
public communication.

The Spens Committee were generous in their recommendations for the provision of languages in the
secondary curriculum. In the secondary grammar
schools Spens recommended the experience of at least
one foreign language for all pupils, with one forty-
five minute period a day in the first year.(74) In
the second year a second modern language (or Latin)

should be on offer, whilst those pupils 'with no
signs of an aptitude for languages' should be allowed to drop them entirely. Spens also suggests, somewhat outside the committee's brief, that a foreign
language should also be provided, 'for suitable pupils', in the modern schools, echoing and strengthening the Hadow Report's recommendation.(75) It is
interesting that whilst, as we have seen earlier,
deploring the dead hand of the universities on the
school curriculum, the Spens Committee breaches its
own principle of a common curriculum to age 13½ by
recommending the introduction of a second foreign
language option in the second year, because otherwise pupils will be 'seriously handicapped by a
later start in a second language if they intend to
proceed to a University'!(76)

Thus at the beginning of the Second World War
we have large numbers of grammar school pupils seriously learning French (nearly all of these, in
fact, though few taking any modern foreign language
other than French), and increasing numbers of modern
school pupils attempting some French in a rather
haphazard way. The grammar school pupils especially
are being taught largely in a formal, unpractical
way with their eyes carefully fixed on university-
oriented examinations, by teachers themselves the
products of the same system and indifferently qualified to cope with any other aims or methodology. The
Second World War and the postwar period with its
staff upheavals, linguistic demands, technological
breakthroughs and secondary reorganisation was in
the space of forty years to effect changes in aims
and methods far greater than any in the period we
have been considering, though blooming from seeds
sown at that time. The established view of language
learning and teaching was to be shattered. Nous
avons changé tout cela! Well ... perhaps not quite;
but that is another story.

NOTES AND REFERENCES

    1.   Report of the Committee Appointed by the
Prime Minister to Enquire into the Position of Modern Languages in the Educational System of Great
Britain (hereinafter Report on Modern Languages),
(HMSO, 1918), p.56, considering which language to
teach, revealingly claims: 'This country, above all
others, should be the home of learning for all the
chief and almost all the minor non-European languages.'

2.   Though the Modern Languages Association
set up subcommittees for Russian and Spanish in 1917
and 1931, they had a negligible impact in terms of
numbers studying the subjects in schools. Deplore it
as we may 'modern languages' in British schools was,
and is, predominantly French with a little German.
3.   See N. Chomsky, Cartesian Linguistics
(Harper and Row, New York, 1966).
4.   See D. Wardle, English Popular Education
1780-1975 (Cambridge University Press, 1976),
pp. 118 ff.
5.   Schools Inquiry Commission, (Taunton
Report) Vol. 6: General Reports of Assistant
Commissioners (HMSO, 1868), p. 599. That Arnold did
not here consider girls is not surprising. Languages
for girls had a different, more decorative function:
they represented a social accomplishment comparable
to music and dancing. And as we shall see, this view
of languages as a frill would continue to affect
their status long after girls' schools, especially,
had begun to take them seriously and teach them effectively.
6.   Board of Education, Report of the Board of
Education for the Year 1908-1909 (HMSO, 1910),
pp. 129-30.
7.   Royal Commission on Secondary Education,
(Bryce Report) Vol. 1: Report of the Commissioners
(HMSO, 1895), p. 284.
8.   Schools Inquiry Commission, (Taunton
Report) Vol. 1: Report of the Commissioners (HMSO,
1868), p. 27.
9.   F. Gouin, L'art d'enseigner et d'étudier
les langues (Paris, 1880), translated as The Art of
Teaching and Studying Languages (Philip and Son,
1892).
10.   'Language teaching must reverse its direction' (Heilbronn, 1886).
11.   E. Hawkins in an addendum to his Modern
Languages in the Curriculum (Cambridge University
Press, 1981) lists no fewer than 19 alternative
names used for the direct (etc.) method.
12.   See his article in F.W. Farrar (ed.),
Essays on a Liberal Education (Macmillan, 1867).
13.   Not entirely positive, this, since they
were to be simultaneously excluded, in favour of the
classics, from the curriculum of the full
university-preparatory secondary schools.
14.   P. Horn, Education in Rural England 1800-
1914 (Gill and Macmillan, Dublin, 1978), p. 253.
15.   Translated into English as How to Teach a
Foreign Language (Allen and Unwin, 1904).

16. Quoted in L.G. Kelly, 25 Centuries of Language Teaching (Newbury House, Rowley, Mass., 1969), p. 381.

17. Quoted in Board of Education, Report of the Consultative Committee on Secondary Education with Special Reference to Grammar Schools and Technical High Schools (hereinafter Spens Report), (HMSO, 1938), p. 29.

18. R.H. Quick, 'The First Stage in Teaching a Foreign Language with Some Account of Celebrated Methods' in American Journal of Education, vol. 26 (1875), pp. 537 ff.

19. Board of Education, Report of the Board of Education for the Year 1906-1907 (HMSO, 1908), p. 68.

20. It is interesting to recall that the last experience of oral and direct method language teaching at the end of the seventeenth century had been with quite small classes.

21. Board of Education, Memoranda on Teaching and Organisation in Secondary Schools: Modern Languages, Circular 797 (HMSO, 1912). This Circular was reissued unchanged after the war, in 1925.

22. Ibid., p. 4.

23. Ibid., p. 6.

24. Ibid., p. 15.

25. Ibid., p. 17.

26. Ibid., pp. 21-3.

27. Board of Education, Memoranda on Teaching and Organisation in Secondary Schools: Curricula of Secondary Schools, Circular 826 (HMSO, 1913).

28. Report on Modern Languages, p. 11.

29. Ibid. The Science Committee also reported in 1918, those on Classics and English in 1921.

30. Ibid., pp. 4-5.

31. Indeed the only French master at Eton is reported as describing himself as 'a mere objet de luxe': Report of Her Majesty's Commissioners Appointed to Inquire into the Revenues and Management of Certain Colleges and Schools, and the Studies Pursued and Instruction Given Therein (Clarendon Report), Vol. 1 (HMSO, 1864), p. 84.

32. Report on Modern Languages, p. 43.

33. Ibid., p. 52.

34. Ibid., p. 55.

35. Ibid., p. 11.

36. Ibid., p. 28.

37. Ibid., p. 19.

38. It is revealing to compare its attitudes with those of the Norwood Report: Board of Education, Curriculum and Examinations in Secondary Schools (HMSO, 1943), produced at a comparable point

in the Second World War. Strongly in favour of French <u>and</u> German, 'at every turn French and German thought and language confront the educated reader and the intelligent citizen' (p. 118), the Norwood Committee feels the need to be concerned with and highly defensive about the position of Latin, both in general, in the chapter on the place and teaching of classics (pp. 119-22), and specifically in relation to French: 'We would suggest, too, that Latin might be the first language more often than is at present the practice' (p. 118).

39. Board of Education, <u>Curricula of Secondary Schools in England</u>, Circular 1294 (HMSO, 1922). See also Board of Education, <u>Report of the Board of Education for the Year 1921-22</u> (HMSO, 1923).

40. It is interesting to compare this with the currently common pre-16 plus allocation of two periods of 70 minutes per week, less than two-thirds that amount.

41. Board of Education, <u>Report of the Consultative Committee on Differentiation of the Curriculum for Boys and Girls Respectively in Secondary Schools</u> (HMSO, 1923), p. 100.

42. Ibid., p. 101.

43. Ibid., p. 102.

44. Board of Education, <u>Report of the Consultative Committee on Examinations in Secondary Schools</u> (HMSO, 1911).

45. Board of Education, <u>Report: Education in 1937</u> (HMSO, 1938).

46. Even at this level the oral examination was optional and candidates had to pay an extra fee in order to sit it.

47. Board of Education, <u>Report on the Position of French in the First School Certificate Examinations (Midsummer, 1928)</u>, Educational Pamphlet No. 70 (HMSO, 1929).

48. Board of Education, <u>The Education of the Adolescent</u> (hereinafter <u>Hadow Report</u>), (HMSO, 1927), p. 87.

49. <u>Spens Report</u>.

50. J.A. Comenius, <u>Orbis sensualium pictus</u> (Leutschoviae, 1658).

51. L. Sauveur, <u>Introduction to the Teaching of Living Languages without Grammar or Dictionary</u> (Schoenhof and Moeller, Boston, Mass., 1874).

52. The first nine such sentences from Lesson 1 read: 1. Wo war es? 2. Wer war hier? 3. Ist sie nicht oben? 4. Nein, sie ist unten. 5. Es war nicht dort. 6. Wo ist es? 7. Wer ist hier? 8. Sie war nicht dort. 9. Wo waren sie gestern?

53.   C. Brenkmann, Hossfield's New Practical Method for Learning the German Language (Hirschfeld Bros., 1909), p. 22.

54.   Linguaphone, for example, began publishing their record courses in the early 1920s.

55.   Flashcards in language teaching were attracting articles in the journals as early as 1916: e.g. A.F. Gianella, 'The Use of Flashcards for Drill in French', Modern Languages, vol. 1 (1916), pp. 96-9.

56.   Board of Education, A Memorandum on the Position of French in Grant-aided Secondary Schools in England, Educational Pamphlet No. 47 (HMSO, 1926).

57.   Ibid., p. 19.

58.   Ibid., p. 28.

59.   Ibid., p. 29.

60.   Ibid., p. 28.

61.   H.E. Palmer, The Oral Method of Teaching Languages (Heffer, Cambridge, 1921), p. vi.

62.   H.E. Palmer, The Principles of Language Study (Harrap, 1921), p. 113.

63.   Kelly, 25 Centuries, p. 62.

64.   That distinction probably belongs to Thomas Prendergast in the 1870s.

65.   Hadow Report, p. 88.

66.   Ibid., p. 214.

67.   Board of Education, Memorandum on the Teaching of Foreign Languages in Certain Types of Schools, Educational Pamphlet No. 82 (HMSO, 1930).

68.   Ibid., p. 7.

69.   Ibid., p. 13.

70.   Ibid., p. 20.

71.   Spens Report, pp. 175-6.

72.   The Jazz Singer was released in 1927.

73.   Spens Report, appendix 3, p. 426.

74.   Ibid., p. 175.

75.   Ibid., p. 182.

76.   Ibid., p. 182.

Chapter Five

THE PERRY MOVEMENT IN SCHOOL MATHEMATICS

MICHAEL PRICE

> [John Perry (1850-1920)] will go down to fame
> as an original and constructive teacher who
> laid the foundation of a new era. He made math-
> ematical teaching practical ... (1)

A major 'crisis' in school mathematics in the early
years of this century became associated principally
with the name of one man: John Perry. By training an
engineer and by inclination an educational reformer
with wide ambitions, he lent his name to the most
significant 'movement' in the history of mathematical education in England prior to the 1960s. As one
appraisal of 'reformed mathematical teaching' by the
1920s put it, 'Professor Perry ... took so prominent a part ... that the reforms, both in geometry
and in other branches of mathematics, are known here
and abroad as the Perry Movement.'(2) What is more,
Perry's inspiration was international in its range,
the movement becoming known as 'Perryismus' on the
Continent (3) and the 'Laboratory Method' in America.(4)
    In the field of curriculum history, the notions
of major crisis and movement in a school subject are
of particular interest. The fact that contemporary
accounts of early-twentieth-century developments in
English school mathematics link such notions with
the name of one particular individual is perhaps
remarkable. Detailed evidence of curricular activity
in this period reveals at least twenty individuals
who made significant contributions to the reform of
school mathematics.(5) However, the Perry movement
involved much more than the activities of one individual, and it is the background, ideology, development and evaluation of this movement which is the
principal concern of this chapter.(6) Much of the
discussion will centre upon Perry himself, though

the possibility of resulting distortion in curriculum historiography is admitted at the outset. Thus,
for example, the opening quotation from the obituary
by Armstrong, taken literally, is historically dubious regarding the contribution of a single individual to major reform in mathematical education.
Nevertheless, it will be argued that the association
of Perry with a 'new era' and with the complex notion of 'practical' mathematics is a fitting one,
which will be central to the analysis of the Perry
movement. The movement's main thrust in relation to
school mathematics can be traced to around 1900, but
Perry's early career and his pioneering work in the
field of technical education are important aspects
of the nineteenth-century background to later, more
general, developments.

MATHEMATICS FOR ENGINEERS

Perry attended classes at the Model School, Belfast,
before taking up a foundry apprenticeship and attending engineering classes at Queen's College, Belfast, where he graduated as Bachelor of Engineering
in 1870. Perry's early workshop experience was an
important moulding feature of his career and he 'attached great importance in his later life to the
fact that his theoretical and practical instruction
thus went on hand in hand'.(7) Perry commenced his
teaching career by accepting a post as second mathematical master and lecturer in physics at Clifton
College (founded in 1862), one of the new propri-
etary schools which took science teaching seriously.
In 1871, at the suggestion of the Headmaster, Dr
Percival, he established a physical laboratory and
engineering workshop, and implemented a novel scheme
of quantitative and mechanical experiments.(8) However, the evidence does not suggest that the mathematics teaching at the College was in any way innovatory at this time. More general initiatives were
beginning to emerge in relation to school geometry,
which was strictly based on editions of Euclid, but
major progress here was not achieved until thirty
years later.(9) In relation to the education of engineers, Perry's move to Japan in 1875 was an important one.
        In Japan, Perry became closely associated with
William Ayrton (1847-1908), particularly in the exciting new field of electrical engineering and in
the education of engineers at Tokyo. Here, Perry and
Ayrton developed the use of graphical methods by

technical students, including the plotting of curves on squared paper.(10) They returned to England in 1879 and, together with Armstrong, they put their Japanese experience to good use in the pioneering development of technical curricula in England at what became Finsbury Technical College.(11) Perry was appointed there as Professor of Mechanical Engineering in 1882. Armstrong subsequently referred to the trio as the 'Finsbury Mohicans', and it was at Finsbury that Perry developed a scheme of 'practical mathematics' which was subsequently to enjoy enormous popularity in technical institutions, which were strongly influenced by the Department of Science and Art, and the Board of Education from 1899.

The emergence of an alternative paradigm for mathematics in relation to the developing needs of engineering and technical education is of great significance. What was required was a much wider and more applicable mathematics curriculum than the conventional 'academic' routine, and one which fully exploited experimental, numerical and graphical methods. This entailed swift progress to provide a working knowledge of a wide range of useful topics in mathematics, as opposed to the laborious academic treatment of the various branches of arithmetic, algebra, etc., following rigorous, pure mathematical lines, with utility neglected. The Department of Science and Art offered an alternative to Euclid from 1859, namely practical plane and solid geometry, which was essentially geometrical drawing, but the Department's pure mathematics, from 1864, followed conventional academic lines in arithmetic, algebra and Euclid. With the burgeoning of technical education, and the growing demand for post-elementary forms of education, the influence of the Department grew rapidly in the late nineteenth century.(12) Significantly, a new subject and syllabus, 'practical mathematics', was first offered by the Department in 1899, in the same year as an Act was passed transferring the Department's operations to the newly created Board of Education. By this time, Perry had left Finsbury to become Professor of Mathematics and Mechanics at the Royal College of Science, South Kensington, from 1896. The publication of new textbooks, based on the Finsbury experience, was another significant development.

In the case of mechanics, a textbook by Perry, Practical Mechanics, was published as early as 1881 and, sixteen years later, this was superseded by his Applied Mechanics. Calculus also warranted a radical new treatment, and Perry's The Calculus for

Engineers was published in 1897. His introductory
lectures on practical mathematics were first published by the Department of Science and Art in 1899.
(13) The American mathematician E.H. Moore subsequently referred to the 'grievous' separation between pure and applicable mathematics in relation to
textbook production and Perry's initiative in particular.(14) In relation to school mathematics generally, it was the progress of the scheme of practical mathematics which brought with it various developments of much wider consequence.

As Perry himself remarked, the subject of practical mathematics was 'exceedingly different from
what used to be the study of the mere mathematician
on the same subjects'.(15) Perry's cutting reference
to 'mere' mathematicians signifies a conflict between the practical users of mathematics and the
higher-status academic mathematicians of Cambridge.
In detail, the elementary stage of practical mathematics as an examination subject was innovatory in
a number of respects when compared with the traditional treatment of the elementary branches of mathematics. In arithmetic, emphasis was placed on decimals rather than fractions, including approxima-
tions, and the use of both logarithmic tables and
slide rules. In algebra, the use of formulae featured prominently, as well as the study of functions
and graphs, using squared paper, and leading to some
early ideas in the calculus. The deductive ideals of
a liberal geometry, based on Euclid, were largely
ignored and replaced by a treatment based on measurement and drawing mixed with arithmetic and alge-
braic methods. Furthermore, the scheme encroached on
some of the traditionally advanced branches of mathematics by including some work in simple trigonometry, three-dimensional geometry and vector methods,
as well as calculus. Overall, the scheme was notable
for its breadth of subject-matter and its mixing of
hitherto separately treated branches of the subject,
as well as for its distinctive methodology.(16) The
success of this subject under the new Board of Education's regulations for further education was quite
extraordinary over the first decade of this century,
and was at the expense of the older-established
stages of pure mathematics developed by the Department of Science and Art.

The Board of Education reported that in 1899
there were only 212 papers worked in the new subject, compared with around 12,500 for practical geometry and 24,000 for pure mathematics.(17) However,
by 1903 a correspondent in the journal Engineering

could refer to 'enormous' progress, and added, 'How else describe the effect at one college in these islands, at which preparation was made for ten or a dozen students in the new mathematics, and to which several hundreds came?'(18) Dissemination was rapid, and in 1909 the new subject was taken by around 6,500 candidates, with around 6,000 for pure mathematics and 3,500 for geometry. The numbers actually attending evening vocational classes in these subjects would have been at least two or three times greater.(19) By 1913, Perry could boast that there were more students of science engaged in practical mathematics than in any other subject, and also that it was more popular with students than pure mathematics, taking the attendance levels through the year as an indicator.(20)

Paralleling the rapidly growing success of this new examination subject, various writers provided suitable new textbooks which followed Perry's lead and reflected his influence.(21) Perry himself acted as an examiner for the Board of Education and also contributed to the Board's provision of courses at South Kensington, which were intended for further education teachers seeking to advance their mathematical competence and teaching methods in the new subject.(22) In summary, Perry's towering personal contribution to curriculum development in this field was accorded the following contemporary tribute:

> It is probably correct to say that nobody has done more to influence the teaching of Mathematics in this country during the last 15 or 20 years than Professor Perry; and in no branch of the work has he brought about greater changes than in the teaching of Mathematics to technical students. Until the introduction of his 'Practical Mathematics', the mathematical teaching of students in Technical Institutions followed, for the most part, the ordinary conventional academic routine ... But all this was changed by the introduction of Professor Perry's 'Practical Mathematics' ... (23)

However, it is important to emphasise the limited scope of the achievements described thus far, in relation to the development of mathematics in education generally.

Technical instruction came to be very widely interpreted after the Acts of 1888-90, and it expanded rapidly in various forms over the last two decades of the nineteenth century, as did the scope

of the influence of the examinations of the Department of Science and Art, which were utilised by
higher elementary schools, grammar schools, pupil-
teacher centres and training colleges, all of which
profited from the system of payment by results.(24)
Significantly, social-class divisions and the association of the Department with the industrial and
working classes meant that the influential public
schools remained antipathetic to and uninfluenced by
its work.(25) The concept of a 'secondary' education
was itself problematic in the 1890s, but the creation of the new Board of Education and subsequent
administrative policy served to sharpen the distinc-
tions between elementary, secondary and technical
education, aligning secondary education with a 'liberal' education along public-school lines, and lim-
iting the influence of the Board's examinations in
science and art to strictly vocational and predominantly part-time evening education.(26) It was the
examinations of the Universities of Oxford, Cambridge and London which exerted the dominant curricular influence on the developing system of secondary schools in the early years of the twentieth
century.(27) The traditional branches of arithmetic,
algebra and Euclid's geometry were the staple ingre-
dients for mathematics in these university examinations for non-specialists, with some differentiation
in the scope of the work examined depending upon
both age and sex. For example, mathematics might involve no more than arithmetic in the case of girls
particularly.(28) The nineteenth-century treatment
of these branches for university examination purposes was strictly 'academic' and in sharp contrast
to the new demands of practical mathematics. But the
scope of the direct influence of practical mathematics as an examination subject was limited by the
general administrative policy and ideological assumptions of a central authority which was also determined not to continue to act as an examining body
for the work of secondary schools under its various
regulations, following the Education Act of 1902.(29)
However, the Perry movement's espousal of practical
mathematics involved much more than examination syllabus reform in mathematics for technical students.
The movement developed and popularised a distinctive
pedagogy for mathematics in the education of <u>all</u>
pupils and students. This pedagogy had associations
with other educational developments during the late
nineteenth century, particularly the kindergarten
movement, the development of manual training and
workshops, and the growth of science teaching with

laboratory work. These roots as well as the association of the movement with technical education and
the working classes are important for understanding
the character and consequences of the major debates
and conflicts concerning secondary school mathematics which loomed large from around 1900. In particular, various connotations of the adjective 'practical' in relation to mathematics emerged and will
need to be considered.

PEDAGOGICAL DEVELOPMENTS

The early pioneering work at Finsbury Technical College placed much emphasis on empirical activity by
the students themselves, with generous provision
made for practical activity in the workshop and
laboratory.(30) Put simply this was the pedagogy of
'learning by doing', the spirit of which was shared
by the kindergarten movement which thrived in the
late nineteenth century and was inspired in particular by the writings of Pestalozzi and Froebel. The
emphasis at Finsbury was part of a much wider and
growing concern for the development of 'practical
education' in various forms, and the protagonists
here exploited the links with infant education and
its championship of the values of self-activity and
sense training.(31) As Richard Wormell (1838-1914),
Headmaster of the Cowper Street School, Finsbury,
pointed out:

> although the educational methods which are
> associated with the name of Froebel have been
> brought very near to perfection in the Kinder-
> garten, they are to a great extent suspended
> when the pupil passes from the Infant School.
> They reappear, however, in the schools and
> colleges devoted to Technical and Experimental
> Science ... It is very desirable that we should
> bridge over the gap ... (32)

In particular, the intrinsic value of workshop and
laboratory methods was justified in terms of 'hand
and eye' training, heurism and motivation:

> The charm of these methods will always be, as
> in the Kindergarten, inherent in their nature.
> They give something to be done by the hand and
> followed by the eye, keeping pace with the
> course of thought and reasoning ... the pupil
> ... is constantly on a voyage of discovery, and

has all the pleasure and stimulus of an original investigation.(33)

Perry himself pointed to the kindergarten's inspiration: 'I feel so strongly about the necessity for
experimental or kindergarten methods of education
being adopted';(34) and he argued that 'a good
teacher will educate the hands and eyes of his pupils'.(35) More generally, the Perry movement in
mathematics drew strength from the wider cause for
practical education, which embraced the promotion of
newer school subjects such as drawing, manual training, science and nature study, as well as a
kindergarten-inspired and less 'bookish' pedagogy.(36) The components of this pedagogy were well
summarised by J.J. Findlay (1860-1940), who spoke to
the College of Preceptors, at a time of 'impending
reforms' in school mathematics:

> Mathematical knowledge, like all other knowl-
> edge, has its foundation in the senses; ab-
> stract thought must be based on concrete ex-
> perience, and in the immature mind must con-
> stantly revert to concrete experience as an aid
> to abstraction ...
> Self-activity. - By 'using' squared paper, by
> measuring, by plotting curves, etc.
> Intuition. - Many mathemathical [sic] truths
> can be apprehended and rationally employed long
> before they can be reduced to formal expression
> in a system of philosophic thought.(37)

As Findlay was quick to point out, 'We are not concerned with some new patent process, to be labelled
the Perry Method. Heaven forbid!'(38) What was new
around 1900 was the application of such principles
in the growing debates concerning school mathematics, and geometry in particular. Findlay also referred to the principle of 'correlation', with particular reference to mathematics and science teaching.
This aspect of pedagogy was a relatively recent concern at the time and it warrants closer scrutiny.
   The links with science education were important
for the reform movement in school mathematics in relation to the debates and developments concerning
both the content of the curriculum and methods of
teaching. In the latter case it is significant that
a German survey of English reforms contrasted as opposites the traditional euklidische Methode with the
newer praktisch-heuristische Methode, which was associated with Perry and Armstrong in particular.(39)

The Perry Movement in School Mathematics

Heurism as a method of teaching science is normally
associated with Armstrong, 'the champion of the
heuristic approach'.(40) By 1902, Findlay could
refer to the 'Armstrong method' as one of a number
of competing pedagogical panaceas which, as he amus-
ingly added, some ignorant teachers 'confound with a
novel device in corporal punishment!'(41) What is
important for mathematics teaching is that elements
of heurism could be transferred from the science
laboratory to the mathematics classroom, particularly in the cases of mensuration and geometry. Such
possibilities were actively pursued in some class-
rooms and exploited in the rhetoric by agitators
such as Armstrong, Perry, Wormell, Findlay and others.(42) For example, W.D. Eggar (1865-1945), a
physics and mathematics teacher at Eton College, acknowledged in his preface to one of the new practical geometry textbooks that:

> This book is an attempt to adapt the experi-
> mental method to the teaching of Geometry in
> schools. The main object of this method, some-
> times called 'heuristic', is to make the stu-
> dent think for himself, to give him something
> to do with his hands for which the brain must
> be called in as a fellow-worker. The plan has
> been tried with success in the laboratory, and
> it seems to be equally well-suited to the Math-
> ematical class-room.(43)

But the links between mathematics and science were
not only related to Armstrong's heurism. More generally, the cause of mathematical reform was furthered
by the growth of school science teaching and the
pressing demands for closer correlation with the
mathematics curriculum.
     Findlay referred to correlation as well as
'self-activity' as 'the stock in trade ... of every
lecturer on education', and in the case of mathematics and science he commented:

> This whole movement is the outcome of the de-
> sire to rank mathematics in its place as the
> handmaid of science ... in close correlation
> with the needs of the science syllabus right
> through the school.(44)

The roots of laboratory work in school physics go
back to at least the 1870s. For example, in 1875,
soon after Perry's departure from Clifton College,
A.M. Worthington developed at the same school a

course of practical work in elementary mensuration
and hydrostatics, which subsequently became adopted
as a standard introduction to practical physics:
'elementary physical measurements', as it became
known.(45) With the support of Armstrong and others,
and through the efforts of the Department of Science
and Art, such an introductory course became widely
disseminated particularly in those elementary and
secondary schools which accepted grants from the
Department up to the turn of the century.(46) These
developments were part of a wider movement towards
more 'modern' curricula, with a growing emphasis on
scientific and technical subjects, in response to
shifting vocational and parental demands, as well as
the pressure exerted by the scientific community,
notably through the British Association for the
Advancement of Science, the lobbying of the practical educationists, and the workings of the Technical
Instruction Act of 1889.(47) These developments held
important implications for the older public and endowed schools, and for the character of their mathematics in particular.

The classical tradition and classical headmasters, who were generally antipathetic to the newer educational climate, continued to exert a strong
hold within the public school sector.(48) However,
the looming crisis for mathematics teaching was well
captured by Professor G.H. Bryan (1864-1928):

> Formerly our schools and colleges were given
> over mainly to the study of classical and lit-
> erary subjects, and mathematics was looked upon
> as a portion of an arts course. The rigid de-
> ductive system was undoubtedly admirably suited
> to the object then held in view. With the de-
> velopment of experimental science new teachers
> have been appointed all over the country for
> physics, chemistry and biology, but next to no-
> thing has been done to meet the greatly in-
> creased demand for mathematical teaching thus
> produced [Bryan's stress]. The same teachers
> who provided efficiently for the teaching of
> mathematics on the classical side have now
> thrust upon them an influx of new pupils having
> quite different requirements. The mathematical
> master is thus placed in the position of a
> 'tweeny-maid' or 'buffer' between opposing
> forces - the classical side and the modern
> side, and between these two stools it will be a
> great credit to him if he does not fall to the
> ground.(49)

Thus correlation with science emerged as yet another important aspect of the Perry movement's pedagogical underpinning.

The importance for major change of the various developments in the pedagogical climate, which have already been discussed, was strongly emphasised by one commentator from the College of Preceptors, who remarked:

> the change was inevitable ... When teachers began to teach science - as well as other subjects - scientifically and with more due regard to the pupils' share in education, when the demands of the laboratory and the workshop, of technical schools and colleges, made themselves felt, reform was bound to come in the teaching of mathematics, as of logic and languages and other subjects. It is part of a general movement.(50)

In all this a wider political and economic concern for Britain's industrial and commercial well-being, particularly in relation to foreign competition, was also exploited in the exhortations of Perry and others, who pointed to the backward state of school mathematics, based on outmoded classical ideals supported by the doctrine of mental discipline, as partly to blame for Britain's alleged decline.(51) This kind of attack is well exemplified by the following interpretation of Perry's thinking in the journal Engineer:

> we in England have quite suddenly become convinced that we are really getting old, and that we must wake up from a 'Rip Van Winkle' slumber in order to avoid Chinese decrepitude and rottenness. Professor John Perry's gallant crusade against orthodox mathematical method is one of the signs of these times ... In England almost alone has there been solid refusal to budge with the times on the part of University mathematical examiners and public school head masters. They have stuck to the literal inspiration of their Euclid, and by their influential stolidity have retarded for more than a full generation the intellectual development of the British race.(52)

The range of curricular exhortation which inspired the Perry movement may be summarised as follows:

1.   Take account of the pupil's motivation and
interests
2.   Base abstract ideas on concrete experience to
promote understanding
3.   Employ activities involving the hand and eye,
and not just the ear, in conjunction with the brain,
and 'graphic(al)' methods in particular
4.   Adopt experimental and heuristic methods:
'Experiment, estimation, approximation, observation,
induction, intuition, common sense are to have honoured places in every mathematical classroom in
which the laboratory method has sway.'(53)
5.   Postpone logical rigour and any early concern
for the foundations, and generally restrict the formal deductive elements, admitting various forms of
'proof'
6.   Simplify, broaden and unify the subject-matter
of mathematics, ignoring traditional artificial divisions
7.   Correlate mathematics with science and laboratory work, and generally relate mathematics to life
and its applications (54)

It is to the strategy and tactics of the 'crusade'
that we must now turn.

PRESSURE FOR REFORM

Meetings, speeches and agitation in the educational
and scientific press around 1900 were important pre-
cursors of more organised pressure-group activity.
Perry had already achieved a breakthrough in 1899,
in connection with mathematics for technical students under the Department of Science and Art's arrangements. However, he held much wider ambitions
for educational reform, not only in the case of engineers, but also in mathematics for pupils in elementary and secondary schools as well as students
in training colleges. As a Correspondent in the
journal Engineering pointed out, Perry regarded his
scheme in mathematics as 'the best method of teaching all children, for whatever life intended', and
furthermore:

> it will be easily realised that the new system
> would from its very nature prove less startling
> to those who are trained to work hand-in-hand
> with Nature, and would therefore be easier to
> introduce to the engineering world than any
> other. Practical mathematics, in fact, is a

system for teaching mathematics to all persons, of all kinds and all ages.(55)

The text of a powerful address by Perry to the Institute of Electrical Engineers was fully reported in The Times in November of 1900. Here brief but scathing reference was made to mathematics which 'ought to be the natural language of the electrical engineer, but at present it was a foreign language'. (56) A more specific attack on mathematics teaching from Perry, including his syllabus for elementary practical mathematics, had already been published in Nature earlier in the year,(57) as had a more general article, 'England's Neglect of Science', which was subsequently adopted as the title of a collection of various published statements by Perry on scientific, technical and mathematical education going back to as early as 1879.(58) As Perry was quick to point out, his views expressed in The Times and elsewhere, to which there had been a number of responses in the press, were far from new, although hitherto they had remained largely unheeded.(59) But from 1900 reaction was much stronger and in the case of mathematics Perry's article in Nature generated some lively correspondence.(60) By this time a new monthly journal from Macmillan, the School World, had also started to publish articles concerning mathematics teaching and to compete with the older periodicals, the Journal of Education and the Educational Times.(61) As Findlay pointed out, many of the ideas being broadcast were far from new and had 'long been familiar, in their main outlines, to the many teachers, "thoughtful teachers", who think for themselves ... the columns of the Educational Times and the Journal of Education contain repeated sketches of reform, worked out in great detail'.(62) He judged that the important thrust came in 1900:

> with articles by Prof. Perry in Nature ... and
> it is my impression that the editors of that
> journal (closely associated with an enterpris-
> ing magazine called the School World, issued
> from the same publishing house) recognized that
> the time was ripe for stirring up both the sci-
> entific world and the teaching world on this
> subject.(63)

Thus agitation was spreading in the educational and scientific press, but more organised activity was a necessary prerequisite for the success of the campaign which had been initiated.(64)

The British Association for the Advancement of
Science had become involved with efforts to reform
geometrical teaching in the 1870s but very little
was achieved at that time.(65) The organisation of
this Association in sections catered primarily for
academic rather than educational matters, the latter
being treated incidentally within particular Sections, and without adequate representation from the
teaching profession itself. It was Armstrong who was
instrumental in the establishment of a new Section L
for Educational Science, which began its work in
1901.(66) In the previous year at the Bradford meeting he was supported to this end by Perry in particular, who 'preached his gospel' concerning educational reform, though his audience was principally
composed of mathematicians and scientists, and his
contribution was not widely publicised.(67) Clearly,
Perry saw the creation of a new Section L, which
might co-operate with existing Sections, as a means
of generating a wider interest and involvement in,
as well as influence upon, both the education of
engineers and mathematical education generally,
through the British Association. Accordingly, in
Section L's first year at Glasgow a joint meeting
was organised with Section A, for Mathematics and
Physics, and the opening address to a wide audience
of around two hundred was given by Perry.(68)
Predictably, Perry launched a strong attack on
the existing state of school mathematics and the
educational system which supported the status quo.
In the interests of the majority of pupils he questioned the deductive ideals of the academic pure
mathematician, which were enshrined in school geometry based on Euclid as a mind-trainer par excellence, and he advocated an alternative practical
pedagogy for a broader and more outward-looking
mathematics curriculum. Regarding curriculum content, he proposed his own scheme of elementary practical mathematics as an alternative paradigm for
school and training college mathematics. Tactically,
the focus on training college requirements in particular is of some interest. Syllabuses and examinations were centrally controlled by the Board of Education, which inherited the Education Department's
responsibilities, as well as those of the Department
of Science and Art. Perry was a member of a Departmental Committee considering syllabus changes for
the training colleges, and he envisaged the possibility of a further breakthrough here in favour of
his scheme of practical mathematics:

> It is to be remembered that courses of instruc-
> tion adopted in training colleges are very
> likely to be adopted in primary schools, in
> continuation schools, and in many secondary
> schools. I have been allowed by the Science and
> Art Department to introduce this method of
> mathematical teaching in many evening science-
> schools and technical colleges ... It is obvi-
> ous, therefore, that what I am doing may have
> far-reaching consequences ... (69)

Consequences there certainly were but major syllabus
reform outside the technical field was more complex
and less easily achievable, given the strength of
the control of the university examining bodies. Predictably, the Board of Education was not prepared
itself to initiate major innovation in mathematics
for the training colleges and chose to wait for a
lead from the universities. Early reactions to
Perry's proposals were multifarious in the extent of
their support.
    A three-hour discussion followed Perry's Glas-
gow address and involved a wide range of interests
in secondary and higher, technical and military education including, notably, A.R. Forsyth (1858-1942),
Sadleirian Professor of Mathematics at Cambridge.
Tensions between the 'liberal' academic perspective
and the more general vocational perspective, based
on the utility of mathematics, clearly emerged, with
Perry exploiting 'declinist' arguments and attacking
the public schools and older universities 'where
there is a deep-rooted scorn for all such scientific
knowledge as may be useful to the nation'.(70) Perry
also strongly argued for anti-elitism in education
and for the interests of the majority of pupils: 'I
hold a brief in the interests of average boys and
men; my strong language and possible excess of zeal
are due to the fact that nearly all the clever men
have briefs on the other side.'(71) Thus, deeper-
rooted issues of social class, status and control in
education were implicit in these early exchanges.
Significantly, Wolff subsequently identified and
sharply contrasted two schools of thought concerning
English reform, personified by Perry on the one hand
and Forysth on the other.(72) However, on pedagogical grounds there was much support for Perry, particularly regarding the value of practical work in
geometry, and 'general assent, even on the part of
the "official" mathematicians, to the idea of "aban-
doning Euclid" - a notable fact'.(73) Other countries had already abandoned Euclid and the position

in England was becoming increasingly untenable.(74)
Perry's radical proposals and relentless exhortation
threw into sharp relief the general deficiencies in
English school mathematics. Tactically, it was examination requirements which acted as the major bar-
rier to early progress for the movement.

The focus on examining bodies was well sharpen-
ed by Professor Love of Oxford who remarked, 'The
future of mathematical teaching in this country is
in their hands.'(75) As one schoolmaster remarked to
Perry:

> you will have to get the [Oxford and Cambridge]
> local examiners, the [Oxbridge] Joint Board,
> the College of Preceptors, and the University
> of London all to agree to issue an alternative
> 'practical mathematics' syllabus before second-
> ary schools can safely move.(76)

In addition, the American D.E. Smith provided Perry
with some penetrating advice concerning major curriculum development:

> The scheme [Perry's] is certainly better than
> the present one. But the obtaining of books,
> the training of teachers, the conversion of
> examiners, these are serious matters, and can-
> not be accomplished in one generation.(77)

As a start, the British Association itself took an
important further initiative.

At the joint request of Sections A and L at
Glasgow, a powerful Committee of the British Asso-
ciation was appointed, with Forsyth as Chairman and
Perry as Secretary. Its terms of reference were:

> To report upon improvements that might be ef-
> fected in the teaching of Mathematics, in the
> first instance in the teaching of Elementary
> Mathematics, and upon such means as they think
> likely to effect such improvements.(78)

Eggar of Eton was the only school teacher representative, but the strong representation of scientific, technical and military interests was clearly
favourable to Perry's cause. Before this Committee
reported, however, there was much other individual
and collective activity in the interests of reform.

Before the end of 1901, and in great haste Macmillan published in one volume Perry's Glasgow address and scheme, details of the discussion, and a

collection of invited written remarks, together with
some further responses from Perry.(79) The Glasgow
meeting and its substance were widely publicised in
the periodical literature, and many individual responses were generated, particularly in Nature and
the School World, the latter providing a 'Special
Mathematical Number' in March of 1902.(80) The columns of the Mathematical Gazette, the organ of the
Mathematical Association from 1894, also began to
reflect the new climate for reform.

As Charles Godfrey (1873-1924), who became a
leading reformer within the public-school sector,
subsequently remarked, 'The Mathematical Association
... awoke as one out of sleep.'(81) Three individual reactions to the Glasgow deliberations were published in the Mathematical Gazette, before the Association took any organised steps.(82) Included was
an interesting 'compromise' syllabus from Godfrey,
based on his work at Winchester College.(83) He pertinently asked, 'After Professor Perry's stimulating
denunciation at Glasgow, many of us must be wonder-
ing how far are we really able to mend our ways at
public schools?'(84) But the conservatism and internal organisation of the Mathematical Association
were ill-suited to speedy exploitation of the situation, and Forsyth approached Godfrey independently
to obtain some general representation of public-
school interests, which might assist the work of the
British Association.(85) Godfrey acted swiftly and
compiled a letter which was signed by twenty-three
predominantly younger schoolmasters from nine leading public schools. The letter was published early
in 1902 in Nature, the School World and the Mathematical Gazette, and also included in the second
edition of Perry's volume, based on his Glasgow initiative.(86) The letter served to strengthen the
British Association's case by providing evidence of
significant support for reform from within the commonly presumed conservative public-school sector.

Various views were exchanged at meetings and in
periodicals during 1902. General educational associations of training college staffs, headmasters and
assistant masters became involved in the debates and
representations concerning school mathematics. There
was some concern that the abandonment of Euclid
might lead to chaos in examinations and curricula,
but the weight of opposition was mounting.(87) The
Mathematical Gazette even published a stylish attack
on Euclid from a pure mathematical standpoint by
Bertrand Russell. He argued that the claim that
Euclid was 'an invaluable training to the youthful

powers of reasoning ... vanishes on a close inspection' because 'His definitions do not always define, his axioms are not always indemonstrable, his demonstrations require many axioms of which he is quite unconscious.'(88) The Mathematical Association itself was also goaded into action early in 1902.

The independent organisation of a letter by Godfrey was an obvious embarrassment and prompted the Mathematical Association to establish its own first Teaching Committee, which worked energetically on the preparation of reports on arithmetic, algebra and geometry during 1902.(89) Geometry was the main concern, but in the event the Association's report was not of great consequence, as Godfrey subsequently pointed out:

> On the eve of our liberation the M.A. published a report on Geometry teaching, a very conservative report, as it was considered impracticable to secure the abolition of the sequence [i.e. Euclid's]. This report became obsolete in 1902 ... (90)

The Committee of the British Association reported to Section L at Belfast in September 1902.

The Report of the Committee was based on seven meetings and the agreed principles were drawn up by the Chairman, Forsyth. It was well publicised and incorporated in the second edition of Perry's volume based on the Glasgow meeting in the previous year. (91) The Committee boldly rejected the need for uniformity in deductive geometry, and argued strongly for curricular freedom and variety, based on new examination schedules, which would give teachers themselves the opportunity to develop school geometry on lines more suited to the twentieth century. The need for practical work in geometry was also supported, and two experimental schemes from Eggar and Perry were appended. Problem solving, and links with arithmetic and algebra were also encouraged. In the case of these two other branches, manipulative excesses and unnecessary complications were deprecated, and correlation between the two branches was favoured, as well as an emphasis on the use of tables, graphical methods and formulae. The Report concluded by suggesting that through pruning and simplification the curriculum could be broadened to include introductory elements of trigonometry, coordinate geometry and even calculus as part of elementary mathematics. Overall, it was a strong and forward-looking statement of principles, which owed

much to Perry, though the status of deductive geometry _per se_ was not called into question. There was
little sympathy with Perry here, who admitted at the
time, 'The view to which I hold most firmly of all
my views about the teaching of mathematics is that
demonstrative geometry ought never to be taught ...
in schools.'(92) Examination reform and the dissemination of new textbooks and teaching aids proceeded
in parallel with the various individual and organised representations, such as the British Association's, which have already been described. The detailed evidence does not suggest any simple causal
chain of events in the implementation of major
change.

EXAMINATION REFORM

Given the complex nature of the idiosyncratic English examination system, syllabus reform was bound
to be far from straightforward in character. The
Department of Science and Art's adoption of Perry's
practical mathematics from 1899 was a significant
development, but it did not influence secondary
schools directly. However, the Department had done
much from the 1870s to disseminate geometrical drawing and instruments for the purpose, through its
examinations in practical plane and solid geometry.
These examinations were utilised by a wide range of
educational institutions in the late nineteenth century, the classics-dominated preparatory and public
schools excepted.(93) It is important to emphasise
that this work was divorced from deductive geometry
based on Euclid. As O. Henrici pointed out, 'Geometrical drawing belongs ... to a branch of Geometry of
which Euclid knew nothing, and where Euclid's propo-
sitions are of little use.'(94) The ancient universities and public schools generally disregarded and
deprecated this utilitarian aspect of geometry. In
1900, D. Mair (1868-1942) of the Civil Service Commission reported in _Nature_:

> A few weeks ago I asked some hundred boys in a
> well-taught school (as present teaching goes)
> to give a certain construction of Euclid's, and
> also to carry out the construction with ruler
> and compasses on a given line. Hardly one fail-
> ed to write out the construction and proof, but
> only one of the hundred carried out the practi-
> cal construction. Clearly our present Euclidian
> teaching has little to do with geometry.(95)

Three years later, a reviewer in <u>Nature</u> remarked:

> A PERSON may be a Cambridge Wrangler, and yet
> unable to make a simple graphical construction
> with accuracy. The ordinary schoolboy's knowl-
> edge of practical geometry is generally worth-
> less or nil ... But this state of affairs is
> being rapidly changed.(96)

Before considering these changes it should be added
that the Department of Science and Art also gave an
early lead regarding deductive alternatives to
Euclid, within its pure mathematical examinations,
which were quite separate from practical geometry.
From the 1880s, the Department permitted the use of
textbooks and sequences of theorems other than
Euclid's, a concession which the university examining bodies had generally refused to grant.(97) The
Civil Service Commission also took some important
early steps, before the universities.
   The Civil Service Commissioners controlled the
examinations for army entrance, which included drawing and measurement tasks in the geometry papers in
the 1890s, and, in 1901, the decisive step of dispensing with Euclid's order was also taken.(98)
These examinations directly influenced some public
schools and, as Godfrey acknowledged, 'gave a most
valuable lead'.(99) He judged the Commission's influence to be a seminal one for mathematics teaching
throughout English public schools.(100) One schoolmaster remarked, 'Whatever faults they [the army
examinations] have had in the past, I know of no
papers which have gone further towards encouraging -
I might almost say <u>enforcing</u> - some of Professor
Perry's proposed reforms.'(101) Major changes in the
universities' examination requirements began in
1902.
   In syllabus reform the Oxford Locals moved
first, followed by London Matriculation, and then
the Cambridge Locals before the end of 1902.(102)
Forsyth was involved with the manoeuvres at Cambridge, which were more difficult and protracted in
the case of the Previous (matriculation) examination. In fact Oxford Responsions (matriculation)
followed the Locals early in 1903, and it was not
until May of the same year that major changes were
announced for the Previous, which was a particularly
important examination for the public schools. Details of the various developments and reactions to
them were published in periodicals such as <u>Nature</u>
and the <u>School World</u>, and also technical journals

such as Engineering.(103) It is clear that the greatest conservatism was at Cambridge, which eventually responded to the combined weight of recommendations for change, reforms in other examinations, and a recognition of 'the widespread desire for reform'.(104) The changes for the Previous were summarised in Nature as follows:

> (1) In demonstrative geometry, Euclid's Elements shall be optional as a text-book, and the sequence of Euclid shall not be enforced. The examiners will accept any proof of a proposition which they are satisfied forms part of a systematic treatment of the subject.
> (2) Practical geometry is to be introduced, along with deductive geometry, and questions will be set requiring careful draughtsmanship and the use of efficient drawing instruments.
> (3) In arithmetic, the use of algebraical symbols and processes will be permitted.
> (4) In algebra, graphs and squared paper work will be introduced; and a knowledge will be required of fractional indices and the use of four figure tables of logarithms.(105)

The Board of Education closely followed the Cambridge Previous in its own syllabus changes for the teacher training colleges, published in the Regulations for 1904.(106) Thus a remarkable breakthrough in examination reform had been achieved in a comparatively short time.

Perry was cautiously optimistic in these early stages of curriculum development:

> because it has occurred in the English way, we know that the reform is real, that it will have a fair chance, that it will go on year after year for many a year to come ... Freedom has been given to teachers, a freedom much sighed for, a freedom which will create enthusiasm. Those who are most determined to make the reform complete are most anxious to proceed cautiously and to smother intemperate zeal.(107)

Furthermore, a commentator in Nature, in referring to the 'movement now in progress throughout the country' added a note of caution: 'we hope to see it carried much farther before crystallisation takes place'.(108) Clearly, textbook production and the dissemination of aids and advice of various kinds were major priorities to support teachers in the

unprecedented and no doubt somewhat bewildering new
climate of freedom for experimentation in the school
mathematics curriculum.

TEXTBOOKS AND TEACHING AIDS

Educational suppliers were quick to exploit the expanding market for geometrical instruments and
squared paper, advertising their products in the
educational press. The output of 'new geometries',
whether preliminary, practical, theoretical, or some
combination of these features, was quite extraordinary in the early years of this century, particularly in the two-year period 1903-4, during which there
appeared around 35 per cent of the total output of
first editions over the first quarter of this century.(109) Many of these textbooks were reviewed in
batches in the periodical literature: it was a highly competitive but potentially very profitable new
market for the educational publishers.(110) The requirements of graphical work in algebra examinations
also produced a swift response from authors and
their publishers.
    The growing importance of graphs in relation to
the new examination requirements is well exemplified
by one teacher's remark concerning London Matriculation:

    Here graphs [author's stress] is the word which
    has caught the popular eye, witness an adver-
    tisement in a morning paper: 'Wanted immediate
    preparation in mathematics for the London Ma-
    tric., graphs necessary'.(111)

A number of publications on graphs, the majority
containing relatively few pages, suddenly appeared
on the market from the end of 1902, as supplements
to existing textbooks on algebra.(112) The contribution of the prolific textbook-writer Hall to what
became known as 'graphical algebra' was compiled on
a seaside holiday at short notice to meet a 'sudden
demand'.(113) It should be emphasised that squared
paper was already being used for a variety of purposes in relation to the education of technical students along lines pioneered by Perry and Ayrton in
Japan in the 1870s.(114) Typically, the new textbooks on practical mathematics from 1899 incorporated a separate chapter on uses of squared paper.
Also, graphical work was being widely exploited in
the science laboratory, particularly in relation to

physical data and the search for functional relationships.(115) What was new was the adoption of
squared paper within school mathematics, and particularly algebra teaching. As Godfrey enthusiastically commented, 'GRAPHS have found their way into
elementary work, and are now recognised as quite the
most valuable instrument in our possession for
awakening interest.'(116) As Perry emphasised, the
nineteenth-century tradition in pure mathematics was
such that 'Simple exercises on squared paper ...
must not be approached until one has wasted years on
higher algebra and trigonometry and geometrical con-
ics, because they belong to the subject of coordinate geometry.'(117) But with the coming of the
new secondary examination requirements, the drawing
of graphs became rife by 1905, and Hall could refer
to a state of 'graphomania', which he claimed was
particularly affecting younger teachers.(118)
Turner's assessment in Perry's obituary for the
Royal Society is a fitting one: 'The broadcasting of
squared paper, though a detail, is a detail of great
importance, and representative of the effects of
Perry's campaign.'(119)
     In the early heady years of reform undoubtedly
the greatest general effects were felt in geometry
teaching. The following lament in the Journal of
Education serves well to sharpen the contrast between the 'old geometry', which followed Euclid's
pure mathematical ideals, and the 'new geometry',
which was inspired by the pedagogical ideals of the
Perry movement:

EUCLID'S ELEMENTS. By AN ANCIENT GEOMETER

FAREWELL! old Euclid: loved of yore, and may be
     loved again,
When our beatific vision sees thy plane
     surface, plain;
Unfettered now, we range without thy limited
     confines;
Thy concept had no breadth at all. We must have
     broader lines.

We shun thy close restrictions, and thy ordered
     sequence, too:
The ancient Greeks might learn to think; we've
     other things to do;
Nor can we stimulate again thy sober mental joy -
Euclidian reasoning 'stupefies the normal
     British boy'.

No more we seek the famous <u>pons</u> when standing
    on the brink -
'Tis but a shallow stream to cross, nor need
    the tiro shrink;
Bring compasses and callipers and geometric
    tools,
And waive eternal principle for briefly stated
    rules.

So we close the battered volume; lay it high
    upon the shelf,
And adopt more modern methods in our eager
    chase for pelf:
Thus one more link is severed, and we hail our
    glad release
From the intellectual thraldom of the glory
    that was Greece.(120)

Justifiably, Godfrey could refer by 1906 to
'The Passing of Euclid', but this did not mean the
abandonment of formal deductive geometry, as Perry
himself had advocated.(121) Rather, the movement
opened up the possibilities for practical and experimental work in geometry, and the relationship
with deductive geometry in <u>some</u> form now emerged as
a major pedagogical issue which was to engage the
mathematics teaching community over the next half
century. In the shorter term, there were some other
important developments and effects associated with
the reform movement.
    Market-capturing labels such as 'practical',
'experimental', 'heuristic' and 'observational' were
exploited by publishers in the titles of new textbooks, particularly in geometry, but also in arithmetic, mensuration and trigonometry.(122) Textbooks
which referred to 'practical mathematics' were principally aimed at the technical and military fields,
but it is clear that authors and their publishers
judged the market to be generally receptive to a
'practical' emphasis in teaching methods, variously
interpreted in relation to the branches of school
mathematics.
    In the cases of arithmetic and mensuration,
teachers of science were already leading the way in
the widely disseminated work on physical measurements in both elementary and secondary schools. In
arithmetic, work on measures was traditionally re-
stricted to computations involving the complex imperial system. However, with simple aids like drawing instruments, scissors, tracing paper, squared
paper, string, sets of cubes and solid models, it

was possible to undertake in the mathematics classroom much of the simpler work in practical physics
and to correlate this with the teaching of such topics as fractions, decimals, length, area and volume,
as well as the use of formulae and graphs.(123)
Such possibilities were exploited at an early stage
by innovators such as Eggar and Findlay, and suitable textbooks were soon produced for this so-called
'practical arithmetic' for younger pupils.(124) It
became a commonplace in many girls' secondary
schools and also in elementary schools, where P.B.
Ballard (1865-1950), an LCC Inspector, judged that
'Far and away the most significant change that has
taken place during the past few years has been the
introduction of what is known in the schools as
practical arithmetic.'(125) In relation to the public schools, the widening curricular interest in
practical measurements was associated with the perhaps surprising development of <u>mathematical</u> laboratories in some schools.
    It was not only adherence to the principle of
correlation with science which serves to explain the
phenomenon of laboratories equipped specifically for
mathematics. A major stimulus was provided by new
examination requirements in mathematics for army entrance, which were announced in 1904, and gave considerable prominence to work in 'practical measurements' as well as demanding practical work in mechanics.(126) A reviewer of textbooks on 'practical
(or experimental) mathematics' in the <u>Mathematical
Gazette</u> acknowledged Perry's inspiration and the
importance of these new army requirements as part of
'a great increase in the attention paid to practical
applications in the elementary parts of the subject'. He added, 'The new requirements have already
produced a crop of text books.'(127) At Harrow, two
laboratories were equipped, for practical measurements and mechanics, in direct response to the new
army entrance requirements.(128) At Winchester,
Godfrey and Bell developed a course on similar lines
in a new mathematical laboratory, and provided a
textbook which owed much to earlier work in practical physics.(129) Similar developments at Clifton
and Oundle, principally to serve military and engineering requirements, were also subsequently reported in the Board of Education's <u>Special Reports</u>, in a
section devoted to 'Practical Mathematics at Public
Schools'.(130) Fawdry of Clifton admitted that 'it
is in great measure due to the demands of these
[army] examinations that the attention of teachers
has been drawn to the advisability of including

practical work in the Mathematics Course'.(131)

In summary, <u>three</u> contrasting interpretations
of 'practical mathematics' have been identified thus
far: a syllabus in mathematics for technical students; laboratory-based work in mathematics; and a
general approach to mathematics teaching following
the pedagogical principles of the Perry movement.
The 'laboratory method', coined in America in connection with the Perry movement, captured the spirit
rather than the letter of the various developments
in England.

Working out the implications of the new pedagogy in classroom terms was an important concern in
the early years of reform. One teacher referred to
the 'very remarkable agreement in favour of practical methods of teaching', but at the same time 'an
equally remarkable disagreement with regard to the
meaning and application of such methods'. He claimed
that the details were being 'hammered out in hundreds of schools'.(132) The School World published
informative articles on the interpretation of 'practical mathematics' and aids for the new approach,
including detailed surveys of available geometrical
instruments, squared paper and mathematical tables
for schools. It was clearly emerging that in 'the
modern method': 'a fairly extensive field of practical mathematics can be covered without the assistance of any elaborate apparatus and without leaving
the class-room for the laboratory'.(133)

Perry was fairly optimistic in the very early
years of major reform. At the British Association in
1902, he delivered another powerful address, this
time to a joint meeting of Section G, for Engineering, and the new Section L. The general focus was
the education of engineers, but he also reflected
upon the encouraging developments in school mathematics, and looked forward to further major
achievements:

> It seems probable that at the end of another
> five years no average boy of fifteen years of
> age will have been compelled to attempt any
> abstract reasoning about things of which he
> knows nothing; he will be versed in experimen-
> tal mathematics, which he may or may not call
> mensuration; he will use logarithms, and mere
> multiplication and division will be a joy to
> him; he will be able to tackle at once any
> curious new problems which can be solved by
> squared paper; and he will have no fear of the
> symbols of the infinitesimal calculus ... Five

> years hence it will be called 'elementary math-
> ematics'. Four years ago it was an unorthodox
> subject called 'practical mathematics' ... (134)

Love of Oxford even went so far as to judge that
Perry's belief that his scheme was not only suitable
for engineers but was also appropriate as a 'means
of culture', and for the future mathematics specialist too, was 'widely held' in the movement's early
stages. However, Findlay's judgement was more sober
and reliable in the event:

> I do not think Prof. Perry and his friends
> quite realize how fragmentary and disjointed
> their own suggestions are, and what a great
> gulf separates their work with adults and
> artisans from that conducted by teachers of
> boys and girls in school classes.(135)

The passing reference to girls was a pertinent one.
As one schoolmistress subsequently pointed out, in
referring to 'a revolt, led by the engineers', the
principal thrust was:

> against the actual methods and material of
> mathematical teaching in the schools which have
> been found too academic and unpractical for the
> needs of real life, that is, the need of boys.
> Euclid is dethroned. Practical Mathematics of
> various kinds is introduced, and school Math-
> ematics is more definitely directed towards the
> demands of careers which do not concern
> girls.(136)

Furthermore, Perry's challenging Belfast agenda was
to involve the mathematics teaching community for
many years beyond his death in 1920. Progress in the
cases of geometry and graphical work was rapid and
general, given the stimulus of major examination reform. However, the particular case of mathematical
tables serves to exemplify the difficulty of implementing general change in other aspects of the
school mathematics curriculum.
      Up to the turn of the century the use of nu-
merical tables in school mathematics was generally
confined to the work of future mathematics specialists, particularly in relation to trigonometry,
which was regarded as an 'advanced' branch of the
subject. Only bulky seven-figure tables were provided for this purpose. It was in relation to science
teaching that the use of simple four-figure tables

of logarithms was under way in schools by 1900.(137)
Significantly also, the Department of Science and
Art published a simple set of tables for use as part
of the scheme of practical mathematics. Perry could
very soon claim:

> since the Science and Art Department has dis-
> tributed its tables of four-figure logarithms
> and functions of angles over the country as
> cheaply as grocers' advertisements, there has
> been a wonderful development in knowledge and
> use of such tables.(138)

The use of tables did filter into secondary school
work, but support for the teaching of logarithms to
younger pupils in secondary mathematics was not generally forthcoming in the early examination reforms,
and over the first decade of this century general
progress in the use of simple tables in mathematics
was gradual.(139) Slowly, tables were being incorporated in arithmetic and algebra as well as practical
mathematics textbooks, and separate booklets of tables were also provided by some publishers.(140)
Largely through the efforts of the Mathematical Association, examination requirements were generally
adjusted by the early 1920s, to acknowledge logarithms as part of a general secondary education.(141)
Thus the victory was virtually complete, but the
battle for this advance had been fought for some
twenty years.(142)
   In relation to the three elementary branches of
arithmetic, algebra and geometry, the movement to
make mathematics teaching more 'practical' was notably successful in its early stages. But optimism
concerning the progress of reform was short-lived
and a significant reaction to the new directions in
mathematics teaching soon set in.

PROGRESS AND REACTION

The issue of correlation, which was one of the reform movement's pedagogical principles, as we have
seen, was the subject of an address by Perry to an
exceptional joint conference between the Mathematical Association and the Federated Associations of
London Non-Primary Teachers in 1908. In some revealing asides, Perry was beginning to show frustration
with the character of reform. For a start, the
changes had not gone far enough for his liking, and
powerful constraints were involved:

130

> The teaching of mathematics still follows the
> old lines; we are compelled by examination sys-
> tems to refrain from suggesting drastic reform,
> and we can only tinker with it ... Will you
> forgive me for saying that, all so excellent as
> the syllabuses of the Mathematical Association
> are, they seem to me to possess too much of the
> orthodox mathematical spirit? There is too much
> hankering after a kind of logical perfection
> which is impossible in the teaching of the av-
> erage boy.(143)

Furthermore, he complained that even where some of
the movement's ideals had received general support,
distortion by teachers themselves was prevalent in
the process of realisation:

> It astonishes me to see how little comprehen-
> sion there seems to be of the proposals made by
> the British Association committees. We recom-
> mended experimental geometry with common-sense
> reasoning, and everybody seems to think that we
> asked for a babyish use of rulers and compasses
> following a series of propositions. We asked
> for interesting work in weighing and measuring,
> and care is taken that all such work shall be
> made as uninteresting as possible. We recom-
> mended some work with graphs on squared paper,
> and some teachers do nothing but graphs, and
> there are dozens of school books to help on the
> craze ... The surprising thing is that many
> teachers seem to have no individuality, no
> originality, nor even the power to think for
> themselves at all.(144)

These were cutting remarks concerning a teaching
force which the evidence will show was generally
ill-equipped to cope effectively with major curriculum development in secondary mathematics.

The period of major reform up to the First
World War coincided with the early stages of expansion for the system of grant-aided secondary schools
under the new Board of Education and LEAs. The increasing demand for academically competent teachers
of mathematics was a long way from being met.(145)
Furthermore, many of the new ideals concerned teaching methods rather than new subject-matter, and such
ideals demanded pedagogical sensitivity and balanced
judgement for their effective implementation. Unfortunately, the need for some form of professional
initial training, to supplement academic

qualifications, was some way from being generally
accepted and in-service training was also only in
its infancy.(146) As regards the teaching force,
circumstances were far from favourable to the Perry
movement. The immediate response of Perry himself
was rather simplistic in relation to English conditions: 'it almost seems that at present we must im-
pose some system of teaching so complete in every
detail that any teacher can follow it exactly'.(147)
More pertinently, he pointed to some major resource
implications:

> Until salaries are doubled and forms halved in
> their number of boys there will be things very
> open to criticism ... It is our duty to ... see
> that [teachers] are better paid, for that is
> the only way in which a greater proportion of
> able men are to be induced to become teach-
> ers.(148)

Clearly, an organisation such as the British Association was ill-equipped to tackle the complexities
of school curriculum development and Perry had come
to realise this.(149) The progress of reform was
also affected by a significant reaction to aspects
of the ideology involved and its consequences for
mathematics in a secondary education.

In relation to the Perry movement, the reaction
came in two principal forms. One concerned the value
of a more practical pedagogy per se; the other concerned the value of practical mathematics as mathematics. In the former case, as HMI Strachan noted,
'At various times the reform movement has been
brought into temporary disrepute by an excessive
devotion to so-called practical work or by alliance
with the extreme heuristic school.'(150) By 1905,
the army requirements had swung dramatically towards
practical work and attracted some of the earliest
criticism. The Mathematical Gazette included a
strongly worded response to the Civil Service Commission's wholesale acceptance of such methods:

> The policy of 'overturn, overturn' has been
> pushed too far: if numerical calculations,
> graphical representations, and geometrical
> drawing are not merely to be an aid, but a sub-
> stitute for a systematic knowledge of the theo-
> ry of Elementary Mathematics, the value of the
> subject as an educational instrument will be
> but small.(151)

The author felt that the new demands only required
of candidates 'a few knoblets of knowledge which
will enable them to solve questions of a strictly
practical and "useful" kind'. Laboratory work was
being 'dignified by the title of "Practical Mathematics"', and was 'somewhat out of place' as part
of mathematics.(152) More general misgivings concerning practical geometry and graphical work were
also being aired at this time. The School World
included a strong critique of the new tendencies,
particularly in geometry where 'exercises which
merely test a pupil's skill in draughtsman's work
are surely for the art room'. In the case of the new
geometry textbooks the author added that 'the majority seem to have been hurriedly turned out for the
sake of inserting something which could be called
practical'. The deductive ideals of pure mathematics
were upheld, for which practical demonstration was
no substitute: 'geometry is not an experimental science' was the claim. Purposeless 'graphomania' was
also deprecated.(153) Before the end of the decade
some of the leading reformers were themselves expressing some concern over the direction of change.
       B. Branford (1868-1944), an Inspector of London
Schools, welcomed the newer tendencies in many
schools where 'the practical and theoretical aspects
of mathematics are co-ordinated and developed', but
he felt it necessary to add:

> It must, however, be admitted that the par-
> ticular type of intellectual discipline obtain-
> able from mathematical study on its formal,
> systematic, and logical side, is in consider-
> able danger of becoming temporarily sacrificed
> during a too extreme swing of the pendulum of
> reform.(154)

Godfrey referred to the recently released 'volume of
pent-up energy' in geometry teaching which had resulted in a tendency to overdo the practical elements. He added:

> But it was soon realized that this would make
> the subject invertebrate, that there must be a
> certain element of severity in every school
> study, and that for the purposes of general
> education geometry must still stand or fall by
> the logical training it gives.(155)

He judged that 'the transitional period is still on
us' and that 'it is still too soon to give a final

opinion'. In relation to numerical and graphical
work in algebra, he commented, 'Following the usual
law, the reform went too far', but that 'The pendu-
lum is now swinging in the opposite direction.'(156)
The need for working out an appropriate balance between the practical and theoretical aspects of mathematics at different educational stages was emphasised by Professor E.W. Hobson (1856-1933) of Cambridge in an address to Section A of the British Association in 1910. He also referred to 'some signs
of reaction against the recent movement of reform in
the teaching of geometry'.(157) There is some evidence of a further hardening of attitude in some
quarters by the First World War. An article 'On
Practical Mathematics in Schools', published in the
Mathematical Gazette in 1914, expressed a hope that:

> the authorities of the Mathematical Association
> will keep in the future, as they have done in
> the past, a firm faith that the primary value
> of mathematical study is not to be found in
> such results as skill with the penny ruler, the
> scissors and the scales, but in the culture
> that all genuine mathematical study has been
> held to give from the days of Plato to those of
> Russell and Whitehead.(158)

After the War, C.H.P. Mayo looked back on his own
experiences as a senior master at Harrow with a
sense of relief. He confessed that he had never had
much sympathy for the extreme swing towards 'materialism' in the form of practical and laboratory work:
'the elementary and pottering experimentation gave
no mental grip, and their value was almost negligible'; it was 'pandering to the spirit of mere
utility in education'. He welcomed the reaffirmation
of a more disciplinary view in mathematics aligned
with 'a strong return to the Classics' as part of
'the revolt from the materialism to which circumstances forced us some twenty or more years ago'.
Significantly, he added, 'the mathematical laboratories at Harrow, hailed almost as the saviour of
the study, are no longer used'.(159)

Reactions to Perry's scheme of practical mathematics as a course in mathematics per se go back to
the turn of the century. An early response in Nature
was typical:

> the syllabus ... is admirably adapted for a
> technical training. In practical mathematics,
> where mental training is of minor importance,

> exigencies of time will compel the teacher to
> omit explanations, or only give them roughly,
> for his chief object is to enable his pupils to
> apply mathematical results, as distinct from
> reasoning, to problems in engineering, science,
> or kindred subjects.(160)

The gulf separating the Cambridge school of mathematicians, led by Forsyth, and the technical institutions, working on Perry's lines, was a major one
to which Perry addressed himself in some early contributions to Nature and the Engineer. He claimed,
'I am constantly being asked to recommend men to
teach mathematics in technical schools and colleges,
and warned that I must not recommend a Cambridge
man.'(161) From a pure mathematical standpoint, the
major bone of contention was that Perry's mathematics involved rapid progress through an ambitious
range of useful content which necessitated a lack of
attention to general principles and systematic theoretical development i.e. it was necessarily shallow
mathematically. Thus, Professor Greenhill referred
to Perry's The Calculus for Engineers as 'a series
of events connected by a slight thread of continuous
theory' which suggested 'a mathematical Pickwick'.
(162) Perry vainly hoped for a mathematical lead
from Cambridge in relation to the higher education
of engineers:

> it is not merely elementary education that is
> going into the melting-pot. Is Cambridge going
> to hold aloof from the little army of men who
> think that the melting and solidifying pro-
> cesses need to be guided? Has Cambridge no in-
> terest whatsoever in the nature of the possible
> crystallisation?(163)

However, Perry's practical mathematics for technical
students thrived and continued to be sniped at by
mathematicians. Addressing the Mathematical Association, Professor Hobson remarked, 'I gather that in
some of the current teaching of practical Mathematics, a kind of perverse ingenuity is exhibited in
evading all discussion of fundamental ideas, and in
the elimination of reference to general principles.'(164) When asked to clarify whether he had in
mind Perry's scheme or laboratory work, he significantly added, 'I think I had both in my mind. I used
the word "practical" to distinguish from the mathematics which deals with principles.'(165) Perry
himself was beginning to show signs of disillusion.

It was, he said, 'perhaps a pity that I gave such a misleading name as practical mathematics to the reformed methods, but I wanted to differentiate them from the orthodox methods'.(166) By now his scheme was even coming into question in the case of the higher education of engineers.

Engineering science had established itself as an alternative to mathematics or natural science as an academic discipline in its own right.(167) At the Fifth International Congress of Mathematicians at Cambridge, Sir William White claimed that the 'preponderance of opinion' favoured the handing over of mathematics for engineers to mathematical specialists, who could provide a broader and deeper theoretical basis for subsequent application. This was a clear rejection of the older tradition of practical mathematics, closely linked with specific applications throughout, which it was felt had inhibited this country's research in particular.(168) Perry reacted strongly to White's 'contemptuous' reference to practical mathematics. White was a member of the governing body at Imperial College, where important changes were in the process of implementation. Perry had been asked to retire, but was reluctant to leave, and claimed, 'The syllabus and methods of teaching are exactly as they have been for seventeen years.'(169) In retrospect, it appears to have been a major failing in Perry's later years that he stubbornly and persistently advocated an inflexible scheme of mathematics, with roots going back to the 1870s, as a panacea in the education of engineers. Perry lost this battle and was forcibly retired in 1913. Ironically, he was replaced by Forsyth of all people, a Cambridge mathematician who shared White's views.(170)

Somewhat belatedly, Perry's published lectures to working men of 1899 were revised and appeared as a textbook, Elementary Practical Mathematics, in 1913.(171) Such a course was now firmly established in evening technical education, but Perry expressed concern for the general misinterpretation of his principles by technical teachers, working through the medium of textbooks which dominated the teaching. Predictably, on pure mathematical grounds, Perry's own contribution was savagely reviewed both by Professor G.H. Bryan (1864-1928) of University College Bangor, in Nature, and anonymously under the title 'The Apotheosis of Practical Mathematics' in the School World.(172) The criticisms were far from new: throughout his life Perry remained too much a practical engineer in outlook and too little a mathematician for the likes of the mathematical community. It is no wonder that he had once confessed to feeling that 'nearly all the clever men have briefs on the other side'.(173)

After the First World War mathematics for technical students continued to be associated with an inferior treatment of the subject. As Professor H.T.H. Piaggio remarked, 'Practical Mathematics ... is regarded very unfavourably by many mathematicians', and 'an evil tradition has grown up that lack of logic makes an argument particularly convincing to practical men'. He added:

> The pioneers in Practical Mathematics were involved in much controversy, and they denounced the ordinary mathematical course with much vehemence ... But the impetus of their attack on academic methods led them to reject the good as well as the bad, and their example has been followed by too many of their followers.(174)

The Mathematical Association first turned its attention to evening technical work in the mid-1920s, and acknowledged the pioneering work which had been done:

> At one time, the presentation was undoubtedly too abstract. This tendency has now disappeared, chiefly owing to the effort of the late Professor Perry. His methods have been adopted very widely. When they were first introduced they aroused great enthusiasm ... (175)

However, the Association's sub-committee judged the early hopes to be 'too sanguine', and reported that 'in the opinion of many, the results obtained are somewhat disappointing'. Overall, their report served to emphasise the pure mathematical deficiencies of such work and argued for a more 'liberal' treatment with less attention to mere 'rule of thumb'.

THE MOVEMENT'S ACHIEVEMENTS

Perry died in 1920 and did not receive at this time general recognition for his role in the reform of mathematical education in both schools and colleges. His Obituary in Nature was written by his old friend Armstrong, at a time when the old Finsbury College was in a serious state of decline.(176) The Perry

movement as such had faded, but to do justice to its
significance for English school mathematics it is
important to consider in summary some of the longer-
term benefits, which have their roots in the earlier
experimentation and pedagogical ideals of the movement.

Given the strong emphasis on teaching methods
in the ideology of the Perry movement, it is of
great significance that 'intuition and experiment'
in mathematics teaching was chosen in 1911 as a major focus for international comparative and evalu-
ative work by the first International Commission on
the Teaching of Mathematics, an off-shoot of the
International Congress of Mathematicians.(177) Such
methods were taken to include the graphical study of
statistics, functions, vectors and statics; the use
of slide rules, mathematical tables and squared paper; approximate methods in computation; geometrical
drawing; practical mensuration and surveying; and
practical astronomy. In this connection, Godfrey
undertook and reported upon a survey of English secondary schools for the Commission. He referred to
such methods as 'the keynote of modern mathematical
education'. In summary, he found:

> The use of graphical methods in elementary al-
> gebra teaching is universal and entirely a
> 20th-century development. Other aspects of the
> same movement are the adoption of descriptive
> geometry by the mathematicians, and the use of
> handy 4-figure tables, and of graphical methods
> in statics, and, though, in these cases, the
> victory is less complete than that of the
> 'graph', it is remarkable and equally mod-
> ern.(178)

The American D.E. Smith summarised corresponding advances in Austria, France, Germany, Switzerland and
the United States.(179)

Pruning and simplification of the content of
secondary school mathematics was an early concern in
reform but, more ambitiously, there was much support
in the rhetoric for the principle of broadening the
scope of the subject, to exemplify its utility in
particular. As Fawdry suggested, 'In brief, the general object of the reform was to make it possible
for all boys of seventeen to leave school with some
knowledge of trigonometry, mechanics, and the calculus.'(180) In the cases of both trigonometry and
calculus the Perry movement brought with it some new
possibilities.

Traditionally, trigonometry was regarded as an 'advanced' branch of secondary school mathematics, which followed a thorough grounding in algebra and Euclid. It was largely a complex symbolic pursuit, whose potential utility was little exploited, and in this form it was quite unsuitable for the majority of pupils who, in any case, never reached this 'promised land'.(181) However, in the early years of this century, a new introductory approach slowly developed which exploited graphical and numerical work, and was supported by the availability of simple four-figure tables. Young naval cadets were involved in some of the early experimentation. New textbooks gradually appeared and their prefaces and contents confirm the inspiration of the Perry movement.(182) For example, Borchardt and Perrott admitted that the 'new trigonometry' was part of a general change 'so largely due to the genius of Prof. Perry'.(183) Through the efforts of the Mathematical Association in particular, what became known as 'numerical trigonometry' slowly gained a firm hold in secondary mathematics for non-specialists between the wars, with examining bodies eventually lending their support to this development.(184) It was a victory akin to that of logarithms, and one which again owed much to the Perry movement.

As with trigonometry, there was no possibility of teaching calculus more widely in schools until alternative approaches to the conventional academic treatment for mathematics specialists had emerged. Again, with the Perry movement there developed alternative treatments of calculus, tailored to this branch's applications, and exploiting numerical and graphical methods. For example, Perry's own textbook on calculus was a radical alternative to the severely analytic approach and it involved major simplification and use of intuition.(185) One commentator in referring to the traditional approach acknowledged that 'Professor Perry in his well-known treatise on the calculus initiated a reaction ...'(186) By 1908, Godfrey could report 'a strong movement at the present day in favour of an early use of the calculus', and the developing interest was particularly strong on the Continent.(187) Indeed, calculus was another chosen focus for the International Commission in the period 1912-14. Some early experimentation in England again involved naval cadets and employed a treatment which Godfrey summarised thus:

the most striking feature ... is that (in development of a suggestion originally due to

Prof. Perry) all the main applications of differentiation and integration are exemplified
without using any function more abstruse than
x^n.(188)

Army and Civil Service examination requirements provided a further early stimulus, but the progress of
this branch in a general secondary education was
very slow, particularly outside the public schools,
where experimentation appears to have been greatest,
principally up to the First World War, but largely
with older pupils. Although much of the momentum for
innovation was lost in the 1920s and 1930s, some
calculus was eventually accepted as an option within
elementary mathematics in the School Certificate examinations, after 1944. It was a belated and partial
victory and, predictably, no reference at this time
was made to the much earlier inspiration of the
Perry movement. The link is a clear and notable one
nonetheless.(189)
    Another longer-term link with the Perry move-
ment concerns the resurrection of the notion of
'practical mathematics' in relation to the mathematics curriculum for older pupils outside the secondary school system. In the period 1903-6, Perry and
Armstrong had also become involved through the British Association in curricular initiatives concerning
mathematics for elementary schools and the encouragement of 'experimental, observational, and practical studies'.(190) But the British Association's involvement here was of little consequence in relation
to the reality of curriculum development in the elementary schools: their final report published in
1906 is strong on exhortation but conspicuously weak
regarding strategies for implementing change.(191)
These efforts faded, but after Perry's death the
relevance of his scheme and pedagogy re-emerged in
the case of mathematics for post-primary pupils
within the elementary school system.
    In the 1920s, the emerging idea of a post-
primary 'modern school' brought with it a concern
for the development of a more useful and less academic curriculum than that for secondary pupils preparing for the School Certificate examinations.(192)
An early master's dissertation in 1928 was significantly entitled 'Practical Mathematics: The Approach
of the Post-Primary Pupil to the Study of Mathematics',(193) and HMI Carson, with reference to modern
school requirements, remarked that 'The subject (or
method) known as practical mathematics, which thirty
years ago did so much for teaching in this country,

is in mind in this connection.'(194) A 1935 Pamphlet
of the Board of Education entitled <u>Senior School
Mathematics</u> encouraged LEAs 'to provide courses for
teachers in Practical Mathematics', which could ignore the constraints of secondary school examinations, as well as 'the need for academic or conventional treatment', and thereby encourage a unified
new approach to the subject, ignoring traditional
subdivisions.(195) Underlying assumptions of status
and social class are embedded in such 'progressive'
thinking concerning the curriculum for pupils in
senior elementary schools and classes. The progres-
sivism here contrasts sharply with the typical conservatism and consolidatory tendencies in mathematics for public and grammar school pupils. What is
more, a lower-status paradigm for school mathematics, with its roots in technical education and with
working-class associations, was now being advocated
as a panacea for the embryonic secondary-modern
school sector: 'parity of esteem' in this regard had
little chance of realisation.(196)

CONCLUSION

At a time when the effects of the Perry movement
were still being strongly felt, a number of personal
tributes were paid to Perry himself for his contribution to reform. For example:

> Of late years a new spirit has come over the
> mathematical teaching in many of our institu-
> tions, due in no small measure to the reforming
> zeal of ... Professor John Perry.(197)

> It is well known that this revolution owes its
> success largely to the indefatigable exertions
> of Prof. John Perry.(198)

> [The utility motive] is the psychological prin-
> ciple which justified 'the dethronement of
> Euclid' and other reforms that owe so much to
> the eloquence, wit, and authority of Prof.
> Perry.(199)

After Perry's death, one writer in the <u>Mathematical
Gazette</u> referred to the 'Perry Controversy' concerning mathematical priorities as 'far from being
settled' and added, 'its importance and its potency
for progress lies in the fact that it is a movement
from outside'.(200) As Howson has shown, Euclid was

'a very English subject' which exceptionally dominated mathematics in a liberal education in England
until the turn of the century.(201) As Godfrey put
it, the time was then 'ripe for change' but 'no
change would come till some wave of public opinion
should carry examiners and teachers together to a
new position ... The needful impulse came from the
engineering profession ...'(202) Thus it was indeed
a 'movement from outside', with Perry himself, an
engineer and certainly not a member of the mathematical establishment, a pioneer in technical education
and a man with working-class affinities coming to
occupy the centre of the stage in the early years of
major reform in English school mathematics. In sharp
contrast, the status quo was linked with the two
ancient universities and the public schools for the
upper classes, where classical elitism and anti-
scientific conservatism were strongest and combined
with a lack of sympathy for practical and technical
education, with its inferior class associations.
Perhaps surprisingly, the Mathematical Association
also shared some of this conservatism initially: its
major work and achievements were to come later.

In the opening years of this century it was
Perry who did much to sharpen the feeling of 'crisis' in English school mathematics by locating discontent within a set of broader and more general
concerns for greater democracy in education, more
consideration of utility in the curriculum and more
serious consideration of pedagogical principles.
Furthermore, he provocatively presented the scheme
of practical mathematics as an alternative to what
he labelled 'academic mathematics' as a paradigm for
schools. These years were also critical ones for the
structure and patterns of administrative control in
the English educational system, with a new system of
secondary schools being shaped and developed from
the existing patchwork through the new administrative policies and functioning of the Board of Education and LEAs. It seems reasonable to conjecture
that such a system in a state of flux was likely to
be particularly receptive to curricular innovation
in the interests of the majority of pupils who were
being admitted to grant-aided secondary schools in
increasing numbers.

The American historian of mathematics Florian
Cajori has judged that the Perry movement 'made at
once a deep and lasting impress, especially in England and America, and then spent itself'.(203) Certainly, Perry's own tactical efforts were only effective in the short term, but it has been a

principal purpose of this chapter to show that the
movement's guiding principles continued for many
years to be reflected in the development of English
school mathematics. As Bryan acknowledged with reference to the possible earlier introduction of calculus 'this and many other equally important changes
owe their inception largely to what has often been
described as the "Perry movement"'.(204) The details
of curriculum development over the first half of
this century were to engage many leading personal-
ities, and the Mathematical Association in particular became centrally involved in much of the work,
but that is another story. A rich legacy from the
Perry movement survived the early reactions to aspects of its ideology and some of the short-term
effects. The character and circumstances of this
movement lend considerable weight to a claim for its
uniqueness as a phenomenon in curriculum history.

NOTES AND REFERENCES

1.   H.E. Armstrong, 'Prof. John Perry F.R.S.',
Nature, vol.105, no.265 (1920), pp. 751-2 (p. 752).
2.   R.C. Fawdry, 'Reformed Mathematical Teaching' in J. Adams (ed.), Educational Movements and
Methods (Harrap, 1924), pp. 129-43 (p. 131). Fawdry
(1873-1965) taught at Clifton College for thirty
years, 1903-33 and Perry had also briefly taught
mathematics and science at Clifton, 1871-4.
3.   G. Wolff, Der Mathematische Unterricht der
Höheren Knabenschulen Englands (Teubner, Leipzig,
1915), pp. 67-84.
4.   J.W.A. Young, The Teaching of Mathematics
in the Elementary and Secondary School, 2nd ed.
(Longmans, New York, 1914), pp. 87-121.
5.   M.H. Price, 'The Reform of English Mathematical Education in the Late Nineteenth and Early
Twentieth Centuries', unpublished PhD thesis, University of Leicester, 1981, pp. 360-4.
6.   For a biographical approach to the period
focused on Charles Godfrey (1873-1924) see A.G. Howson, A History of Mathematics Education in England
(Cambridge University Press, 1982), pp. 141-68. For
a critical discussion of Howson's treatment see M.H.
Price, 'Utility or Mental Discipline in Mathematics
Education?', Studies in Science Education, vol.11
(1984), pp. 102-8.
7.   H.H.T. [Turner], 'John Perry - 1850-1920',
Proceedings of the Royal Society, series A, vol.111
(1926), pp. i-vii (p. i).

8.   Ibid., pp. iv-v. The workshop and laboratory at Clifton were not the first of their kind. There had been an earlier initiative at Rossall.

9.   The early efforts to reform school geometry centred on the Association for the Improvement of Geometrical Teaching. For discussion of the limited nineteenth-century achievements, and the continuing dominance of Euclid in England see W.H. Brock, 'Geometry and the Universities: Euclid and his Modern Rivals 1860-1901', History of Education, vol.4, no.2 (1975), pp. 21-35; M.H. Price, 'Mathematics in English Education 1860-1914: Some Questions and Explanations in Curriculum History', History of Education, vol.12, no.4 (1983), pp. 271-84; A.G. Howson, 'Euclid: "a very English subject"' in Sciences et Techniques en Perspective, forthcoming.

10.   J. Perry, England's Neglect of Science (Fisher Unwin, 1900), pp. 102-3. For a general discussion of the significance of squared paper and graphical methods in relation to the Perry movement see W.H. Brock and M.H. Price, 'Squared Paper in the Nineteenth Century: Instrument of Science and Engineering, and Symbol of Reform in Mathematical Education', Educational Studies in Mathematics, vol.11 (1980), pp. 365-81.

11.   W.H. Brock, 'An Experiment in Technical Education', New Scientist, 22 November 1979, pp. 622-3. Importantly for major curricular innovation, Finsbury was free from external examination pressures.

12.   H. Butterworth, 'The Science and Art Department Examinations: Origins and Achievements' in R. Macleod (ed.), Days of Judgement (Nafferton, Driffield, 1982), pp. 27-44.

13.   Department of Science and Art, Practical Mathematics: Summary of Six Lectures Delivered to Working Men by Professor John Perry (HMSO, 1899).

14.   E.H. Moore, 'On the Foundations of Mathematics' in National Council of Teachers of Mathematics, The First Yearbook: A General Survey of Progress in the Last Twenty-Five Years (New York, 1926), pp. 32-57 (pp. 39-40). This Presidential Address to the American Mathematical Society was first published in 1903.

15.   J. Perry, 'Practical Mathematics', Correspondence, Nature, vol.90, no.2237 (1912), pp. 34-5 (p. 35).

16.   J. Perry, 'The Teaching of Mathematics', Nature, vol.62, no.1605 (1900), pp. 317-20. The scheme is reproduced in Howson, A History of

Mathematics Education in England, pp. 222-4.

17.   Board of Education, *Report of the Board of Education 1899-1900*, Vol.2 (HMSO, 1900), p. 35.

18.   Correspondent, 'The Reform in Mathematical Education', *Engineering*, 19 June 1903, pp. 803-5 (p. 803).

19.   H.T. Holmes, 'Elementary Mathematics in Evening Schools', *Mathematical Gazette*, vol.5, no.84 (1910), pp. 200-2 (p. 200).

20.   J. Perry, *Elementary Practical Mathematics* (Macmillan, 1913), pp. vii-viii.

21.   See, for example, the early output of Frank Castle, who came under Perry's direct influence at South Kensington, and whose textbooks were very successful for Macmillan: F. Castle, *Workshop Mathematics* (Macmillan, 1900); F. Castle, *Practical Mathematics for Beginners* (Macmillan, 1901); and F. Castle, *A Manual of Practical Mathematics* (Macmillan, 1903). For a review of various textbooks see J.E. Boyt, 'Reviews. Practical (or Experimental) Mathematics', *Mathematical Gazette*, vol.3, no.56 (1906), pp. 294-300.

22.   Board of Education, *Report of the Board of Education for the Year 1903-1904* (1904), p. 18, *1907-1908* (1909), p. 81, *1911-1912* (1913), p. 136, *1924-1925* (1926), p. 153 (HMSO). The Board did not provide in-service courses for secondary school teachers specifically until 1916.

23.   P. Abbott, 'The Preliminary Mathematical Training of Technical Students' in Board of Education, *The Teaching of Mathematics in the United Kingdom Part II*, Special Reports on Educational Subjects Vol.27 (hereinafter *Special Reports Vol.27*), (HMSO, 1912), pp. 10-26 (p. 10).

24.   Butterworth, 'The Science and Art Department Examinations'.

25.   Royal Commission on Secondary Education, (*Bryce Report*) Vol.9 (HMSO, 1895), pp. 404-15.

26.   For detailed discussion of these administrative developments and their consequences see A.S. Bishop, *The Rise of a Central Authority for English Education* (Cambridge University Press, 1971); also P.H.J.H. Gosden, *The Development of Educational Administration in England and Wales* (Basil Blackwell, Oxford, 1966).

27.   Board of Education, *Report of the Consultative Committee on Examinations in Secondary Schools* (HMSO, 1911), particularly ch. 1.

28.   Price, 'The Reform of English Mathematical Education', pp. 42-50.

29.   R.J. Montgomery, *Examinations* (Longmans,

1965), pp. 88-90.
30.   Brock, 'An Experiment in Technical Education', p. 623.
31.   R.J.W. Selleck, The New Education 1870-1914 (Pitman, 1968), p. 203.
32.   R. Wormell, 'Mathematics' in P.A. Barnett (ed.), Teaching and Organisation with Special Reference to Secondary Schools (Longmans, 1897), pp. 78-97 (pp. 82-3). Wormell's school accommodated some of the early classes run by Ayrton and Armstrong, before the new College was built on the adjoining playground.
33.   Ibid., p. 83.
34.   J. Perry, 'The Force of One Pound', Nature, vol.55, no.1412 (1896), pp. 49-51 (p. 51).
35.   J. Perry (ed.) British Association Meeting at Glasgow, 1901: Discussion on the Teaching of Mathematics (Macmillan, 1901), p. 27.
36.   Selleck, The New Education, pp. 102-51.
37.   J.J. Findlay, 'The Teaching of Elementary Mathematics: Impending Reforms', Educational Times, vol.55, no.492 (1902), pp. 184-7 (p. 185).
38.   Ibid., p. 185.
39.   Wolff, Der Mathematische Unterricht, pp. 119-21.
40.   W.H. Brock, 'From Liebig to Nuffield: A Bibliography of the History of Science Education, 1839-1974', Studies in Science Education, vol.2 (1975), p. 75. See also W.H. Brock, H.E. Armstrong and the Teaching of Science 1880-1930 (Cambridge University Press, 1973).
41.   Findlay, 'The Teaching of Elementary Mathematics', p. 185.
42.   Ibid., and see R. Wormell, 'Unstable Questions of Method in the Teaching of Elementary Science', Educational Times, vol.53, no.470 (1900), pp. 240-3; R. Wormell, 'The Essentials of the Teaching of Geometry', Journal of Education, no.392 (1902), pp. 210-12.
43.   W.D. Eggar, Practical Exercises in Geometry (Macmillan, 1903), p. v. Eggar was a founder member of the Association of Public School Science Masters in 1900: see D. Layton, Interpreters of Science (John Murray/ASE, 1984), pp. 1-32.
44.   Findlay, 'The Teaching of Elementary Mathematics', p. 185.
45.   R.C. Fawdry, 'Practical Mathematics at Clifton College' in Board of Education, The Teaching of Mathematics in the United Kingdom Part I, Special Reports on Educational Subjects Vol.26 (hereinafter Special Reports Vol.26), (HMSO, 1912), pp. 400-2

(p. 400).
46.   W.D. Eggar, 'The Co-ordination of the
Teaching of Elementary Mathematics and Physics',
School World, vol.3, no.34 (1901), pp. 361-3 (p. 361);
E.W. Jenkins, From Armstrong to Nuffield: Studies in
Twentieth-Century Science Education in England and
Wales (John Murray, 1979), pp. 30-3.
47.   Findlay, 'The Teaching of Elementary Mathematics', p. 184; Jenkins, From Armstrong to Nuffield, pp. 252-5.
48.   G.M. Minchin, Review of Perry, England's
Neglect, Nature, vol.64, no.1653 (1901), pp. 226-8
(p. 227).
49.   G.H. Bryan, 'The British Association Discussion on the Teaching of Mathematics', School
World, vol.4, no.39 (1902), pp. 88-91 (p. 90).
50.   College of Preceptors, 'The Teaching of
Elementary Geometry', Educational Times, vol.56,
no.511 (1903), pp. 465-7 (p. 465).
51.   Selleck, The New Education, pp. 78-101.
Such political arguments for major reform in curricula, as exploited by the practical educationists
in particular, are referred to as 'declinism' in
W.H. Brock, 'The Knowledge that Is Most Worth',
Studies in Science Education, vol.7 (1980), pp. 171-
7 (p. 172).
52.   R.H. Smith, 'Reform in Mathematical Education', Engineer, vol.93, 7 February 1902, pp. 129-30
(p. 129).
53.   Young, The Teaching of Mathematics, p. 105.
54.   Price, 'Mathematics in English Education',
p. 284.
55.   Correspondent, 'The Reform in Mathematical
Education', p. 803.
56.   The Times, 9 November 1900.
57.   Perry, 'The Teaching of Mathematics'.
58.   Perry, England's Neglect.
59.   Ibid., p. v.
60.   See correspondence on 'The Reform of Mathematical Teaching' in Nature, vol.62, nos.1608,
1610, 1611, 1613 (1900), pp. 389, 436, 466, 523; and
O. Heaviside, 'The Teaching of Mathematics', Nature,
vol.62, no.1614 (1900), pp. 548-9.
61.   See, for example, the series of articles
on the teaching of algebra and geometry, by Professors Mathews and Minchin respectively, and the resulting correspondence concerning the latter in
vol.1 of the School World (1899).
62.   Findlay, 'The Teaching of Elementary Mathematics', p. 184.
63.   Ibid., p. 184. Macmillan, the publishers

The Perry Movement in School Mathematics

of Nature and the School World, was also a major publisher of mathematics textbooks, including practical mathematics.

64. Interestingly, the columns of the Mathematical Association's journal the Mathematical Gazette, which started in 1894, remained unruffled by these early individual initiatives.

65. For a discussion of the failure to achieve major reform in the earlier period and the sharp contrast with the developments in the 1900s see Price, 'Mathematics in English Education'.

66. On the background concerning Section L see P. Collins, 'The Origins of the British Association's Education Section', British Journal of Educational Studies, vol.27, no.3 (1979), pp. 232-44.

67. H.A. Moylan, 'Prof. Perry, F.R.S., and the Teaching of Mathematics', Journal of Education, no.378 (1901), pp. 39-40 (p. 39).

68. R.F. Muirhead, 'The Teaching of Mathematics', Mathematical Gazette, vol.2, no.29 (1901), pp. 81-3 (p. 81).

69. Perry, British Association Meeting at Glasgow, p. 1.

70. J. Perry, 'Reform of Mathematical Education', Engineer, vol.93, 28 February 1902, p. 203.

71. Perry, England's Neglect, p. 49.

72. Wolff, Der Mathematische Unterricht, pp. 67-84.

73. Muirhead, 'The Teaching of Mathematics', p. 82. For a brief summary of the Glasgow proceedings see Nature, vol.64, no.1667 (1901), p. 592.

74. National Education Association and American Federation of Teachers of the Mathematical and Natural Sciences, Final Report of the National Committee of Fifteen on Geometry Syllabus (New York, 1912), pp. 5-32.

75. A.E.H. Love, Review of Perry, British Association Meeting at Glasgow, Nature, vol.65, no.1690 (1902), pp. 457-8 (p. 458).

76. W.P. Workman, in a written remark in Perry, British Association Meeting at Glasgow, p. 77.

77. Ibid., in a written remark, p. 91.

78. Ibid., p. ix.

79. Ibid.

80. School World, vol.4, no.39 (1902).

81. C. Godfrey, 'The Passing of Euclid', Cornhill Magazine, new series, vol.21 (1906), pp. 72-7 (p. 76). The Association for the Improvement of Geometrical Teaching changed its name to the Mathematical Association in 1897. It had strong associations with the public schools and two ancient

148

universities, particularly Cambridge. Socially and
ideologically it was distanced from the wider concerns of the Perry movement in its early stages: see
Price, 'The Reform of English Mathematical Education', pp. 88-95, 107-13.
    82. Mathematical Gazette, vol.2, no.30 (1902),
pp. 105-11.
    83. Ibid., p. 107.
    84. Ibid., p. 106.
    85. Price, 'The Reform of English Mathematical
Education', pp. 107-9.
    86. Ibid., pp. 108-10; and see Perry, British
Association Meeting at Glasgow, 2nd ed. (1902), pp.
106-11.
    87. Price, 'The Reform of English Mathematical
Education', pp. 110-13.
    88. B. Russell, 'The Teaching of Euclid',
Mathematical Gazette, vol.2, no.33 (1902), pp. 165-7
(p. 165).
    89. Price, 'The Reform of English Mathematical
Education', pp. 111-13.
    90. C. Godfrey, 'Geometry Teaching: The Next
Step', Mathematical Gazette, vol.10, no.145 (1920),
pp. 20-4 (p. 20).
    91. Mathematical Gazette, vol.2, no.35 (1902),
pp. 197-201; School World, vol.4, no.46 (1902), pp.
389-92; Perry, British Association Meeting at Glasgow, 2nd ed. (1902), pp. 112-23.
    92. J. Perry, 'The Teaching of Mathematics',
Correspondence, Nature, vol.65, no.1691 (1902), pp.
484-6 (p. 486).
    93. Butterworth, 'The Science and Art Depart-
ment Examinations'.
    94. O. Henrici, Elementary Geometry: Congruent
Figures (Longmans, 1879), p. ix.
    95. D. Mair, 'The Reform of Mathematical
Teaching', Nature, vol.62, no.1608 (1900), p. 389.
    96. 'School Geometry Reform', Nature, vol.68,
no.1755 (1903), pp. 147-8 (p. 147).
    97. C.A. Rumsey, 'Recent Developments in Math-
ematical Examinations', School World, vol.5, no.49,
pp. 10-13 (p. 11). Examination papers are reproduced
in B.S. Hitchens, 'Mathematics and Higher Grade
Schools', unpublished MEd dissertation, University
of London, 1978, pp. 71-8.
    98. Rumsey, 'Recent Developments in Mathemati-
cal Examinations', p. 11.
    99. Godfrey, 'The Passing of Euclid', p. 76.
    100. C. Godfrey, 'Methods of Intuition and Ex-
periment in Secondary Schools' in Special Reports
Vol. 26, pp. 429-38 (p. 431).

101. E.M. Langley in Perry, British Association Meeting at Glasgow, p. 44.

102. For a detailed discussion of examination syllabus reform see Price, 'The Reform of English Mathematical Education', pp. 115-20.

103. See, for example, Rumsey, 'Recent Developments in Mathematical Examinations', and Correspondent, 'The Reform in Mathematical Education'; also, Correspondent, 'The Reform in Mathematical Education', pt 2, Engineering, 21 August 1903, pp. 237-8; J. Perry, 'Mathematics in the Cambridge Locals', Nature, vol.67, no.1726 (1902), pp. 81-2.

104. 'Mathematical Reform at Cambridge', Nature, vol.68, no.1756 (1903), pp. 178-9 (p. 178).

105. Ibid., p. 179.

106. Board of Education, Regulations for the Instruction and Training of Pupil-Teachers (HMSO, 1904), pp. 23-4; Board of Education, Regulations for the Training of Teachers and for the Examination of Students in Training Colleges (HMSO, 1904), pp. 29-31.

107. Perry, 'Mathematics in the Cambridge Locals', p. 82.

108. 'Mathematical Reform at Cambridge', p. 179.

109. See Price, 'The Reform of English Mathematical Education', pp. 120-1, where the Subject Indices and General Catalogue of the British Museum, a copyright deposit library, are used to measure the output of school textbooks.

110. Mathematical Association, Index to the Mathematical Gazette Volumes I-XV (Bell, 1933), pp. 106-60. See also the monthly School World and 'School Geometry Reform'; J. Harrison, 'School Geometry Reform', Nature, vol.67, no.1747 (1903), pp. 577-8.

111. C.H. French, 'New London Matriculation Syllabus in Mathematics', School World, vol.4, no.46 (1902), pp. 363-6 (p. 365).

112. Price, 'The Reform of English Mathematical Education', p. 121.

113. H.S. Hall, A Short Introduction to Graphical Algebra (Macmillan, 1902).

114. Brock and Price, 'Squared Paper in the Nineteenth Century'.

115. W.H. Salmon, 'Squared Paper', School World, vol.5, no.53 (1903), pp. 169-70.

116. C. Godfrey, 'The Teaching of Mathematics at Preparatory Schools', School World, vol.4, no.44 (1902), pp. 288-91 (p. 289).

117. Perry, England's Neglect, p. 46.

118. H.S. Hall, 'The Use and Abuse of Graphs',

Correspondence, School World, vol.7, no.76 (1905), pp. 158-9 (p. 159).

119. H.H.T., 'John Perry', p. v.

120. S.C., 'Euclid's Elements by an Ancient Geometer', Journal of Education, no.450 (1907), p. 32.

121. Godfrey, 'The Passing of Euclid'.

122. British Museum, Subject Index of Modern Works Added to the Library of the British Museum in the Years 1901-1905, 1906-1910, 1911-1915 (1906, 1911, 1918).

123. Eggar, 'The Co-ordination of the Teaching of Elementary Mathematics and Physics'.

124. Findlay, 'The Teaching of Elementary Mathematics', p. 186; A. Consterdine and S.O. Andrew, Practical Arithmetic (John Murray, 1905).

125. P.B. Ballard, 'The Teaching of Mathematics in London Public Elementary Schools' in Special Reports Vol.26, pp. 3-30 (p. 12); ibid., L. Story, 'The Organisation of the Teaching of Mathematics in Public Secondary Schools for Girls', pp. 543-59 (p. 550).

126. A. Lodge, 'Mathematics in the Army Entrance Examinations', School World, vol.6, no.72 (1904), pp. 452-4.

127. Boyt, 'Reviews', pp. 294-5.

128. A.W. Siddons, 'Practical Mathematics at Harrow School' in Special Reports Vol.26, pp. 403-9.

129. G.M. Bell, 'Practical Mathematics at Winchester College' in Special Reports Vol.26, pp. 427-8; C. Godfrey and G.M. Bell, Note-book of Experimental Mathematics (Arnold, 1905).

130. R.C. Fawdry, 'Practical Mathematics at Clifton College' and F.W. Sanderson, 'Practical Mathematics at Oundle School' in Special Reports Vol.26, pp. 400-2, 410-26.

131. R.C. Fawdry, 'Laboratory Work in Connection with Mathematics', Mathematical Gazette, vol.8, no.116 (1915), pp. 36-9 (p. 36).

132. R.H. Bayliss, 'Practical Mathematics', School World, vol.7, no.78 (1905), pp. 214-6 (p. 214); G.H. Wyatt, 'Equipment for the Teaching of Practical Mathematics', School World, vol.7, no.78 (1905), pp. 216-8; W.D. Eggar, 'Mathematical Instruments for School Use', School World, vol.5, no.55 (1903), pp. 247-8; Salmon, 'Squared Paper', and G.A. Gibson, 'Mathematical Tables', School World, vol.7, no.78 (1905), pp. 201-3.

133. Bayliss, 'Practical Mathematics', p. 216.

134. J. Perry, 'The Education of Engineers' in British Association for the Advancement of Science, Report of the Seventy-Second Meeting: Belfast 1902

(John Murray, 1903), pp. 711-29 (p. 719).

135. Findlay, 'The Teaching of Elementary Mathematics', p. 184.

136. S.A. Burstall, 'The Place of Mathematics in the Education of Girls and Women' in Special Reports Vol.26, pp. 575-81 (p. 576).

137. Price, 'The Reform of English Mathematical Education', pp. 231-3; C. Godfrey, 'The Teaching of Mathematics in English Public Schools for Boys', Mathematical Gazette, vol.4, no.71 (1908), pp. 250-9 (p. 253).

138. Perry, British Association Meeting at Glasgow, p. 25.

139. Price, 'The Reform of English Mathematical Education', pp. 234-5. The requirements of the Cambridge Previous were an exception, but directly affected only older pupils, predominantly in public schools. See also Godfrey, 'Methods of Intuition and Experiment', p. 436.

140. Wolff, Der Mathematische Unterricht, p. 157. The tables of Godfrey and Siddons, first published in 1913, enjoyed enormous success for over forty years.

141. Price, 'The Reform of English Mathematical Education', p. 236.

142. By contrast, the educational use of slide rules made little headway: ibid., pp. 236-8.

143. J. Perry, 'The Correlation of the Teaching of Mathematics and Science', School World, vol.10, no.120 (1908), pp. 459-64 (p. 461).

144. Ibid., p. 463.

145. W.C. Fletcher, 'The Position of Mathematics in Secondary Schools in England' in Special Reports Vol.26, pp. 90-103.

146. Price, 'The Reform of English Mathematical Education', pp. 69-81.

147. Perry, 'The Correlation of the Teaching of Mathematics and Science', p. 463.

148. Ibid., p. 464.

149. The Mathematical Association became the most important organisation in relation to the tactical details of curriculum development in public and secondary school mathematics, following the early years of major upheaval. An evaluation of its work is beyond the scope of this chapter, though the tension between the educational ideals of the Mathematical Association and those of the Perry movement is notable: see Price, 'The Reform of English Mathematical Education', pp. 138-82.

150. J. Strachan, 'Mathematics' in J. Adams (ed.), The New Teaching (Hodder and Stoughton,

1918), pp. 195-229 (p. 197).

151. F.E. Robinson, 'Mathematics for Army Candidates', Mathematical Gazette, vol.3, no.58 (1906), pp. 336-8 (p. 336).

152. Ibid., p. 338.

153. A.C. Jones, 'Practical Mathematical Exercises and Graphs', School World, vol.7, no.80 (1905), pp. 287-90 (p. 288); and see Hall, 'The Use and Abuse of Graphs'.

154. B. Branford, A Study of Mathematical Education (Clarendon Press, Oxford, 1908), pp. vii-viii.

155. Godfrey, 'The Teaching of Mathematics in English Public Schools', p. 256.

156. Ibid., pp. 256-7.

157. British Association for the Advancement of Science, Report of the Eightieth Meeting: Sheffield 1910 (John Murray, 1911), pp. 521-2.

158. J.E.A. Steggall, 'On Practical Mathematics in Schools', Mathematical Gazette, vol.7, no.110 (1914), pp. 287-94 (p. 294).

159. C.H.P. Mayo, Reminiscences of a Harrow Master (Rivingtons, 1928), pp. 132-7.

160. W.F. Beard, 'The Reform of Mathematical Teaching', Nature, vol.62, no.1611 (1900), p. 466.

161. Perry, 'The Teaching of Mathematics', Correspondence, p. 486.

162. J. Perry, 'Cambridge Mathematics', Correspondence, Nature, vol.67, no.1739 (1903), pp. 390-1 (p. 390).

163. Ibid., p. 391.

164. E.W. Hobson, 'The Democratization of Mathematical Education', Mathematical Gazette, vol.6, no.97 (1912), pp. 234-43 (p. 239).

165. Ibid., p. 243.

166. Perry, 'Practical Mathematics', p. 34.

167. B. Hopkinson, 'The Relation of Mathematics to Engineering at Cambridge' in Special Reports Vol.27, pp. 327-39.

168. W.H. White, 'The Place of Mathematics in Engineering Practice', Nature, vol.90, no.2238 (1912), pp. 95-6 (p. 95).

169. Perry, 'Practical Mathematics', pp. 34-5.

170. Wolff, Der Mathematische Unterricht, p. 83.

171. Perry, Elementary Practical Mathematics.

172. G.H. Bryan, 'Prof. Perry's Practical Mathematics', Nature, vol.91, no.2283 (1913), pp. 551-3; 'The Apotheosis of Practical Mathematics', School World, vol.15, no.176 (1913), p. 314.

173. Perry, England's Neglect, p. 49.

174. H.T.H. Piaggio, 'Mathematics for Evening Technical Students', Mathematical Gazette, vol.12,

no.171 (1924), pp. 161-3 (pp. 161-2).
175. Mathematical Association, The Teaching of Mathematics to Evening Technical Students (Bell, 1926), p. 9.
176. Armstrong, 'Prof. John Perry F.R.S.'. Curiously, his obituary for the Royal Society, H.H.T., 'John Perry' did not appear until 1926.
177. D.E. Smith, 'Intuition and Experiment in Mathematical Teaching in the Secondary Schools' in International Congress of Mathematicians, Proceedings of the Fifth International Congress of Mathematicians, Vol.2 (Cambridge University Press, 1913), pp. 611-32.
178. Godfrey, 'Methods of Intuition and Experiment', p. 437.
179. Smith, 'Intuition and Experiment'.
180. Fawdry, 'Reformed Mathematical Teaching', p. 133.
181. Strachan, 'Mathematics', p. 218.
182. Price, 'The Reform of English Mathematical Education', pp. 309-11.
183. W.G. Borchardt and A.D. Perrott, A New Trigonometry for Schools (Bell, 1904).
184. Price, 'The Reform of English Mathematical Education', pp. 311-15; G.StL. Carson, 'England' in National Council of Teachers of Mathematics, The Fourth Yearbook: Significant Changes and Trends in the Teaching of Mathematics throughout the World since 1910 (New York, 1929), pp. 21-31.
185. J. Perry, The Calculus for Engineers (Arnold, 1897).
186. C.S. Jackson, 'Calculus as a School Subject' in Special Reports Vol.26, pp. 365-80 (p. 369).
187. Godfrey, 'The Teaching of Mathematics in English Public Schools', p. 259.
188. C. Godfrey, 'Mathematics in English Schools', Science Progress, vol.6 (1912), pp. 161-80 (p. 178).
189. Price, 'The Reform of English Mathematical Education', pp. 315-21. There is also a more tenuous connection between the Perry movement's opposition to the rigid nineteenth-century separation of the branches of mathematics and the development of alternative 'unified' secondary mathematics courses after 1944. The new alternative syllabuses bore a striking resemblance to Perry's scheme of 1899. See ibid., pp. 289-98.
190. Ibid., pp. 127-8.
191. British Association for the Advancement of Science, 'The Teaching of Elementary Arithmetic' in School World, vol.8, no.92 (1906), pp. 301-5.

192. Board of Education, The Education of the
Adolescent (HMSO, 1926).
193. L.J. Frobisher and R.R. Joy, Mathematical
Education: A Bibliography of Theses and Dissertations (Mathsed Press, Leeds, 1978), p. 2.
194. Carson, 'England', p. 30.
195. Board of Education, Senior School Mathematics, Educational Pamphlet No.101 (HMSO, 1935),
pp. 3-4.
196. O. Banks, Parity and Prestige in English
Secondary Education (Routledge and Kegan Paul, 1955).
197. Hobson in British Association, Report of
the Eightieth Meeting, p. 521.
198. Bryan, 'Prof. Perry's Practical Mathematics', p. 551.
199. T.P. Nunn, 'The Aim and Methods of School
Algebra Teaching', Mathematical Gazette, vol.6,
no.95 (1911), pp. 167-72 (p. 171). See also Abbott's
tribute (n.23).
200. H.B. Heywood, 'The Reform of University
Mathematics', Mathematical Gazette, vol.12, no.175
(1925), pp. 322-30 (p. 326).
201. Howson, 'Euclid: "a very English subject"'.
202. Godfrey, 'The Teaching of Mathematics',
p. 252.
203. F. Cajori, A History of Elementary Mathematics, 2nd ed. (Macmillan, New York, 1917), p. 290.
204. G.H. Bryan, 'Practical Mathematics', Correspondence, Nature, vol.90, no.2238 (1912), p. 68.

Chapter Six

SCIENCE FOR PROFESSIONALS: SCIENTIFIC METHOD AND
SECONDARY EDUCATION

EDGAR JENKINS

By the time the Taunton Commissioners reported in
1868, the curriculum of the English grammar school
had been the subject of lively controversy for well
over half a century. The challenge to the supremacy
of the classics mounted in the 1790s by, among others, Mary Wollstonecraft and the Edgeworths, had
continued in the following century in, for example,
Bentham's Chrestomathia, in the writings of George
Combe, in the lectures of Thomas Huxley and, above
all, in the first of Herbert Spencer's essays on
education published between 1854 and 1859.(1) Spencer's answer to the question 'What knowledge is of
most worth?' was unambiguous and provocative and his
eloquent and aggressive advocacy of science ensured
that his views were discussed widely. However, during the later 1860s, the nature of the debate about
the inclusion of scientific subjects in the grammar
school curriculum changed. The conflict of studies
began to abate and the ardent protagonism of Spencer
and the vigorous response of his opponents gradually
gave way to a greater perception of the complexity
of the problems of curriculum reform and to a broader and more rational analysis of the issues involved.
In 1864, the report of the Clarendon Commissioners,
although confirming the importance of a classical
education, acknowledged its contemporary short-
comings and, in describing the exclusion of natural
science from the education of the higher classes in
England as 'a plain defect and a great practical
evil', offered some hope that the position of scientific education in the leading public schools
might be improved.(2) Only three years later, the
British Association for the Advancement of Science,
in a report 'On the Best Means for Promoting Scientific Education in Schools', was able to assert that

there was 'already a <u>general</u> recognition of Science
as an element in liberal education'. In support of
this assertion, it cited the encouragement of science given 'to a greater or less degree, by the English, Scotch and Irish Universities', its recognition as an 'optional study by the College of Preceptors', its inclusion in the schedule of local examinations conducted by the Universities of Oxford and
Cambridge and its partial incorporation within the
curriculum of several public schools.

THE BRITISH ASSOCIATION AND THE SCHOOLING OF SCIENCE

The British Association report of 1867, which was
widely circulated and publicised and remained an
important point of reference for advocates of scientific education for at least half a century, suggested that the case for teaching science in secondary schools rested upon a number of distinct grounds.
First, science offered an excellent means of mental
training by 'providing the best discipline in observation and collection of facts, in the combination
of inductive and deductive reasoning, and in accuracy of both thought and language'. Secondly, the inclusion of science within the curriculum could 'remedy some of the defects of the ordinary school education' both by appealing to the 'many boys' (<u>sic</u>)
on whom the usual non-scientific studies produced
'very slight effect' and by contributing a valuable
element to the education of those who showed a 'special aptitude for literary culture'. Thirdly, the
methods and results of science had 'so profoundly
affected all the philosophical thought of the age'
that an educated man was 'under a very great disad-
vantage' if he remained unacquainted with them. Additionally, it was claimed, the teaching of science
could be justified on the ground that even a 'moder-
ate acquaintance' led to a 'very great intellectual
pleasure' in after life. Finally, science should be
taught because it affected materially 'the present
position and future progress of civilization' i.e.
scientific knowledge was useful. This five-point
rationale was accompanied by an important distinction drawn between scientific <u>information</u> and scientific <u>training</u>; in other words, between general
literary acquaintance with scientific facts and the
knowledge of methods that may be gained by studying
the facts at first hand under the guidance of a competent teacher. While both of these aspects were
recognised as important, the principal benefit of a

157

scientific education was regarded as the 'scientific habit of mind': a habit described as of 'incalculable value whatever ... the pursuits of after life'.(3) The distinction drawn in the report between 'content' and 'process' and the relative importance ascribed to these two aspects of scientific education provide a useful framework for the discussion of the practice and rationale of school science teaching both within, and beyond, the period with which this study is concerned.

Also of significance in the report is the emphasis placed upon mental training and intellectual discipline. Such an emphasis suggests a different and somewhat more homogeneous curriculum rationale than that evident earlier in the nineteenth century when, for some, science had provided a means of reconciling an understanding of the natural world with the teaching of the bible or, for others of a more radical persuasion, offered a weapon with which to fight authoritarianism, dogma or superstition. In particular, the feeble acknowledgement given in the 1867 report to the usefulness of scientific knowledge stands in marked contrast with the views prevalent at the time of the founding of the British Association itself in 1831, when science was widely disseminated and learnt precisely because of its utility and its justification depended, in some sense or other, upon the manner in which it served the public.(4)

What brought about this narrowing of the perception of the educational function of science? At the tactical level, utilitarian arguments could clearly be given little prominence in presenting the case for science teaching in schools concerned with the liberal education of English gentlemen. In addition, the claim that a scientific education provided the best discipline in observation and in the combination of inductive with deductive reasoning enabled its advocates to argue for its inclusion in the curriculum on grounds precisely parallel to those invoked to support the teaching of classics, a subject of high status and long established within public schools. Thus it was, perhaps surprisingly, the Clarendon Commissioners who claimed that the study of science 'quickens and cultivates directly the faculty of observation ... the power of accurate and rapid generalization and the mental habit of method and arrangement'. However, science itself had also undergone a number of important changes. In particular, it had become increasingly professional in its practice and organisation. By the time the

Devonshire Commissioners were appointed in 1870, to enquire into the relationships between scientific education and the advancement of science (the terms of the enquiry are significant), the processes leading to the professionalisation of science were well under way. Indeed, the British Association, through its annual meetings, served as an important public forum within which 'men of science examined anew who they were and what they wanted'.(5) Essential to this growing professionalisation of science in the nineteenth century was the freedom of the scientific community to control as far as possible the direction of scientific research and, more particularly, to pursue such research within the constraints necessarily imposed by overtly and immediately utilitarian considerations. According to Kuhn, this freedom, with its consequent insulation of the scientific community from society and its attendant notion of 'pure science', was essential to the development of the modern scientific enterprise.(6) It remained possible, of course, for individuals or organisations to deploy utilitarian arguments in appealing to governments for financial support but in general, the benefits to be offered were unspecified, long-term and, to a large degree, unpredictable. The case for scientific education presented in the British Association report of 1867 in terms of mental training and the 'scientific habit of mind' was, therefore, more than an elegant means of meeting the requirements of a liberal secondary education and of encouraging the future well-being of the emerging profession of science. It was part of the tacit 'social contract' developed in the mid-nineteenth century between the professional scientific community and the society of which it formed an increasingly powerful and influential part.(7)

The immediate origins of the 1867 report lie in the annual meeting of the Association held in Nottingham in the previous year when several speakers had addressed the issue of school science teaching and the Biology Section had considered a paper by the Reverend F.W. Farrar entitled 'On the Teaching of Science at the Public Schools'.(8) Farrar, a teacher of classics at Harrow who was elected to Fellowship of the Royal Society in 1866, argued that science called into play different faculties of mind from those involved with the study of classics and he identified the difficulties facing those seeking to incorporate science within the curriculum of public schools. Apart from the already severe pressure on the timetable, there were no well-developed and

suitable schemes of study in science and few satisfactory textbooks to support them. In addition,
there was no general agreement among the advocates
of school scientific education about which branch or
branches of science were appropriate to the needs of
the secondary and public schools. It was in an attempt to overcome some of these difficulties that
the 1867 report was produced by a committee of the
Association, established at Farrar's request.

Using the distinction it had drawn between scientific information and training, the committee suggested that the former, embracing elementary astronomy, geology, natural history and physiology
need not be circumscribed by any syllabus and might
be left to the 'discretion of the masters who teach
them'. Scientific training, on the other hand, could
be assured only by the systematic teaching of experimental physics, elementary chemistry and botany,
with the latter, because of its direct relationship
to everyday experience, admitting 'pre-eminently of
being taught in the true scientific method'. The inclusion of elementary chemistry among the subjects
advised by the committee is of some interest. Among
the members of the committee was J.M. Wilson, an assistant master at Rugby and Fellow of St John's,
Cambridge, who contributed an essay on the teaching
of natural science in schools to a volume edited by
Farrar and published in 1867. In Wilson's view,
chemistry was 'not a good subject for lecture instruction to beginners in science' since the subject, although possessing the advantage of being
'rather amusing', was 'very deficient' as an exercise in reasoning.(9)

EXAMINATIONS, RESOURCES AND METHODS

By 1870, therefore, the future of secondary school
science teaching was cast firmly in an instrumental,
pre-professional role and, despite Wilson's objec-
tions to chemistry, a degree of consensus had emerged about the subjects to be included within the
science curriculum. However, many important and more
practical matters remained to be determined: there
were courses to be constructed, examinations developed, textbooks written, teachers prepared and suitable teaching methods to be devised. For each of
these aspects of science education there were, of
course, some precedents to which reference could be
made. The Universities of Oxford and Cambridge had
conducted 'local' examinations since 1858, the

system of examinations organised by the Royal Society of Arts had been in operation since 1854 and the
Department of Science and Art had introduced its
full scheme of examinations in science in 1860, in
which year it subsidised 30 classes and 1,340 pupils, mostly in private and endowed schools.(10) The
work of the South Kensington Department expanded
greatly during the late nineteenth century, especially after the introduction of organised science
schools in 1872. Although much of this work involved
the more senior pupils in public elementary schools
established under the legislation of 1870, some of
the Department's science schools were associated
with the smaller endowed grammar schools for whom
the science examinations represented something of a
financial lifeline. Finally, and of seminal importance for the future of secondary school science education, there were the developments which had taken
place during the 1850s in the teaching and examining
of science at undergraduate level at the Universities of Oxford, Cambridge and London.(11)

Publishers and potential authors were quick to
respond to the remarkable expansion in the provision
for science teaching which took place during the
later years of the nineteenth century. Although it
is difficult to establish which texts were actually
used widely in schools, there can be little doubt
that publishing ventures such as Longman's London
Science Series or Macmillan's Science Primers were
highly successful.(12) Most textbooks were intended
for use by particular groups of students such as
those preparing for the examinations of the Department of Science and Art or the Matriculation examination of London or other universities. However,
scrutiny of a range of appropriate texts of a comparable level indicates that the differences in contents were marginal rather than substantial so that,
for example, a textbook of elementary inorganic
chemistry would have met the needs of students preparing for examinations set by several different examining bodies. Many of the science texts intended
for school use were written by practising teachers,
some of whom relied on the major works or advice of
authors engaged in the professional practice of science. Thus the various works of Francis Jones, a
teacher of chemistry at the Manchester Grammar
School, owed much to his experience as a Junior Dem-
onstrator in Roscoe's laboratory at Owens College.(13)
Very few school teachers of science were, of course,
professionally trained. Such training did not become
the norm for graduates until well after the Second

World War and was not made compulsory for new graduates in science and mathematics until as recently as 1983.

What of the methods by which science was taught in the years immediately after 1870? Discussions of the methodology of science teaching raise a number of problems, although there have been some attempts at classification e.g. by Brock and Fowles.(14) Different approaches to the teaching of science are likely to involve a number of common elements such as the taking of notes or classroom discussion and, in the historical context, the problem of sources is particularly severe. However, it seems clear that, at least in the years leading up to 1870, the method used most widely for teaching science in secondary schools was the so-called 'lecture demonstration'. Perhaps modelled upon the technique employed earlier in the century by Davy and Faraday in their lectures at the Royal Institution, this involved supporting an exposition of the subject matter with a series of suitable demonstration experiments. The work in physical science at Eton in the early 1860s extended over two or three years and was based upon lectures said to be 'principally experimental'. At Charterhouse in the same period, the rudiments of inorganic chemistry were taught by lectures which were 'always experimental' and, at Rugby, some electricity was taught by lectures illustrated by experiments and diagrams. The role of pupils during these lecture demonstrations was not necessarily passive. At Charterhouse and Rugby, for example, boys were questioned to probe their understanding. The work covered during lecture demonstrations was often supplemented by requiring pupils to read the relevant parts of textbooks. This 'textbook work' was one of the methods used to teach geology, mechanics and chemistry at King Edward VI School, Birmingham, in 1868 and it seems to have been the only means of conveying scientific information at Harrow, where pupils prepared for examination by reading and learning several pages of an elementary text of physical science.(15)

In these circumstances, the frequent complaints made by the science examiners of, for example, the Oxford and Cambridge Joint Board or the Department of Science and Art that candidates' work revealed a serious lack of first-hand familiarity with scientific equipment, materials and procedures were inevitable. To remedy such a defect required capital and recurrent expenditure on the construction and maintenance of school science laboratories. The extent to which the necessary funds were provided is indicated by the claim made in 1902 that of 1,165 laboratories then used for school science teaching, some 1,100 had been built since 1877.(16) Initially, much of the money had come from the Department of Science and Art which, from 1868, offered grants for the construction of laboratories and the purchase of equipment. Later in the century, the funds available under a Local Taxation (Customs and Excise) Act - the so-called whisky money - enabled many Technical Instruction Committees to provide the facilities necessary to support the practical teaching of science. Within the public schools, there was also progress in the provision of science laboratories, although this was more rapid in institutions such as Rossall, Wellington, Christ's Hospital and the grammar schools at Manchester and Bradford than in schools like Eton and Harrow or those modelled most closely upon them. Almost all of the earliest laboratories were equipped for the teaching of chemistry, rather than physics, although the pioneering work of John Perry and, later, of A.M. Worthington at Clifton College represent distinguished exceptions. By 1904, the Regulations of the newly established Board of Education, governing the work of grant-aided secondary schools in England and Wales, ensured not only that science was a compulsory part of the secondary curriculum but that provision was made for it to be taught on a practical basis.

The programme of school science laboratory building which marked the last quarter of the nineteenth century was encouraged and sustained by the introduction of practical examinations, by the publication of a large number of practical texts and by the development of scientific apparatus specifically for teaching purposes. In chemistry, the emphasis was upon simple preparative exercises and upon volumetric and systematic qualitative analysis, with the courses modelled closely upon those provided at undergraduate level within the universities. Practical courses in physics and the appropriate texts to support them were somewhat slower to develop than their chemical counterparts, partly because physics was less developed as a profession than chemistry. Among the earliest practical physics texts to be published were those by Worthington, Stewart and Gee, and Glazebrook and Shaw.(17) As far as biology was concerned, this was accommodated in the schools in the form of botany, animal physiology and, to a lesser extent, zoology and agricultural science. Huxley, dissatisfied with much of the teaching of

botany and zoology and aware that the work of
Schleiden, Schwann, Schultze and von Mohl had revealed the cellular, protoplasmic nature of life
common to plants and animals, encouraged the teaching of biology in schools and, in 1874, the subject
was added to the list of those approved for grant-
earning purposes by the Department of Science and
Art. Huxley and Martin's A Course of Practical Instruction in Elementary Biology was published in
1875 but, despite Huxley's endeavours, biology
failed to secure a place in the secondary school
curriculum in the nineteenth century and even at
Eton, where Huxley was a governor, the subject was
abandoned shortly after its introduction in 1881.

Some of the earliest practical texts, especially in chemistry and physics, set the pattern for
much that was to follow, particularly in the manner
in which experimental results were to be recorded.
Worthington's A First Course of Physical Laboratory
Practice (1886) included a prototype set of rules
for pupils working in the laboratory, of which the
following illustrates the point:

> The form in which the experiment is to be re-
> corded should be got ready beforehand so that
> as soon as an observation is made it can be re-
> corded in the right place in the form.(18)

The earliest laboratory manuals also reflected
the growing importance attached to the conduct of
practical work by the pupils themselves. This emphasis, initially more marked and evident much earlier
in chemistry than in physics, followed developments
which had taken place in the provision of undergraduate courses in science within the universities.
More broadly, it reflected the increasing professionalisation of science and, in particular, of the
training of its future practitioners. The pre-
professional and professional functions of scientific education within the secondary schools and universities respectively were intimately linked and
practical training at the laboratory bench was an
integral and necessary part of each. Such training
at either level is necessarily expensive and it is
not self-evidently either the most interesting or
the most successful way of providing pupils with a
liberal scientific education.(19) The fact that it
has survived all criticism and remains a distinctive
feature of secondary school science education in the
United Kingdom owes much to the influence of H.E.
Armstrong, whose advocacy of the heuristic approach

strengthened the pre-professional aspects of secondary school science and, simultaneously, provided it
with a powerful, beguiling and more generous rationale founded upon a training in scientific method.

H.E. ARMSTRONG AND TRAINING IN SCIENTIFIC METHOD

Armstrong began his campaign to reform school science teaching in a lecture delivered to an International Conference on Education held in South Kensington in 1884. As a Fellow of the Royal Society,
Secretary of the Chemical Society and, in the following year, President of the Chemistry Section of
the British Association, Armstrong had a wide range
of professional contacts and was able to exert considerable influence. He used the Association as a
platform for his developing ideas and, from 1890 onwards, engaged in most of the activities now associated with curriculum development: addressing meetings, writing articles for the educational press and
conducting in-service courses for teachers. His account of the Heuristic Method of Teaching or the Art
of Making Children Discover Things for Themselves
was published in 1898.(20)
    When Armstrong became President of the newly
formed Section L (Educational Science) of the British Association in 1902, there were several signs
that his heuristic campaign had met with considerable success. A large number of schools had been
equipped with laboratories to support the practical
teaching of science and Armstrong had shown that
large classes and the requirements of external examinations were not incompatible with heuristic
methods of teaching. A small nucleus of teachers had
been trained to use these methods and some adver-
tisements for teaching appointments even specified
that a knowledge of the 'Armstrong Method' was 'desirable' or 'essential'. By 1907, the heuristic approach 'with modification' was 'very general' in the
public schools, although it is clear that other
'methods' were also in use. At Berkhamsted, for example, lectures were used to teach senior pupils on
the science side. At Harrow, an early course on mensuration was followed by lectures which, in the case
of chemistry, were 'somewhat heuristic' and, to a
certain extent, followed 'Armstrong's method of
dealing very completely with some one substance'. At
Clifton in 1907, laboratory work was generally independent of lecture work in science, a situation
which also prevailed at Gresham's School until the

work was reorganised so that 'if a boy is doing heat theoretically, he will also be doing it practically'.(21)

By 1908, laboratory classes were almost universal in maintained secondary schools and Armstrong's heuristic method was 'widely used', particularly when teaching chemistry to younger pupils. In many instances, pupils were introduced to the topic to be studied by means of a general class discussion or by writing answers to questions set in advance of the laboratory work 'in order to focus the ideas of the class upon its purpose'. Pupils produced written accounts of their work, notes made by the pupils being the widely accepted practice. The Board of Education was critical of some of these accounts. 'While accurate as mere description', they often failed to identify the assumptions which had been made or to elaborate the relationship between the observations and the conclusions drawn from them.(22)

Unlike some reformers, Armstrong did not provide his would-be followers with a comprehensive and coherent account of his beliefs. The Teaching of Scientific Method and Other Papers on Education, first published in 1903, was a compilation of speeches and articles which lacked 'system and co-ordination' and served only to add to the ambiguity of some of Armstrong's strongly expressed pronouncements. For Armstrong, the principal purpose of a scientific education was to teach pupils the 'scientific method'. By his own admission, his interest in the practice of scientific method was originally literary and owed much to his reading at school of Trench's Study of Words, a book which he claimed made him 'critical and anxious to get behind meanings'. Another seminal experience was his involvement in 1880 in a patent dispute about a process for the production of salicylic acid: 'The display of judicial method, the stringent examination and cross-examination of every particular came to me as the acme of scientific thought.'

For Armstrong, scientific method was the methodical, logical use of systematised knowledge. This interpretation is confirmed by his choice of 'textbooks'. Herbert Spencer's Essays on Education and Charles Kingsley's Scientific Lectures and Essays were to be followed by a liberal course of detective literature, 'beginning perhaps with Edgar Allan Poe's The Murder in the Rue Morgue'. Armstrong's view of science is similar, therefore, to that expounded by Huxley in 1854: 'Science is nothing but trained and organized common sense, differing from the latter only as a veteran may differ from a raw recruit.' For Huxley, the 'vast results obtained by Science' were won by 'no mental processes other than those which are practised by every one of us, in the humblest and meanest affairs of life'. Huxley admitted no distinction between the sciences 'on the grounds of method' and, like Armstrong, used a detective analogy to emphasise his point. Huxley's view of scientific method was derived from J.S. Mill's System of Logic, as he readily acknowledged, and Armstrong, in turn, confirmed his own debt to Huxley: 'if ever a man sought to mould himself upon another - it is I'. Characteristically, Armstrong added that, although he owed much to the inspiration and support of the Spencer-Huxley 'school', it was mainly 'after the event' and he was particularly critical of Huxley for failing to develop the scientific method in education.(23)

Armstrong was by no means alone in his assumptions about the nature of science and scientific method. Such assumptions underlay both W.K. Clifford's classic exposition, The Common Sense of the Exact Sciences, first published in 1885 and Karl Pearson's more influential text, The Grammar of Science, which appeared in 1892. Two quotations will illustrate the claims made for science and scientific method:

> The classification of facts, the recognition of their sequence and relative sequence is the function of science, and the habit of forming a judgement upon these facts, unbiased by personal feeling, is characteristic of the scientific frame of mind. The scientific method ... is not peculiar to one class of phenomena and to one class of workers ... We must carefully guard ourselves against supposing that the scientific frame of mind is a peculiarity of the professional scientist.
>
> ... the material of science is co-extensive with the whole life, physical and mental, of the universe.(24)

Others were ready to share Pearson's view and, where possible, to act accordingly. Lesley Stephen, the political economist, argued for a scientific theory 'which defined the limits within which institutions might be modified by any proposed change'. The sociologist Benjamin Kidd included 'politics, history, ethics, economics and religion' within his 'science

of life'. Lord Acton initiated the Cambridge Modern
History series to 'meet the scientific demand for
completeness and certainty' and J.B. Bury, Acton's
successor in the Regius Chair at Cambridge, used his
inaugural lecture in 1903 to assert that history was
a science 'no more and no less'. The British Science
Guild, established in 1905, sought 'to apply the
methods of science to all fields of human endeavour'
and the Educational Science Section which Armstrong
forced upon the British Association in 1900 was an
explicit attempt to align education with the physical sciences.

By the early twentieth century, Armstrong's
view of science as 'systematised knowledge' and of
the scientific method as a 'game' whose rules could
be taught and applied had become philosophically
unacceptable. The fundamental obscurity of the apparently simple foundations of Newtonian mechanics
was exposed by Mach and Hertz, and Einstein's theory
of relativity raised the important question of how
science could claim to progress by accumulating
knowledge if major advances seemed to require the
destruction of previously held theories. The concept
of science implicit in heurism could not account for
developments such as thermodynamics or quantum theory, any more than it could accommodate Newton's assertion that a body is at rest only because there
are forces acting upon it or Galileo's 'rape of the
senses' in advocating a heliocentric universe. As
the concepts and imagery of science moved further
and further from 'common sense', it became increasingly difficult to argue that pupils 'not only may
but must be put absolutely in the position of an
original discoverer'.

Armstrong's view of science and of scientific
method also contained an inherent educational paradox. In arguing simultaneously that the scientific
method was not confined to natural science and that
the chief function of science teachers was to teach
scientific method, Armstrong was close to denying
science any educational advantage over other subjects in the curriculum and to surrendering the
claim of science teachers to a special existence.
This paradox was recognised by a committee appointed
by the British Association in 1917 to enquire into
the position of science in secondary schools. The
committee found the paradox to rest upon the false
assumption that the method of science could be regarded as separable from the matter: 'The scientific
method is an abstraction which does not exist apart
from its concrete embodiments.'(25) The term

'concrete embodiments' is an unfortunate one and the committee's conclusion takes the paradox no nearer to resolution unless scientific method is given a more generous interpretation than that implicit in Armstrong's 'game'. Nonetheless, the committee's conclusion that it was possible to use scientific method only when dealing with scientific matters was essentially correct. The paradox inherent in science as organised common sense can be resolved only by a recognition that the logical and imaginative operations of science are conducted with what Ravetz has called 'intellectually constructed things and events' and not with the objects of common sense experience.(26) Although these intellectual constructs are designed to relate as closely as is possible to the inaccessible reality of the external world, they are not, as Armstrong's scientific method seemed to imply, identical with it.

It follows that some aspects of 'scientific method' cannot be taught and that an appreciation of the procedures of science requires that students be introduced to these intellectually constructed 'things and events'. As heurism lost its philosophical support, therefore, an increased emphasis was placed on the acquisition of scientific knowledge as an educational objective. This drift from 'process' to 'content' was encouraged by the findings of the experimental psychologists whose investigations undermined the notion of transfer of training upon which heurism rested. 'Accuracy does not transfer; neatness does not transfer; observation does not transfer'; nor, it might be added, does scientific method. It was also supported by the experience of the First World War which highlighted a widespread ignorance of common scientific facts. Napier Shaw, a former director of the meteorological department, complained of the difficulty of teaching army officers the rudiments of weather forecasting when they had 'no more knowledge about the air than a clodhopper's experience'.(27) Arthur Smithells, who served as chemical adviser in charge of anti-gas training in the Home Command, lamented that 'a vast number and probably the majority of ... casualties [during gas attacks] had been sustained as a result of ignorance of the elements of natural science on the parts of officers and men'.(28) This ignorance of the ABC of everday science meant that 'heroism became a substitute for intelligence'.

Those concerned to promote science and scientific education were quick to take advantage of the opportunity which the War presented to advance their

cause. The dependence of British manufacturing industry upon the scientific and technological expertise of other countries was given prominence and the
so-called 'Neglect of Science' Committee, established in February 1916, campaigned to raise the status
of science in the leading public schools by advocating its incorporation within the entrance examinations of the Universities of Oxford and Cambridge,
the competitive examinations of the Home and Indian
Civil Service and the admission procedures to Sandhurst, then 'probably the only military institution
in Europe where science was not included in the curriculum'.(29) The Association of Public School Science Masters (APSSM),(30) which had been instrumental in establishing the 'Neglect of Science' Committee, made its views on secondary school science
teaching known to the Thomson Committee, established
by the government in August 1916 'to enquire into
the position occupied by Natural Science in the Educational System of Great Britain'.(31) The British
Association added its opinions on secondary school
science education in a report published in 1917.

Nonetheless, when asked by the classicists and
humanists in the summer of 1916 to define the aims
of science teaching, the APSSM found itself in some
difficulty. A seven-hour meeting of the Association's General Committee on 7 October 1916, failed
to produce a satisfactory statement and Archer
Vassall, the Association's chairman, was left to
consolidate the points which had been made.(32) The
obstacles to presenting the case for science as a
humanising study were considerable. Such a case
could not be argued solely in terms of the acquisition of scientific knowledge and it was no longer
possible to proclaim the near-universal applicability of scientific method. Overtly utilitarian arguments were also suspect, despite the role of science
in the War and revelations by the British Science
Guild and others of the continuing scientific inad-
equacy of much of British industry. Moreover, there
was some concern within the scientific community
that if utilitarian arguments were pressed too
strongly, the value of science would be measured
simply by its practical utility. In addition, the
APSSM itself had no clearly formed views on the kind
of science teaching most appropriate for the increasing number of secondary school pupils up to the
age of 16, for many of whom 'general science' seemed
more suitable than a conventional course in 'formal
science' designed with the pre-professional function
of school science principally in mind.

The way forward was indicated by Richard Gregory whose book, Discovery or the Spirit and Service of Science published in 1916, offered an eloquent prescription for the future of school science education. Science was to be taught, not because it provided a training in scientific method, but because it represented 'an intellectual outlook, a standard of truth and a gospel of light' and illustrated the nobility of scientific aims and the spiritual aspects of scientific endeavour. To this end, science should be studied in more effective relation with life and things as they are in the everyday world rather than, in Smithells's phrase, 'as it is dealt with by "professionals" in seminaries'. It is hardly surprising that Gregory warmly welcomed the Thomson Committee's forceful reassertion of the humanising influence of the proper study of science:

> How valuable [science] may be in training the judgement, in stirring the imagination and in cultivating a spirit of reverence, few have yet accepted in full faith.(33)

There was, of course, opposition: from Armstrong who asserted that 'The "damned boy" needs drilling. We forget this and ever twaddle of playing on his interests'; and from H.H. Turner, a former President of the APSSM, who challenged the possibility of a 'science for everybody'.(34) However, the forces which had initiated the science-for-all movement during the First World War were too strong to be resisted and there remained only the formidable problem of translating lofty ideals into practical proposals.

FROM PROCESS TO CONTENT? GENERAL SCIENCE AND BIOLOGY

The most detailed prescription for a broad secondary school science course in which 'the humanising method' was 'the vital point' was undoubtedly general science. Although elements of this curriculum innovation may be detected in Huxley's Physiography and in developments in other countries, particularly the United States, the more immediate origins of general science lay in two pamphlets, The Aims of Science Teaching in General Education and Science for All, published by the APSSM in 1916 as part of the 'Neglect of Science' campaign. General science was given a more precise formulation by the Oxford and Cambridge Examination Board in 1921 when it was

added to the list of subjects included within Group
III for the purposes of the recently established
School Certificate examination. By 1932, six examination boards had introduced papers in general science into their School Certificate examinations and
a similar paper formed part of the army entrance examination conducted by the Civil Service Commissioners. However, the provision of syllabuses and papers
by the examination boards is a misleading measure
of the schools' enthusiasm for general science. In
1925, a Board of Education Report noted that the advocacy of general science by the Science Masters'
Association (SMA), the successor to the APSSM, 'had
had little or no influence on the work of Secondary
Schools generally'.(35) In 1928, a report produced
on behalf of the British Association was sharply
critical of the general science syllabus and examination of the Oxford and Cambridge Joint Examination
Board and, by the mid-1930s, it was clear to the SMA
that a fundamental review of its general science
proposals was necessary.

Various aspects of this review have been well-
documented and need not be repeated here.(36) However, attention should be drawn to the decision of
the general science sub-committee of the SMA to con-
stitute two working groups. The first group was
charged with the production of a list of topics, A,
based upon 'things a boy wanted to know, the questions a boy [sic] wants to be answered'. The second
group, operating independently, selected a few very
important scientific ideas and worked outwards from
these to a second list, B, which exemplified them.
The material common to the A and B lists was used as
the 'backbone' of a new general science syllabus
which was completed by the addition of such content
as was necessary for an adequate understanding of
the core material. Unfortunately, the report of the
sub-committee does not reveal in detail how the
fundamental principles of the 'B men' related to
particular items in the general science syllabus and
the reason given for the omission of this detail is
far from convincing. The SMA's proposals were presented in 1938 as The Teaching of General Science,
following publication and discussion of an interim
report two years earlier.

Despite differences of opinion about its nature
and scope and doubts about its adequacy as a prelude
to more specialised sixth form courses, general science offered a means of broadening the scientific
education available to pupils and it was introduced,
in a variety of ways, into many secondary schools,

particularly towards the end of the 1930s. Between
1922 and 1930, the percentage of all candidates offering general science as a subject in the School
Certificate examinations rose by only 0.1 to 2.7. It
reached 6 per cent by 1936, 11.4 per cent by the
following year and increased to 23 per cent by
1942.(37)

However, insofar as general science represented
no more than a broadening of the secondary school
curriculum, its position was, to some degree, undermined ultimately by the development of biology as an
independent school subject. When the Thomson Committee reported in 1918, biology in boys' secondary
schools was represented almost exclusively by nature
study, taught to younger pupils, and by botany and
zoology taught to the few senior pupils intending to
study medicine. In secondary schools for girls,
botany was the dominant and, occasionally, the only
science taught, although it was becoming increasingly common to study the plant as a living organism
rather than present it as a herbarium specimen to
the class. However, the Thomson Committee asserted
that physics and chemistry should continue to be the
fundamental subjects of the secondary school science
curriculum and its report fell short of recommending
the introduction of a systematic course in biology
for all pupils up to the age of sixteen in secondary
schools.

Despite conferences and meetings organised by
the British Association and the SMA, and the courses
provided by the Board of Education and a number of
LEAs, biology remained 'disgracefully neglected' by
the secondary schools throughout the 1920s. By 1929,
when over 81 per cent of the secondary schools in
England and Wales were preparing pupils for Higher
School Certificate examinations, biology as a subject was taught in only 16 per cent of them. This
position changed markedly during the 1930s when
boys' schools which had hitherto taught little or no
biology began to introduce it as an examination subject and, in the secondary schools for girls, biology gradually replaced botany in the curriculum. By
1931, all eight examination boards examined biology
at School Certificate level, although there was considerable variety both in the form of the examination and in the contents of the syllabuses.

This variety reflected both the diversity of
biology as an emergent discipline and the corresponding different traditions which had developed in
biological education, of which those associated with
natural history and medicine were perhaps the most

firmly established. During the early twentieth century, advances in genetics and in plant and animal
physiology began to exert pressure on the biological
curriculum and, in the years immediately following
the First World War, ecological and field studies
also grew in importance. In addition, during the
interwar period, there were several organisations,
each with a direct and distinct interest in biological education, which not only encouraged the teaching of biology in schools but also exerted some influence upon the manner of its accommodation within
the curriculum. These included organisations as diverse as the Church of England Moral Welfare Council, the Marriage Guidance Council, the Central
Authority for Health Education, the Eugenics Society, the British Social Hygiene Council, the Association for Education in Citizenship and, because of
its statutory interest in the health of pupils, the
Board of Education. Economic considerations also assumed increased importance as the employment opportunities for qualified biologists, particularly in
the Empire overseas, began to expand, although the
recommendations in 1933 of the Chelmsford Committee,
set up to inquire into the education and supply of
biologists, were, in large measure, undermined by
the economic events of two years earlier.(38)

However, the fact that the common interest
among a diverse range of organisations in advancing
biological education rested upon more particular and
primary commitments, such as citizenship or health
education, encouraged the development of different
types of biology courses, intended for different
social purposes and, in some instances, directed towards meeting the needs of a particular social
class. For example, most of the concern about nutri-
tion and health education in the 1930s was directed
at pupils attending public elementary, rather than
secondary, schools. Similarly, the commitment of the
British Social Hygiene Council or the Association
for Education in Citizenship was essentially to social biology with an emphasis upon such matters as
race, diet and various aspects of social policy,
e.g. public health and housing. This emphasis was
markedly different from that which characterised existing examination courses in biology in secondary
and public schools. These derived ultimately from
the requirements of the pre-medical curriculum, with
its emphasis upon anatomy, morphology and dissec-
tion, and reflected the pre-professional function of
secondary school science education.

In emphasising the importance and value of

biological knowledge as a basis for personal and social action, social biology offered a different and
radical interpretation of the educational function
of school science. In this respect, it had much in
common with general science which, in Gregory's
phrase, was 'science for all and not for embryonic
engineers, chemists ... or biologists'.(39) Significantly, both general science and social biology were
to suffer the same fate. They came to be associated
with girls, with 'less-able' pupils and, after 1944,
with the secondary modern rather than the grammar
schools. The pre-professional function of the grammar school was simply too powerful to enable such
radical innovations to be accommodated in any other
way. A more generous interpretation of school biology was not possible until the discipline itself had
advanced sufficiently to encourage the presentation
of the complex of function, form, development and
genesis as a coherent whole; until the employment
prospects of those with biological qualification had
expanded greatly; and until the pre-professional
function of secondary education had been, to some
extent, attenuated by its accommodation within a
system of comprehensive schools. As far as general
science was concerned, the uneasy, and perhaps
fundamentally unsustainable alliance of 'alternative
functions of scientific education', implicit in the
roles of the A and B groups, was insufficient to allow the subject to survive in the postwar grammar
schools committed to the pre-professional training
of scientists in numbers greater than at any time in
history.

CONCLUSION

What assessment may be made of secondary school science education in the period 1870-1940? As far as
the maintained secondary schools are concerned, the
position of science in the curriculum was secured by
the Regulations of the Board of Education, issued
annually. By the early twentieth century, science
was also accommodated within those public schools
which had responded to parental or other pressure to
introduce 'modern subjects' into their curricula,
although its status relative to other, longer-
established disciplines was often subordinate. Much
of the science taught in secondary and public
schools was taught in practical classes, conducted
in laboratories, although not necessarily along the
heuristic lines advocated so fervently by Armstrong.

Such practical teaching was increasingly supported
by suitable apparatus, sometimes developed solely
for educational rather than initially for investiga-
tional/research purposes, and by the provision of
large numbers of science texts.

However, early-twentieth-century science education was narrow in content. In boys' schools, the
science curriculum usually consisted of chemistry
and such elements of physics as heat, light and
sound, and mechanics. In girls' schools, botany and,
to a much lesser extent, chemistry were the principal science subjects taught. In secondary and public
schools of all types, biology was reserved for the
small numbers of senior pupils intending to train
for the medical profession. During the latter half
of the period with which this book is concerned,
there was a considerable broadening of the secondary
school science curriculum. The diverse elements of
physics were combined into a single subject, largely
for pedagogical convenience; biology became more
widely taught and, like general science, became
established as an important subject in the School
Certificate examination. However, this broadening of
the science curriculum did little to undermine the
differentiation of the scientific education of the
sexes established in the mid-nineteenth century. Indeed, it may even have made it more marked. Such
differentiation, determined in large measure by per-
ceptions of the future roles of men and women in society, was also actively encouraged by the flexibility permitted both by the Board of Education's Regulations for Secondary Schools (40) and by the Group
arrangements governing the School Certificate examinations introduced in 1918.(41)

The broadening of the science curriculum in the
interwar years also failed to undermine the assumption that the principal purpose of a secondary
school science education was to introduce pupils to
the grammar and syntax of the scientific disciplines
i.e. to provide the rudiments of a scientific training. Innovations such as general science or social
biology, constructed upon a radical and more generous interpretation of the educational function of
science which gave the personal development of the
pupil priority over the future well-being of the scientific disciplines, could not hope to flourish in a
system of secondary schools, closely linked to the
universities and cast firmly in a pre-professional
role. Where such a role was perceived as of dimin-
ished or even no importance, as in the education of
girls or 'less-able' pupils, or in schools providing

alternative forms of post-elementary education, such innovations could be, and often were, received more hospitably. Although expressed in different terms at different times, and supported by different educational psychologies,(42) the commitment of secondary school science education to a training in the methods of science remained secure, surviving not only the excessive claims of heurism and changes in the relationships between science, technology and society but also ambiguities about the nature of science and doubts about the validity of such concepts as general or transferable skills and attitudes. That commitment enabled secondary science education to share and transmit the assumptions about the nature of science and scientific activity implicit in the schooling of the scientific disciplines in the nineteenth century. Science was essentially a male activity, scientific knowledge was presented as neutral, objective and value-free and scientific method, however defined, was offered not merely as the best, but, by implication, the only, means of establishing 'secure' knowledge or even 'truth'. The enduring effectiveness of that schooling is clear from the recent assertion in an official policy statement that 'The essential characteristic of education in science is that it introduces pupils to the methods of science.'(43) Given this assertion, it will be surprising if secondary school science education proves able to meet the educational responsibilities which have been placed upon it.

NOTES AND REFERENCES

1.   H. Spencer, Education: Intellectual, Moral and Physical (Williams and Norgate, 1861).
2.   Report of Her Majesty's Commissioners Appointed to Inquire into the Revenues and Management of Certain Colleges and Schools, and the Studies Pursued and Instruction Given Therein (Clarendon Report), Vol.1 (HMSO, 1864), pp. 28-33.
3.   British Association for the Advancement of Science, Report of the Thirty-Seventh Meeting: Dundee 1867 (John Murray, 1868), pp. xxxix-liv.
4.   G.H. Daniels, 'The Pure-Science Ideal and Democratic Culture', Science, vol.156, no.3783 (1967), p. 1700.
5.   For the British Association, see R. MacLeod and P. Collins (eds.), The Parliament of Science: The British Association for the Advancement of Science 1831-1981 (Science Reviews Ltd.,

Middlesex, 1981). For the Association and science
education, see especially ch. 7: D. Layton, 'The
Schooling of Science in England, 1854-1939', ibid.,
pp. 188-210.

6.   T. Kuhn, The Structure of Scientific Revolutions, 2nd ed. (University of Chicago Press,
1970), p. 164.

7.   D. Layton, 'Science Education and Values
Education - An Essential Tension?' in J. Head (ed.),
Science Education for the Citizen (British Council/
Chelsea College, 1982), p. 103.

8.   British Association for the Advancement of
Science, Report of the Thirty-Sixth Meeting:
Nottingham 1866 (John Murray, 1867), pp. 72-3.

9.   J.M. Wilson, 'On Teaching Natural Science
in Schools' in F.W. Farrar (ed.), Essays on a Liberal Education (Macmillan, 1867), p. 283.

10.   M. Argles, South Kensington to Robbins:
An Account of English Technical and Scientific Education since 1851 (Longmans, 1964), p. 21.

11.   See, for example, ch. 8 of R. MacLeod
(ed.), Days of Judgement: Science, Examinations and
the Organization of Knowledge in Late Victorian England (Nafferton Books, Driffield, 1982). This chapter, by R. MacLeod and R. Moseley, is a study of the
development of the Natural Science Tripos introduced
at Cambridge in 1851. According to MacLeod, the Tripos 'established standards of merit and achievement
which became, with the examinations of London and
the Scottish universities, a distinctive hallmark of
British science'. MacLeod also reports Liebig's
opinion, expressed to the Oxford University Commissioners in 1851 that the only way 'to promote the
effectual study of the natural sciences' was 'to
introduce them as subjects of examination' and
claims that, by the mid-nineteenth century, Liebig's
opinion 'summarised received wisdom'. The Honours
School of Natural Science was instituted at Oxford
in 1850 and the London science degree in 1860.

12.   W.H. Brock, 'From Liebig to Nuffield: A
Bibliography of the History of Science Education,
1839-1974', Studies in Science Education, vol.2
(1975), p. 75.

13.   F. Jones, The Owens College Junior Course
of Practical Chemistry (Macmillan, 1872); A Junior
Course of Practical Chemistry (Macmillan, 1872).

14.   W.H. Brock, 'Prologue to Heurism' in His-
tory of Education Society, The Changing Curriculum
(Methuen, 1971); G. Fowles, Lecture Experiments in
Chemistry (Bell, 1937).

15.   Schools Inquiry Commission, (Taunton

Report) Vol.3 (HMSO, 1868).

16. W. de W. Abney, Presidential Address to
Section L in British Association for the Advancement
of Science, Report of the Seventy-Third Meeting:
Southport 1903 (John Murray, 1904), p. 868.

17. R.E. Shepherd, 'Individual Practical Work
in the Teaching of Physics in England: A Study of
Its Origins and Rationale', unpublished MPhil thesis, University of Leeds, 1979, appendix 2.

18. A.M. Worthington, A First Course of Physical Laboratory Practice (Rivingtons, 1886), p. 11.

19. Implicit in the notion of pre-professional
scientific education is the assumption that science
is taught largely for the benefit of science rather
than to encourage the personal development of the
learner. For the importance of this distinction in
elementary education in the mid-nineteenth century,
see D. Layton, Science for the People: The Origins
of the School Science Curriculum in England (Allen
and Unwin, 1973). For a scientist's criticisms of
the enduring emphasis on laboratory work in school
science, see F.R. Jevons, The Teaching of Science
Education, Science and Society (Allen and Unwin,
1969), pp. 146-9.

20. For Armstrong, see W.H. Brock (ed.), H.E.
Armstrong and the Teaching of Science, 1880-1930
(Cambridge University Press, 1973). The title of
Armstrong's compendium indicates the essence of his
heuristic approach which was that the 'beginner not
only may but must be put absolutely in the position
of an original discoverer'. However, according to
Armstrong, this did not mean that he expected a pupil to discover everything for himself and Armstrong's
supporters have gone to some lengths to emphasise
this point. See, for example, C.E. Browne, Henry
Edward Armstrong (Christ's Hospital, 1954) and G.
van Praagh (ed.), H.E. Armstrong and Science Education (John Murray, 1978).

21. Board of Education, Report on Science
Teaching in Public Schools Represented on the Association of Public School Science Masters, Educational Pamphlet No.17 (HMSO, 1917), p. 20.

22. Board of Education, Report of the Board of
Education for the Year 1909-1910 (HMSO, 1911), p. 79.

23. For further discussion, see E.W. Jenkins,
From Armstrong to Nuffield: Studies in Twentieth-
Century Science Education in England and Wales (John
Murray, 1979), pp. 48 ff.

24. K. Pearson, The Grammar of Science (Scott,
1892), pp. 6-7 and 15.

25. British Association for the Advancement of

Science, Report: 1917 (John Murray, 1918), p. 134.

26. J.R. Ravetz, Scientific Knowledge and Its Social Problems (Clarendon Press, Oxford, 1971), p. 110.

27. N. Shaw, The Lack of Science in Modern Education with Some Hints of What Might Be (1916), p. 8.

28. A. Smithells, 'The Ways of Chemistry' in supplement to The Listener, 26 February 1930, p. ii. See also A.J. Flintham, 'The Contribution of Arthur Smithells, F.R.S. (1860-1939) to the Development of Science Education in England', unpublished MEd thesis, University of Leeds, 1974.

29. The Neglect of Science: Report of Proceedings of a Conference held in the Rooms of the Linnaean Society, Burlington House, Piccadilly, on Wednesday, 3 May 1916 (1916).

30. For the APSSM, see D. Layton, Interpreters of Science: A History of the Association for Science Education (John Murray, 1984), especially ch. 1. Established in 1901 and reconstituted in 1919 as the Science Masters' Association, the APSSM, 'by concentrating on limited educational objectives, avoiding trade union concerns, and assimilating its interests to those of external and powerful groups such as the Royal Society', was able to achieve 'over two decades a controlled growth in both membership and occupational authority', (ibid., p. 32).

31. For the Thomson Committee, see E.W. Jenkins, 'The Thomson Committee and the Board of Education', British Journal of Educational Studies, vol.21, no.1 (1973), pp. 76-87, and J.M. Feheney, 'The Thomson Report (1918): A Critical Evaluation', unpublished MEd thesis, University of London, 1976.

32. Layton, Interpreters of Science, p. 197.

33. Report of the Committee Appointed by the Prime Minister to Enquire into the Position of Natural Science in the Educational System of Great Britain (HMSO, 1918), para. 4. For Gregory, see W.H. Armytage, Sir Richard Gregory (Macmillan, 1957). Armytage describes (pp. 68-9) Gregory's book as an 'eloquent and effective plea for the abandonment of the view that scientific and humanistic studies were mutually antipathetic' and 'a synthesis of the arguments [Gregory] had been steadily advancing in Nature, The School World, Cornhill, Fortnightly, Sunday at Home and other magazines'.

34. Flintham, 'The Contribution of Arthur Smithells'; Layton, Interpreters of Science, p. 201.

35. Board of Education, Report of an Enquiry into the Conditions Affecting the Teaching of

Science in Secondary Schools for Boys in England (HMSO, 1925). See also, School Science Review, vol.7, no.26 (1925), p. 70.

36. Layton, Interpreters of Science, ch. 9; Jenkins, From Armstrong to Nuffield, ch. 3.

37. By 1943, it seems likely that about 40 per cent of the secondary schools in England and Wales presented candidates for examination in general science at School Certificate level, although the manner in which the teaching of the subject was organised varied greatly. However, the position of general science as an examination subject was not sustained in the educational system developed after 1944 and, after reprinting The Teaching of General Science in 1960, the Science Masters' Association made no further attempt to argue the case for the innovation which it had earlier advocated with such zeal.

38. For details see Jenkins, From Armstrong to Nuffield, pp. 129-30.

39. British Association for the Advancement of Science, Report of the Ninetieth Meeting: Hull 1922 (John Murray, 1923), p. 207.

40. E.W. Jenkins, 'Science Education and the Secondary School Regulations 1902-1909', Journal of Educational Administration and History, vol.10, no.2 (1978), pp. 31-8.

41. R.J. Montgomery, Examinations: An Account of their Evolution as Administrative Devices in England (Longmans, 1965), pp. 133-5.

42. Armstrong's heurism, for example, rested upon a faculty psychology and its implicit notion of the transfer of training. In contrast, general science owed much to T.P. Nunn's three motives of 'wonder, utility and systematisation', derived from the assumption that the interest of children in science exhibited a rhythm corresponding to the rhythm of its history. Nunn's ideas, which also influenced the Spens Committee's report, had obvious implications both for the sequencing of topics within a school science course and for the strategy whereby they should be taught. See T.P. Nunn, Education: Its Data and First Principles (Arnold, 1920) and A.N. Whitehead, The Rhythm of Education (Christophers, 1922).

43. Department of Education and Science and Welsh Office, Science 5-16: A Statement of Policy (HMSO, 1985), para. 11.

Chapter Seven

THE ROYAL GEOGRAPHICAL SOCIETY AND GEOGRAPHY IN
SECONDARY EDUCATION

WILLIAM MARSDEN

From its founding in 1831, the Royal Geographical
Society was seen to epitomise the vigour and prowess
that made Victorian England strong and content with
itself. To Londoners of the time, the RGS 'shone as
the abode of peace, prosperity and renown'.(1) For a
number of reasons, geographical societies prospered
after the Napoleonic wars.

> Peace prevailed, if not uninterruptedly, for a
> hundred years after Waterloo and freed men to
> roam the world both in body and mind. Energies
> that had previously been absorbed in wars and
> internal troubles could be expended in colonial
> ventures and settlement on remote frontiers,
> and geographical exploration was their accom-
> paniment. Also, patriotic pride ... stimulated
> citizens to take a keen interest in the inter-
> nal geography of their own countries.(2)

No body was more likely to flourish in these circumstances than the RGS, located as it was in the
world's largest city, the seat of the most extensive
empire, and a meeting place for scientists and explorers. At its inaugural meeting, the object of the
Society was declared to be 'the promotion and diffusion of that most important and entertaining branch
of knowledge, GEOGRAPHY'. The Society took on the
responsibilities of collecting and collating the
data pouring in from all over the world, of building
up a library and assembling a complete collection of
maps, of helping travellers and scientific explorers, and of establishing links with geographical
societies abroad and other scientific societies at
home.(3)
    At this stage there was no formal commitment to
the promotion of geographical education. This was to

come later. But it will be argued in this chapter
that the indirect impact of the RGS in its formative
years was equally important in building up the image
of geography as a vital component in the school curriculum as was the subsequent more direct intervention. The prestige accorded to the Society as a
result of its dissemination of new knowledge about
the world, the well-publicised scientific exploration it sponsored, and the famous names associated
with it, could not but establish it as a powerful
pressure group for geographical education once it
had decided that this was part of its responsibility. While the efforts of the RGS were far from
being confined to one level of education, this study
will concentrate on the secondary rather than elementary or university spheres. Its impact on elementary schooling, while not entirely absent, was
peripheral. It was of course greatly concerned with
establishing geography in the universities, but its
work in this area has been well documented elsewhere.(4) On the other hand, its labours to promote
geography in schools have received less attention,(5) at least in recent times.(6)

CONTEXTS: EXPLORATION, IMPERIAL EXPANSION, THE RGS
AND GEOGRAPHICAL EDUCATION

The attributes of quintessential RGS man were delin-
eated in W.R. Hamilton's (7) Presidential Address of
1838:

> the real geographer becomes at once an ardent
> traveller, indifferent whether he plunges into
> the burning heats of tropical deserts ... or
> launches his boat on the unknown stream ... or
> endures the hardship of an arctic climate ...
> Buoyed up in his greatest difficulties by the
> consciousness that he is labouring for the good
> of his fellow-creatures, he feels delight in
> the reflection that he is upon ground hitherto
> untrodden by man - that every step he makes
> will serve to enlarge the sphere of human know-
> ledge - and that he is laying up for himself a
> store of gratitude and fame.(8)

In support of this concept of the geographer as
explorer, scientist and citizen, the RGS from its
foundation provided grants for overseas expeditions.
In evidence to the Devonshire Commission in 1873 its
President emphasised that almost every traveller to

partially known countries came first to the Society
to get information and consult its unrivalled
collection of maps.(9) Supplementing these facilities, the RGS had also published a guide, Hints to
Travellers, that was to go through many editions.
The Society's medals carried great prestige, being
awarded to such famous explorers as Captain Robert
Fitzroy of HMS Beagle in 1837, and David Livingstone
in 1855, whose scientific expedition of 1866 was
under the auspices of the RGS.(10)

The heady association of such names with dis-
coveries of mysterious new lands, dubious inhabit-
ants and dangerous animals,(11) combined with a
widening public interest in less hazardous forms of
travel to less distant lands, whether for work or
leisure, were heaven-sent opportunities on which the
promoters of geographical education could seize. The
translation of the values of RGS man to school level
made geography potentially second only to religious
instruction as a subject of 'benefit to mankind'.(12)

The most obvious vocational spin-off of geography, however, was seen to be in military affairs.
The victory of the Germans over the French in the
Franco-Prussian War, for example, was presented as
testimony to the superiority of geography teaching
in German schools.(13) The message was not lost on
the RGS and its Inspector of Geographical Education,
J. Scott Keltie who, in compiling intelligence for
his Report in the early 1880s visited not only
continental institutions of geography and education,
but also the Ministry of War and the War Academy in
Berlin, and the Ministry of War in Paris. Battles
were now being won, apparently, not so much on the
playing fields as in the geography rooms: 'if the
fate of the nation may depend upon a battle, a
battle may depend on a knowledge of geography'.(14)
There was also the vicarious pleasure of being able
to follow knowledgeably the news from the ubiquitous
foreign fronts. The impoverishment of the unini-
tiated was driven home:

> for how can such a man follow the fortunes of
> our troops... with the keen intelligence of one
> whose geographical knowledge enables him, as it
> were, to go side by side with them from one
> battlefield to another? (15)

The RGS similarly made maximum capital out of what
it described as an 'incisive article' by the Military Correspondent of The Times in 1905, which attacked the Civil Service in general and the War

Office in particular for the neglect of geography, alleging that the lessons of the Franco-Prussian and Boer Wars had not been learned.(16)

The military dimension was just one part of a broader utilitarian justification for geography in education. It was also presented as necessary in the promotion of commerce, territorial expansion, and colonial administration abroad. Additionally, social concord at home could be fostered by reducing the burden of the poor by encouraging them to emigrate to the colonies. A correspondent to the RGS urged that by 'giving to the Poor better knowledge of Geography and utilising oversurplus population, our objects would probably be effected'.(17)

The leading proponents of geographical education habitually included in their cases for its inclusion in the curriculum its utilitarian advantages:

> Geography, properly taught, may be said to teach us how to appraise the value of a country, just as a surveyor appraises the value of an estate. The knowledge which it yields is as profitable to the man of business ... as it is to the statesman ... (18)

Herbertson reinforced this view of Ravenstein in extolling the value of geography as 'of supreme significance in administrating a colony, in planning a campaign, or in controlling a large business',(19) while Fairgrieve was later to argue, albeit not as 'a point that need be pressed', that 'geography pays'.(20)

More fundamental than these utilitarian arguments, however, was the imperial ideology which could be wrapped round geography. First the teachers had to be convinced. Yoxall's text for pupil teachers pulled no punches:

> THE EMPIRE. The United Kingdom is the ruling centre of vast possessions; valour and enterprise, conquest and colonisation, have won to British sway an Empire on which 'the sun never sets'. Our Empire extends to every zone and parallel, and shares in every continent and sea. It comprises one-sixth of the globe and one-fourth of the human race.(21)

In his introduction to a textbook entitled Round the Empire for the Use of Schools, Lord Rosebery drew the attention of teachers to the purpose of the

book and their responsibility to remind their children that they inhabited an empire, and to use
geography as a means of character building:

> If we and they are narrow and selfish, averse
> to labour, impatient of necessary burdens,
> factious and self-indulgent; if we see in pub-
> lic affairs not our Empire but our country, not
> our country but our parish, and in our parish
> our house, the Empire is doomed.(22)

The interpenetration of the spirit of exploration, imperial values and academic promotion, and
the application of these to geographical education,
was personified in Douglas Freshfield,(23) a famed
mountain explorer, a Fellow and later Honorary Secretary of the RGS. His summoning call in his 1886
paper on 'The Place of Geography in Education' is
unblushing in its chauvinism:

> Shall we English who inherit so large a part of
> the world not acquaint ourselves with our in-
> heritance and the conditions under which we can
> retain and make the most of it? What has been
> the fate of our race? To be the greatest rulers
> and merchants and colonisers the world has ever
> seen ... Probably in the future ... we may find
> ourselves the centre of a vast confederation
> strong enough to ensure the peace of the world,
> to maintain a pax Britannica which neither Slav
> nor Latin will venture to dispute. Do you think
> we are educating children for this high destiny
> ... by comparative ignorance of the earth's
> structure, of the natural laws by obedience to
> which they may go forth and win peaceful vic-
> tories and fill up the void places of our
> planet? (24)

Among Sir Halford Mackinder's claims to fame
were not only his championship of the cause of
geographical education, and his pre-eminence as a
geopolitician,(25) but also his patriotic engagement
in the practical affairs of empire, as member of the
Visual Instruction Committee of the Colonial Office,
and also Chairman of the Imperial Shipping Committee
and Imperial Economic Committee.(26) A unifying imperial philosophy characterised all his work. A major commitment in his educational writing lay in
producing texts for countries of the Empire so that
their children, particularly through the medium of
visual instruction, would gain a 'just impression'

of the United Kingdom.(27) From an early stage, English textbook publishers took up the responsibility of producing suitable materials for colonial markets, and not least India.(28)

Mackinder was particularly worried by India. Arguing that geography was equally important in a period of consolidation as of extension of Empire, he saw it as necessary in 'exorcising the devils' of ignorance and prejudice overseas, as in India, where they were impeding the progress of the Raj in its efforts to secure 'a new sense of Indian unity'.(29) His objectives were as explicit as those of Freshfield:

> Let our teaching be from the British standpoint, so that finally we see the world as a theatre for British activity. This, no doubt, is to deviate from the cold and impartial ways of science. When we teach the millions, however, we are not training scientific investigators, but the practical striving citizens of an empire which has to hold its place through the universal law of survival through efficiency and effort.(30)

THE DISCIPLINE: THE RGS, NEW PARADIGMS OF GEOGRAPHY AND GEOGRAPHICAL EDUCATION

Nineteenth-century exploration and colonial expansion not only excited popular interest. They also generated a major information explosion,(31) the basis of a new description of the earth. But the information came in a huge, undifferentiated mass. A more cogent initial collection of data, based on accurate trigonometrical, topographical, geological and botanical surveys, was clearly a necessary precursor to a revitalised geographical science. The concept of the scholar-scientist explorer gained weight.(32) Geography could not be confined simply as 'a delineation of the Earth', or as an 'easy' and a 'homely acquirement', in Hamilton's words, but must be amplified into a complex study drawing on a whole series of other disciplines. 'Physical Geography' was to be the immediate beneficiary. Mary Somerville's celebrated text, Physical Geography (1848) epitomises this development. Its authoress eagerly incorporated the new scientific material disseminated by the RGS and its journal.(33) Its success would arguably have been greater but for the early split of geography into a physical dimension, tied to geology, and a political one, tied to history, and symbolised by the division of the British Association into a Section C, devoted to Geology and Physical Geography, and a separate Geography Section (E), for long the responsibility of the RGS.(34)

Following the lead of William Hughes,(35) who opposed the division of the subject,(36) Francis Galton, Honorary Secretary of the RGS between 1857 and 1863, sought integration not only within the subject but also, through the medium of geography, between subjects. He declared that geographers 'with one voice' saw their subject as more than a mere collection of facts about the earth's surface, the stuff of political geography. It had become a liberal science, which should seek to borrow from all the sciences, and function as a linking discipline.(37) Unfortunately, Galton's geographical prizes scheme, designed to promote geography in the public schools, appeared subversive, so far as this integrationist spirit was concerned, in donating separate prizes for physical and political geography, for reasons discussed later.(38)

Sir Archibald Geikie, one of the most eminent geologists of the time and a notable geographical educationist,(39) presented geography as an integrative subject in an invited address on 'Geographical Evolution' to the RGS in 1879:

> It ever looks for a connection between scattered facts, tries to ascertain the relations which subsist between the different parts of the globe, their reactions on each other and the general economy of the whole ... It traces how man, alike unconsciously and knowingly, has changed the face of nature, and how, on the other hand, the conditions of his geographical environment have moulded his progress. With these broad aims, geography comes frankly for assistance to many different branches of science ... (40)

Similar thinking was to be found in the interventions of T.H. Huxley in the realm of geography.(41) He defined a new field of earth science, Physiography, which, in Stoddart's view, transformed the way in which the earth's features were studied in Britain. Physiography became a popular subject in the schools taking the examinations of the Department of Science and Art, and helped to shift opinion at the British Association and, for a time, at the RGS, towards a new emphasis on physical geography.(42)

But the imbalance between the limited intellectual stature of the publicists for the political side of the subject, often concerned with writing elementary school textbooks, and earth scientists such as Geikie and Huxley, who were among the academic giants of the time, was of concern to those at the RGS who saw their subject either being split into two, or at least being shifted too far in one direction. A decisive change occurred in the mid-1880s. Prior to 1870 the great geologist, Sir Roderick Murchison, had been four times President of the RGS. During the 1870s Geikie and Huxley had produced their influential texts. The trend seemed to be in the direction of physical geography. But from the time of the Keltie Report of 1886 the tensions between the earth scientists and the RGS establishment became overt. The break was perhaps triggered by Geikie's lukewarm response when asked by Keltie to support the RGS campaign to establish chairs of geography at Oxford and Cambridge. While a strong supporter of geography in schools, he argued that at university level the subject would more appropriately be regarded as a branch of geology, and should be taught within departments of geology (by special lecturers in geography). The emerging establishment at the RGS was less than happy with this line of thinking. Mackinder's definitions diverged from those of Geikie. Thus on the appearance of The Teaching of Geography, published by Macmillan in 1887, and arguably one of the best methodological texts in the history of the subject, Mackinder, though in general reviewing the book respectfully, was at pains to criticise Geikie's overbroad sweep, introducing to the human side of the subject, on which he was less at home, many topics which 'even the most grasping geographer would scarcely claim as his'.(43) Similarly, after Geikie's rebuff to Keltie, Freshfield somewhat testily referred to geologists as 'perhaps the most forward of the would-be "chuckers-out" of geography from the Hall of Education'.(44) Then Markham, President of the RGS, took the bull by the horns and tried to forge an agreement on the precise limits between physical geography and geology, at a joint meeting of Sections C and E of the British Association in 1893.(45) The geologists were sceptical and Geikie, in the Chair, concluded that they would be unsympathetic to any drawing of tight boundaries, as the tasks of the two subjects were inextricably interwoven.(46) The political implication was that a distinct line of division would have made more

clear-cut the case for separate chairs of geography
in the universities. This Geikie had already opposed.

Thus the influence of the earth scientists and
the cause of physical geography lost ground at the
RGS in the late 1880s and 1890s. An active pressure
group at the same time lobbied to shift the Society's objectives from the promotion of exploration
to the promotion of geographical education. Its
success was clinched by the appearance of a new and
independent star on the horizon: Halford Mackinder.

Having gained a 1st in Natural Science and a
2nd in Modern History at Oxford, Mackinder was well
equipped to manufacture a new synthesis. As a young
man of twenty-six he presented to the RGS in 1887
one of the most significant papers in the history of
British geographical thought, 'On the Scope and
Methods of Geography'. Posing the question, 'Can
geography be rendered a discipline instead of a mere
body of information?' he was clearly referring to
the prior low reputation of its political dimension.
He was categorical that any division into physical
and political geography would be against the subject's best interests. While geography as topography
had been unanimously rejected by the cognoscenti,
the solution was not to be found in offloading
political geography and regarding what remained as a
mere linker of the natural sciences. Geography
should be seen as a more significant cultural
bridge, between the sciences and the humanities:
'Lop off either limb of geography and you maim it in
its noblest part ... Its inherent breadth and many-
sidedness should be claimed as its chief merit.'(47)

Mackinder's paradigm was to underwrite a new
regional geography, and helped to establish his
fortunes. From being a successful Oxford Extension
Lecturer he was made the first Reader in Geography
at that university in 1887. Like other major academics of his day he was also concerned with the subject's educational applications, and was resolved to
translate this concern into concrete activity.(48)
His definition of geography as a bridging subject
was seen as equally appropriate to its development
in schools: 'the regional basis should in the main
be adhered to, for distribution is of the essence of
geography, and imparts to regional geography a unity
not possessed by physical geography'.(49)

Mackinder was the most weighty but not the
first protagonist favouring this bridging role.
Freshfield too had been perturbed by those who
framed a schooling based solely on physical science,

and at the same time by the reactionary stance of
the classicists, blind to alternative curricula:
'between the rival camps of educationists, it seems
to me that geography steps in as the mediator and
uniter'.(50)
    If Mackinder was the catalyst, Herbertson pro-
vided the synthesis for a revived geography, whether
at school or university level. His identification of
the 'major natural regions of the world' as the
'higher units' of study, or what we would call today
the 'key ideas', established regional geography as
the dominant paradigm.(51) The new scheme was presented as having educational as well as geographical
merit, for instead of the world being compartmen-
talised into hundreds of political divisions, it
could be more intelligently studied through the
framework of a dozen or so natural regions, concep-
tualised on the basis of their physical attributes:
climate, vegetation and soil.(52) The academic concept was translated for school use in the Herbert-
sons' amazingly successful Senior Geography, originally published in 1907, which remained in print
until 1952 (53) and was designed to abolish 'the
distinction between physical and political geography
... drawn by older text-books'.(54)
    Thus the shifting definitions at the frontiers
were directly and authoritatively disseminated by
Mackinder, Herbertson and their disciples as advice
and in materials for geography teachers in schools.
This 'new geography' was viewed as a distinct advance in providing in the first place a more cogent
mechanism for the structuring of curriculum units;
in the second, a more liberal education by bridging
with other disciplines: 'Knowledge ... is one. Its
division into subjects is a concession to human
weakness';(55) and, in the third, as developing more
complex intellectual skills of potential value in
the practical affairs of adult life: 'of thinking in
terms of the map, of visualizing intricate correlations, of ordering complex masses of fact'.(56) But,
as we shall see, the pundits were more certain in
their grasp of the subject paradigms than of the
pedagogics.

PEDAGOGY: FROM 'CAPES AND BAYS' TO THE 'HIGHER
UNITS'

    In my day there were many boys at public
    schools who acted consistently, and not alto-
    gether unsuccessfully, on the principle that

whatever was not a city in Asia Minor was an
island in the Aegean Sea.(57)

All the major figures in the field, whether
within or without the RGS, therefore took the view
that geography was more than a mere description of
the world and, in educational terms, required more
than a mere effort of memory. The cram approach had
acquired the tag of 'Capes and Bays' geography. The
genre was linked with the notion of an implicit
order and harmony in the universe, whose compendious
description would attest to the glory of the divine
creation. Like other subjects, geography in Britain
was seen as subservient to religious instruction, an
imperative which had far from died out by the School
Board period. Thus in a review of the Reverend T.
Milner's A Universal Geography in Four Parts:
Historical, Mathematical, Physical and Political,
published in 1876, attention was drawn to the
author's penchant for giving everything a Protestant
Christian twist. The 'Garden of Eden' was assumed to
have had a topographical placing, though the 'exact
spot' was undetermined: 'Each division of the work
ends with a passage pointing out the wisdom, good-
ness and power of the Creator.'(58) Even in the most
neutral listing of facts a moral and social control
element could be infiltrated, and catechetical techniques reinforced the prescriptive pedagogy derived
from religious instruction.(59)

A different slant existed at secondary level,
though one equally reducing geography to a service
function. Here it became the adjunct of classical
education, resulting in a concentration on the so-
called 'historical geography' of the Mediterranean
and the Near and Middle East. Huxley was dismissive
of the joint Christian/classical pincer movement
which gave so much priority to 'Jewish history and
Syrian geography'.(60) Professor Pillans, with pre-
tensions as an educationist, sought to improve the
dusty image with which classical geography had been
associated. He saw geography's role as helping to
'connect the writings of the Classics with impressions and associations that will add to the profit
and pleasure of perusing them'.(61) Therefore to
stimulate interest in the detail he introduced 'impressive associations and striking peculiarities'.
(62) 'Capes and Bays' became more erudite:

On the DURIUS [...Duero (in Spanish) Douro (in
Portuguese)], near the source ... stood
Numantia, which Florus calls Hispaniae Decus.

It sustained a fourteen years' siege against
the Romans, and was taken at last by Scipio
Africanus Minor. At the mouth stood Calle, or
Porto Calensis, whence the Kingdom of Portugal
derives its name. Calle is now Oporto, and from
this comes the word 'Port', as applied to wine
shipped from that harbour.(63)

A third influence sustaining 'Capes and Bays'
geography, and the one most connected with the work
of the RGS, was the widely-held objective of keeping
children up-to-date with the expansion of knowledge
about the world. Even those who accepted the importance of advancing the academic credibility of geography did not deny that a basic description of the
world had to be given some priority. But except in
the delineation of the most formal physical features
the description was rarely a neutral one. The 'impressive associations and striking peculiarities'
advocated by Pillans were deployed to drive home
moral lessons and, through blatant stereotyping and
caricaturing, to furnish an eagerly digested cel-
ebration of the superiority of the Christian and of
the British way of life.
The Reverend J. Goldsmith's (64) textbook of
1813 was a model in terms of its confident message,
its clear-cut pedagogy, and the popular appeal of
its disparaging punch lines:

The climate of Turkey in Asia is delightful and
salubrious; but that dreadful scourge of mankind, the plague, is rendered doubly destructive in this wretched empire, from the native
indolence of the Turks, and from their super-
stitious belief in predestination.(65)

The Turks were negatively matched only by Papists
and African savages in the collective unconscious of
English textbook writers and teachers, who were
indeed only reflecting the official views purveyed
by such journals as The British Colonial Empire,
which as late as 1892 was concluding:

The majority of our Colonies have been re-
claimed from their primitive state by peaceful
British Colonists; at most we have dispossessed
a few wandering tribes of savages still in a
state of barbarity.(66)

Thus Miss Sturgeon's approach, in a sample lesson
for the Manchester Geographical Society in 1887

seems almost innocent:

> The people of Turkey are not called Turkeys as
> you would naturally suppose - they are called
> Turks. We will now leave Constantinople and
> cross the Black Sea. I cannot tell you why it
> has such a gloomy name, as it is certainly not
> black either in colour or character ... (67)

On occasions, the more extreme manifestations of
jingoism provoked some revulsion, as when the reviewer of an anonymous geography text of 1871 con-
demned as 'mischievous' the contrasting national
stereotypes of the English: 'a happy people because
they are well treated by the Queen and the great
Lords', as against the Scotch: 'fond of drinking';
the Portuguese: 'idle' and prone to do 'everything
badly'; and the Italians, who met once a year 'to
kiss the Pope's great toe. Do you laugh? It would be
better to cry.'(68)
    It may be conjectured that these caricatures
infused considerable human interest into the study
of 'Capes and Bays'. In addition, a number of ingen-
ious gambits were resorted to as means of varying
the monotonous diet. The School Board Chronicle
reviewers were generally critical of some heavy-
handed endeavours. Thus the Reverend Alexander
MacKay's attempt in his Geography in Rhyme of 1873
to use doggerel as an aide-mémoire was criticised as
'a burlesque of knowledge rather than a handbook of
learning'. 'Children must not be approached as if
they were idiots ...':

> Glamorgan lying further east
> With measureless coalfields
> An inexhaustible supply
> Of iron it also yields.(69)

An allergic reaction was also provoked by J.E.
Taylor's Geological Stories: A Series of Autobio-
graphies, and his novel tactic of allowing objects
to talk in the first person singular. Thus a piece
of granite explained itself: 'There are few rock
substances on the surface of the globe which have
received more discussion and been more investigated
than myself.' The reviewer found a more lucid and
informative summary emerging when, to his relief,
the lump of coal stopped being talkative and 'the
stones ceased to prattle'.(70)
    The limited intellectual expectations of the
'Capes and Bays' approach, more varied though it was

than is sometimes presented, were a source of embarrassment to those, not least in the RGS, seeking to
upgrade the academic status of geography. The approach had to be authoritatively rejected, and in
particular as a means of converting the headmasters
of the public schools to the cause of geography.
They had hitherto been reluctant to accept the subject into their curricula in large part because of
its image as demanding 'little more than an effort
of memory', and by definition more appropriate to
the elementary school.(71) Freshfield was convinced
that it was up to the RGS to take the initiative:
'We have ... left as long as it seemed expedient the
cause of geographical education in the hands of the
educational bodies. The result has been unsatisfac-
tory ...'(72)

Although this might have been a just condemnation of the reactionary state of school practice,
the blame could hardly be laid at the door of educational theory. There had been long-standing and
pedagogically progressive advice available to geography teachers, in particular in the 'heimatskunde
[sic] approach', popular on the Continent. This was
defined for Keltie on his intelligence-gathering
visit to the Continent for his Report. For example,
in a directive for its use in Austrian schools, it
was agreed that geography's purview was the world as
a whole, but accepted that pupils had direct acquaintance only with their home portion of it. It
was this immediate environment, which lay open to
their observation and was part of their experience,
that had to be the starting point of study: 'The
neighbourhood, then, must serve as a measure and
standard of comparison for the distant, offering as
it does an image of the same arrangement and the
same relations.'(73)

Though not widely practised in England, the
principles behind the study of the local area had
long been understood by methodological experts in
this country, from Wyse, who in 1836 wrote of geography's rudiments being 'already learned in the
daily walk';(74) to HMI Moseley, for whom the first
step in a child's education should be 'to teach him
to observe';(75) to Jelinger Symons, who advocated
what was later known as the concentric approach,
going 'step by step, from the best known to the less
known', the latter to be taught as 'a series of
vivid pictures';(76) to Fitch, who reinforced
Symons: 'we should begin with what is known and what
is near, and let our knowledge radiate from that
centre until it comprehends what is larger and more

remote';(77) to Bain, who argued that it was 'from
some commanding eminence that a pupil should receive
first impressions of Geography';(78) and to Laurie,
who ruled: 'Teaching, like charity, should begin at
home.'(79)

There were obvious links between the heimatskunde approach within elementary geography and 'the
science of common things', as practised in this
country by a Hampshire teacher, Richard Dawes.(80)
The translation of the method into more sophisticated school texts was, however, the achievement of
the two previously mentioned scientists, Geikie, in
his Science Primers on Geology and Physical Geography in the series edited by Huxley.(81) Somewhat
less convincingly, Huxley deployed local study and
experimental techniques to lead students 'from the
firm ground of experience... to remoter objects and
to the less readily comprehensible relations of
things', starting off from the vantage point of
London Bridge.(82)

But just as the progressive techniques of
Richard Dawes were compromised when translated into
the mass teaching situation by non-specialist staff
in elementary schools,(83) so the very demanding
presentation of Huxley created problems in the secondary sector, where his Physiography text was a
standard work, as we have seen, for the Department
of Science and Art examinations. Here too teachers
were insufficiently comprehending of the fundamental
scientific principles involved and even made, according to DSA examiners, 'false and misleading
statements to their pupils', forced to adhere slav-
ishly to the text, typically read out to the class
'without explanation or illustration'.(84)

Huxley's Physiography had also run into difficulties with an emerging science education establishment,(85) and the developing criticism was not
inconvenient in the context of the RGS's realisation
that emphasis on physical geography need no longer
be an index of academic respectability. In this
light, Freshfield took the opportunity of sniping at
the quality of the diagrams in Physiography,(86)
while Herbertson later insisted that geography was
not 'physiography plus topography'.(87) Respectability was achieved, as we have seen, through the new
synthesis of regional geography, the world's natural
regions becoming the 'higher units' of study, to be
further discussed in the concluding section.

DIRECT INVOLVEMENT: THE RGS AND GEOGRAPHICAL
EDUCATION

So far as elementary schooling was concerned, the
stance taken in the Keltie Report was that there had
been a marked advance from the time when Moseley
found geography taught in only one Midlands school
in three, in the 1840s, to the situation in the
1880s when it had become one of the most popular
subjects in the elementary curriculum. Notwithstand-
ing the known inadequacies in terms of quality,
Keltie was able to absolve the RGS from too heavy a
responsibility for this sector, which he concluded
was in 'a healthy condition of progressive evolution'.(88)
    Keltie was more anxious about 'the great cha-
otic mass of English middle-class schools' where the
position of geography was 'far from satisfactory',(89) and particularly so if it was accepted
that it was an especially important subject for
those later referred to by Herbertson as 'the di-
recting classes ... usually educated in secondary
schools'.(90) The first intervention in this area
had been Galton's prize scheme to encourage geography teaching in the public schools.(91) In response
to intelligence from those schools, it was deemed
that the scheme had to be flexible and offer the
boys freedom to 'follow their favourite studies',
which meant separating prizes for physical and political geography.(92) The scheme was not, however,
a success, largely because of the absence of specialist teachers in so many public schools. Two
schools, Liverpool College and Dulwich College, won
almost half the medals awarded.(93) The Headmaster
of Dulwich argued that the failure resulted from
awarding only a limited number of prizes and not
publicising a fuller honours list, which would have
widened the incentive.(94) Less impressed with the
scheme, which he saw as 'encouraging the cramming of
a boy who has a receptive capacity', the Headmaster
of Eton suggested that the RGS should rather be
giving priority to the establishment of geography in
universities, which would in turn stimulate the
subject in the public schools.(95)
    The education lobby in the RGS had also come
round to this conclusion. It had unsuccessfully
approached the universities of Oxford and Cambridge
on three occasions in the 1870s, maintaining that
the introduction of this revived subject would both
benefit the universities and society in general and
'give a much needed impetus to the progress of the

art of teaching geography in schools, which is at present imperfectly developed'.(96)

Prior to 1880, therefore, the educational interventions of the RGS had borne little fruit. It was resolved to adopt a more systematic approach to the attainment of three objectives: the establishment of chairs in universities; the training of specialist teachers; and the promotion of new appliances for geography teaching.(97) In 1884, Keltie was appointed as the Society's Inspector of Geographical Education, with the task of preparing a detailed report on its state, with suggestions for improvement.(98)

This influential Report summarised the aims of geography teaching, the 'state of the art' in the discipline and the position of geography in different types of school, its relations with other subjects, the RGS prize schemes, apparatus, maps and textbooks, the Oxford and Cambridge Local Examinations, the examinations of the Department of Science and Art, geography in the universities, and a wide survey of geographical education on the Continent, which demonstrated its superiority over what was on offer in England and Wales. Keltie's pessimistic conclusion was that apart from in elementary schools, girls' high schools and isolated middle-class schools, 'geography in this country is almost entirely neglected as a subject of education'. In the universities it was nil, and in the public schools very nearly nil.(99)

The Report contained an extensive and informative set of appendices, of which the replies of the headmasters of public schools to Keltie's questionnaires, and the detail of geographical methods and programmes used in continental schools, were and are of particular interest. The publication of the Report was associated with a pioneering exhibition of educational appliances for geography teaching held in London at the end of 1885, at which major lectures were given by E.G. Ravenstein, J. Bryce, Professor H.N. Moseley, and Keltie himself, the text being reproduced in the Report.(100)

The 'appliances' displayed included textbooks and atlases, globes, wall maps, small sheet maps, telluria and planetaria, hardware models and relief maps, and geographical and ethnological pictures. The exhibition was then lent to the Manchester Geographical Society early in 1886, followed by the Scottish Geographical Society.(101) Requests for its loan were received from other provincial centres. On its return it was agreed to select and set in order

those items useful for sending round to schools,
with an explanatory pamphlet.(102) Help for schools
became more practical as, for example, in the RGS's
list of instructions to teachers for the construction of wall maps.(103) The Manchester Geographical
Society similarly committed itself to initiatives of
this type.(104)

In the eleven years following the Keltie Report
the RGS spent over £6,000 on geographical education,
including support for the Readership in Geography at
Oxford, finally established in 1887, for lecture-
ships in Cambridge and Manchester, and contributions
to university and extension work in Oxford and
London. Travelling scholarships were introduced as
well as prizes for training college students, with
the intention of stimulating interest in geography
among students being trained for the elementary
sector.(105) Both Markham and Herbertson were to
stress the importance of improving the quality of
teachers at the 6th International Geographical Congress held in London in 1895.(106)

During this period of support for the promotion
of geographical education, however, there had been
intense in-fighting between contending pressure
groups in the RGS establishment. The education lobby
was led by Galton and Freshfield, and was confronted
by a 'traditionalist' group spearheaded by Markham.
Sir Clements Markham had been Honorary Secretary of
the Society, 1863-88, and became its President in
1893, a position he held until 1904. He was the most
influential figure at the RGS after Murchison's
death. He was, as Mill put it, 'by nature strongly
drawn to the tradition of the past, and required
time and tactful persuasion to turn his mind to new
ideas'.(107)

A private memorandum left by Markham on 'The
History of Expenditure on Education' by the Society
was unequivocal in its condemnation of much of this
spending.(108) His axiom was that the RGS must have
a share in the control over any expenditure involved
in grants to other bodies. This had not generally
happened. He derided Galton's public school prizes
scheme, the travelling scholarships, the prizes for
training colleges, and 'the tiresome interruption of
the business' of the Society at the meetings at
which these awards were presented. He was critical
of the malign influence of those he categorised as
the 'doctrinaires', defined as short on experience,
as 'objectors general', and as dispensing opinions
on every subject whether they knew about it or not.
Freshfield was the chief culprit, responsible for

expenditure 'recklessly lavished'.

Markham also pinned blame on the 'weak rule' of previous Presidents, who had allowed the 'doctrinaires' to gain the upper hand. In a section headed 'The Doctrinaires Rampant', he bewailed the gathering influence of Galton and Freshfield under first Strachey, and then Grant Duff, the first 'bearded President' who looked like 'a little Chinese God ensconced in the Presidential Chair', and allowed Freshfield to gain 'complete sway' and introduce policies which starved exploring and subsidised educational schemes. On the other hand, Markham applauded the Keltie Report as 'full and valuable'.

On becoming President in 1893, Markham resolved to curb the educational expenditure of the RGS. In a Memorandum entitled 'On the Future Educational Policy of the Council', he stressed that the educational expenditure of more than £650 per annum was more than the Society could bear: 'It cripples our legitimate work ... ' While praising the efforts of Mackinder, he insisted that the grants to universities could not be regarded as permanent subsidies. In any case, the object of establishing geography as a permanent subject had not been achieved. Most of Mackinder's students, for example, were in Oxford's Honours School of Modern History.(109) Markham's proposed policy was to shift the emphasis to courses of instruction for travellers and for potential teachers of geography in secondary schools, for he agreed that the chaotic situation in the public schools continued to require the Society's attention. He therefore favoured Mackinder's idea of a Geographical Institute at the University of London.(110)

In these more public statements Markham moderated his approach and his language, and demonstrated at least a cautious commitment to geographical education, so long as expenditure was controlled and under a tight central rein. The clash of personality and of policy with Freshfield may be argued to have been indirectly of benefit to geographical education. The two came into open conflict over the cause célèbre of admitting ladies as Fellows.(111) Freshfield and his supporters were in favour, but after a bitter and by no means one-sided contest, the traditionalists won the day. Disillusioned with the conduct of the Society, Freshfield resigned as Honorary Secretary.(112)

Concurrent with these developments, a group of teachers and others was meeting in Oxford with the limited objective of arranging postal exchanges of

lantern slides between schoolmaster friends.(113)
Out of this meeting grew the Geographical Association, to which Freshfield transferred his alle-
giance. He was the Association's first President
and later indicated that one of the reasons he had
wanted to see ladies as Fellows at the RGS was because so many were engaged in geographical education.(114) The Geographical Association would provide them with facilities denied them elsewhere.(115)
In fact co-operative relationships were quickly established between the Association and the RGS, which
gave the new body its blessing, recognising its
complementary function: its ability to focus more
effectively on educational matters, leaving the
Society to concentrate on its traditional activities.(116) Freshfield was at pains to draw attention
to the complementarity in his introduction to the
first volume of the Association's journal, The Geographical Teacher, which appeared in 1902.(117)
        Another example of fruitful continuity was
personified by H.R. Mill, Librarian of the RGS, who
was one of those present at the preliminary committee meeting of the Geographical Association in 1893,
and was elected its Chairman.(118) The author of the
RGS's Hints to Teachers on the Choice of Geographical Books (1897), Mill presented its rights to the
Geographical Association on condition that a new
edition was prepared. This was undertaken by
Herbertson, Unstead and MacMunn.(119)
        While there were some mild exchanges of concern
about the overlap of material for the respective
publications of the two societies, The Geographical
Journal and The Geographical Teacher, there was
general agreement on the lines of demarcation.(120)
While articles on geographical education continued
to appear in the former, these tended to be in the
nature of overviews and position statements rather
than the detail of advice on classroom practice that
its readers expected of the latter.
        It must be said, however, that the RGS went
further than its implicit limits as guardian of
suitable content would have suggested, as in its
syllabuses for geography in elementary and secondary
schools published in the early 1900s, which were
presented as 'authoritative guidance in regard to
the methods and courses of study most applicable to
the end in view'.(121) Mackinder's secondary programme was also far from confined to advice purely
on the geographical content of the syllabus, claiming to be characterised by careful planning and
progressive development of the quality of work.(122)

Like Herbertson, Mackinder not only imposed a tight
content structure. He also applied his pedagogical
opinions, in which area, it could be argued, he was
less than sure-footed. His experience (though it had
been confined to university and extra-mural work)
'suggested that the best way was not to teach the
facts first and then the principles, but to combine
the two, and teach the facts while emphasising the
principles'. He accepted that he was not referring
to the most elementary pupils, but he believed that
his system, properly diluted (my stress), would be
applicable to them also.(123)
    Despite its initial attractions, Herbertson's
scheme of natural regions, a paradigm which had been
the major beneficiary of the RGS's rejection of
physical geography as the preferred academic emphasis of the subject, was in time to reveal fatal
flaws.(124) At the academic level, it ultimately
contributed to a declining academic image for the
subject, its correlations between climate, soil,
vegetation and human responses displaying little
explanatory power and contributing to deterministic
analyses.(125)
    At school level, there were even greater dan-
gers in the condensed, inert, technical language
which in pseudo-authoritative sentences and phrases
provided pithy, generalised summaries, but no vivid
picture or true analysis, of huge tracts of the
earth's surface.(126) While Herbertson claimed
awareness that 'the best logical order is not necessarily the best pedagogical order'(127) it was the
former that prevailed in his textbooks, which he
hoped would furnish a true and beneficial synthesis
between the sciences and humanities.(128) Concerns
of this sort were indeed raised at the time. Thus
A.J. Cooper, 'Mistress of Method' to the Oxford
Delegacy for the Training of Secondary Teachers,
acknowledged that the scheme was a major advance on
crude political divisions, but in effect expressed
reservations as to whether what was a suitable basis
for the systematization of knowledge for advanced
students was as readily translatable to the cogni-
tive levels of pupils of school age as Herbertson
imagined. She shrewdly appreciated that there were
detailed aspects of 'spatial relation' which 'might
be obscured by Dr. Herbertson's treatment'.(129) As
was the case with Huxley, the problem of the dissemination of advanced knowledge 'down' the educational ladder, though not unrecognised, was not
appreciated as requiring a similar level of sophisticated expertise as was taken for granted in the

content area. Little attention was paid, for example, to the inherent mismatch between the technical
language of the science and the vernacular language
of the pupil in the classroom.(130) There was indeed
less pedagogical underpinning in the new textbooks
based on the framework of the world's natural regions than had been evident in Geikie's much earlier
introductory primers in geology and physical geography.

In appraising the influence of the RGS on the
development of geographical education, whether in
schools or universities, it is clear that its significant achievements were largely the responsibility of a few redoubtable educational protagonists
who were, within the limitations of their background, relatively progressive thinkers, with the
initiative and determination to pursue their cause
in an institutional environment that might not have
been expected to give priority to such matters. The
RGS functioned both as catalyst and midwife for
geographical education, leaving the Geographical
Association to nurse the infant subject into a
healthy existence in schools, and particularly the
secondary schools with which it has since been predominantly linked. Success was never fully achieved
in many public schools and some high-status grammar
schools, however, where geography remained a lower-
status subject on the modern side, a soft option for
failed physicists and classicists. By and large,
however, its place as a core subject in the curriculum was secure by the First World War. It had
gained increasing official recognition, the Board of
Education having issued regulations, and the London
County Council an approved syllabus, in geography,
the latter in association with the RGS, in the first
decade of the century. There remained much to be
done in the Civil Service sector, although the subject had at least been accepted in examinations for
the lower grades.(131)

CONCLUSION

By the time Keltie addressed the Geographical Association in 1914 on thirty years of progress in geographical education since the time he was appointed
the RGS's Inspector, membership of that Society had
grown to over 5,000, and that of the youthful Geographical Association had passed 1,000. Despite the
brake put on by Markham, the Society had expended by
1924 not less than £20,000 on educational grants to

the universities alone.(132) In pursuit of its educational ends the RGS had capitalised on its public
esteem as a guardian of the spirit and purpose of
empire. It had presided over a revolution in the
content, balance and presentation of the discipline,
filtered into the school sector through exhibitions
of appliances, formal advice circulars, and through
the activities of Mackinder, Herbertson and their
followers, in textbook writing, lecturing to teachers, and methodological papers.

Present on the occasion of Keltie's address
were Freshfield and Mackinder, a reunion of three
dominating influences associated with the RGS and
later the Geographical Association, the architects
of the revolution in geographical education which it
can be claimed the period experienced. As we have
seen, they were creatures of their time and of their
particular backgrounds. They were primarily concerned with enhancing the status of their subject,
with establishing it in the ancient universities and
the public schools, and with adapting it to the
national and imperial interest. The strategy had
been, as both Freshfield and Mackinder had agreed,
'to attack the old Universities' through the instrument of the RGS and 'the comparative wealth at its
disposal'.(133) Once geography was established as a
university discipline and could be used for matriculation, its place in the curriculum of the secondary
school could be justified.

On the question of the diffusion of approved
subject matter and conceptual frameworks into school
geography, the procedures were crude. Curriculum
material was inevitably handed down from above.
Subject content and structures were new, and were
being created outside the school system. There was
no obvious substitute for what would today be rejected as a centre-periphery model of dissemination
in a situation in which there were few specialist
teachers. The content was likely to be academic in
its orientation and the pedagogy suspect. But it was
felt strongly at the time that the educational trend
was progressive in the shift from the memorisation
of gazetteer-type knowledge, to an emphasis on the
appraisal of relationships between people and
places.

As we have seen, the more pupil-centred
heimatskunde approach was shunted into a siding,
inadvertent victim of a powerful and novel academic
paradigm, one seen to have the crucial advantage of
uniting the two branches of geography, by drawing on
perspectives from the earth sciences and humanities

in a manner Hughes and Galton had advocated from the 1850s. Absence of an associable pedagogic framework, however, led inexorably to a new cycle of factual recall learning, despite the more sophisticated content and advances in textbook and visual aids production. In this the requirements of the examination system, which the proponents of geography in secondary schools had regarded as a necessary precursor to the subject's wide acceptance, were implicated. By this stage the RGS had, by and large, left the campaigning to others, to revert to its earlier, more characteristic activities. It had proved to be an important influence in exploiting its political and academic prestige and its considerable resources to gain for a popular but intellectually suspect subject credibility in the higher reaches of the educational system.

NOTES AND REFERENCES

1.   H.R. Mill, The Record of the Royal Geographical Society 1830-1930 (Royal Geographical Society, 1930), p. 74.

2.   J.K. Wright, 'The Field of the Geographical Society' in G. Taylor (ed.), Geography in the Twentieth Century (Methuen, 1953), pp. 547-8.

3.   Journal of the Royal Geographical Society of London, vol.1 (1832), pp. vii-viii.

4.   See D.R. Stoddart, 'The RGS and the Foundations of Geography at Cambridge', Geographical Journal, vol.141, no.2 (1975), pp. 216-39; D.I. Scargill, 'The RGS and the Foundations of Geography at Oxford', Geographical Journal, vol.142, no.3 (1976), pp. 438-61; and L.M. Cantor, 'The Royal Geographical Society and the Projected London Institute of Geography 1892-1899', Geographical Journal, vol.128, no.1 (1962), pp. 30-5. The London initiative was not in the event successful.

5.   There is a brief paper: E.W. Gilbert, 'The RGS and Geographical Education in 1871', Geographical Journal, vol.137, no.2 (1971), pp. 200-2.

6.   See, in addition to Mill, Royal Geographical Society, pp. 247-52, C.R. Markham, 'The Fifty Years' Work of the Royal Geographical Society', Journal of the Royal Geographical Society, vol.50 (1880), pp. 1-254; also J.S. Keltie, 'Thirty Years' Progress in Geographical Education', Geographical Teacher, vol.7, no.38 (1914), pp. 215-27.

7.   Hamilton was a diplomat whose exploits included taking part in the securing of the Rosetta

Stone and Elgin Marbles for the British Museum. See
Mill, Royal Geographical Society, pp. 38-9.
   8.   W.R. Hamilton, 'Address', Journal of the
Royal Geographical Society of London, vol.8 (1838),
pp. xxxix-xl.
   9.   Third Report of the Royal Commission on
Scientific Instruction and the Advancement of
Science, Parliamentary Papers XXVIII (1873; C.868),
pp. 262 and 266 (Minutes of Evidence 12,550-1 and
12,591).
   10.   For fuller discussion, see Mill, Royal
Geographical Society, especially pp. 87-9 and 113-
32; also J.S. Keltie, 'Some Geographical Problems',
Geographical Journal, vol.10, no.3 (1897), pp. 308-
23 (p. 309).
   11.   See, for example, Mill, Royal Geographical
Society, p. 89: 'In 1866 a traveller from West
Africa told stories of a giant ape called the goril-
la which excited much controversy and disbelief.'
   12.   RGS Correspondence Files, 1871-1880
Block, Letter from W. Parker. At this first of many
references to the RGS archives it is appropriate to
acknowledge the great help given by the Society's
archivist, Christine Kelly. For a useful introduction to these materials, see C. Kelly, 'The RGS
Archives: A Handlist', Geographical Journal,
vol.141, no.1 (1975), pp. 99-107.
   13.   See, for example, 'The Neglect of
Geography in Our Higher Schools, and the Remedy',
School Board Chronicle (hereinafter SBC), 26 August
1871, p. 51.
   14.   Report of the Proceedings of the Royal
Geographical Society in Reference to the Improvement
of Geographical Education (hereinafter Keltie
Report), (John Murray, 1886), pp. 10-11 and 35-6.
   15.   Miss M.K. Sturgeon, 'The Teaching of Elementary Geography - a Practical Lesson, with Models', Journal of the Manchester Geographical Society,
vol.3 (1887), pp. 83-95 (p. 85).
   16.   'Geography and Education', Geographical
Journal, vol.25, no.1 (1905), pp. 17-22.
   17.   RGS Correspondence Files, 1871-1880
Block. See also Keltie Report, pp. 80, 83 and 180.
   18.   E.G. Ravenstein, 'The Aims and Methods of
Geographical Education' in Keltie Report, pp. 163-81
(pp. 165-6).
   19.   A.J. Herbertson, 'Recent Discussions on
the Scope and Educational Applications of Geography',
Geographical Journal, vol.24, no.4 (1904), pp. 417-
27 (p. 427); also A.J. Herbertson, 'On the Importance of Geography in Secondary Education and the

Training of Teachers Therein' in H.R. Mill (ed.), Report of the Sixth International Geographical Congress Held in London 1895 (John Murray, 1896), pp. 83-95 (pp. 84-5); and J. Bryce, 'The Importance of Geography in Education', Geographical Journal, vol.19, no.3 (1902), pp. 301-13 (pp. 310-11).

20. J. Fairgrieve, Geography in School (University of London Press, 1926; 1937 ed.), p. 7.

21. J.H. Yoxall, The Pupil Teachers' Geography, 2nd ed. (undated), p. 30.

22. Lord Rosebery, 'Introduction' to G.R. Parkin, Round the Empire for the Use of Schools, quoted in review in SBC, 26 May 1894, p. 603.

23. See T.G. Longstaff, 'Douglas Freshfield 1845-1934', Geographical Journal, vol.83, no.4 (1934), pp. 257-62; and L.J. Jay, 'Douglas Freshfield's Contribution to Geographical Education' in W.E. Marsden (ed.), Historical Perspectives on Geographical Education (International Geographical Union/University of London Institute of Education, 1980), pp. 43-53.

24. D.W. Freshfield, 'The Place of Geography in Education', Proceedings of the Royal Geographical Society, new series, vol.8, no.11 (1886), pp. 698-718 (p. 701).

25. See, for example, his seminal paper delivered at the RGS in 1904: H.J. Mackinder, 'The Geographical Pivot of History', Geographical Journal, vol.23, no.4 (1904), pp. 421-37.

26. See W.H. Parker, Mackinder: Geography as an Aid to Statecraft (Clarendon Press, Oxford, 1982), pp. 34 and 51.

27. E.W. Gilbert, 'Seven Lamps of Geography: An Appreciation of the Teaching of Sir Halford J. Mackinder', Geography, vol.36, pt 1 (1951), pp. 21-43.

28. See, for an Indian viewpoint, S.G. Garsole, 'The Impact of British Geographical Writings on School Textbooks in Marathi: Maharashtra (India)' in H. Haubrich (ed.), Perception of People and Places through Media, Vol.2 (International Geographical Union/Pädagogische Hochschule, Freiburg, 1984), pp. 644-55.

29. H.J. Mackinder, 'The Teaching of Geography from the Imperial Point of View, and the Use Which Could and Should Be Made of Visual Instruction', Geographical Teacher, vol.6, no.30 (1911), pp. 79-86 (pp. 79-80).

30. Ibid., p. 83.

31. See T.W. Freeman, A Hundred Years of Geography (Duckworth, 1961), p. 178.

32. See Baron F. von Richthofen, 'The Impetus and Direction of Geography in the Nineteenth Century', Geographical Journal, vol.23, no.2 (1904), pp. 229-32.

33. M. Oughton, 'Mary Somerville 1780-1872' in T.W. Freeman and P. Pinchemel (eds.), Geographers: Biobibliographical Studies, Vol.2, (Mansell, 1978), pp. 109-11 (p. 110).

34. J.N.L. Baker, 'Mary Somerville and Geography in England' (1948), reprinted in The History of Geography: Papers by J.N.L. Baker (Blackwell, Oxford, 1963), pp. 51-71, (p. 63).

35. Hughes is a much quoted, but historically somewhat obscure figure. He lectured at King's College, London. See J.E. Vaughan, 'William Hughes, F.R.G.S. (1818-1876) as Geographical Educationist' in Marsden (ed.), Historical Perspectives, pp. 66-79.

36. W. Hughes, Geography: What It Is and How to Teach It, (Philip and Son, 1870).

37. F. Galton, 'Notes on Modern Geography' in Cambridge Essays 1855 (J.W. Parker, 1855), pp. 79-109 (pp. 82-3).

38. See Baker, History of Geography, p. 64.

39. See W.E. Marsden, 'Archibald Geikie 1835-1924' in Freeman and Pinchemel (eds.), Geographers, Vol.3, pp. 39-52.

40. A. Geikie, 'Geographical Evolution', Proceedings of the Royal Geographical Society, new series, vol.1, no.7 (1879), pp. 422-43 (pp. 422-3).

41. See D.R. Stoddart, 'Darwin's Impact on Geography', Annals of the Association of American Geographers, vol.56 (1966), pp. 683-98.

42. D.R. Stoddart, '"That Victorian Science": Huxley's Physiography and Its Impact on Geography', Transactions of the Institute of British Geographers, vol.66 (1975), pp. 17-40 (pp. 17-18).

43. H.J. Mackinder in a review of Geikie's The Teaching of Geography in Nature, vol.36 (1887), p. 506.

44. Freshfield, 'Place of Geography', p. 704.

45. 'The Limits between Geology and Physical Geography', Geographical Journal, vol.2 (1893), pp. 518-34 (pp. 519-20).

46. Ibid., pp. 533-4.

47. H.J. Mackinder, 'On the Scope and Methods of Geography', Proceedings of the Royal Geographical Society, new series, vol.9 (1887), pp. 141-73 (pp. 141-2, 145 and 159-60).

48. See RGS Correspondence Files 1887-1910, Letter from H.J. Mackinder to J.S. Keltie dated 3 March 1891.

49. 'Geographical Education at the British Association', Geographical Journal, vol.22, no.5 (1903), pp. 549-53 (p. 549), in a summary of Mackinder's address at the joint session of the Geography and Education Sections at the Southport meeting of 1903.

50. Freshfield, 'Place of Geography', pp. 699-70; Keltie, 'Thirty Years' Progress', p. 220, and Bryce, 'Importance of Geography', p. 301, also followed this line.

51. A.J. Herbertson, 'The Major Natural Regions of the World', Geographical Journal, vol.25, no.3 (1905), pp. 300-10.

52. See T. Pickles, The World (J.M. Dent, 1939 ed.), p. 35.

53. See L.J. Jay, 'A.J. Herbertson: His Services to School Geography', Geography, vol.50, pt 4 (1965), pp. 350-61 (p. 356).

54. A.J. and F.D. Herbertson, The Senior Geography (Clarendon Press, Oxford, 1925 ed.), p. iii.

55. Mackinder, 'On the Scope and Methods', p. 154.

56. 'Geographical Education at the British Association' (1903), p. 551.

57. Freshfield, 'Place of Geography', p. 702.

58. Review in SBC, 15 July 1876, p. 67. Other examples could be quoted.

59. For useful background on and examples of the religious infusion of various elementary subjects see J.M. Goldstrom, Education: Elementary Education 1780-1900 (David and Charles, Newton Abbot, 1972).

60. T.H. Huxley, 'A Liberal Education: And Where to Find It' in Science and Education: Essays by T.H. Huxley (Macmillan, 1895), pp. 76-110 (p. 87).

61. J. Pillans, Elements of Physical and Classical Geography (Blackwood and Sons, Edinburgh, 1854), p. iii.

62. J. Pillans, Outlines of Geography, Principally Ancient, with Introductory Observations on the Systems of the World and on the Best Manner of Teaching Geography (A. and C. Black, Edinburgh, 1847), p. 27.

63. Pillans, Elements, pp. 1-3.

64. See J.E. Vaughan, 'Aspects of Teaching Geography in England in the Early Nineteenth Century', Paedogogica Historica, vol.12, no.1 (1972), pp. 128-47; also A.P. Brigham and R.E. Dodge, 'Nineteenth Century Textbooks of Geography' in G.M. Whipple (ed.), The Teaching of Geography, 32nd Year-

book of the National Society for the Study of Education (University of Chicago Press, 1933), pp. 3-28, for background on textbooks of this period.

65.   Rev. J. Goldsmith, An Easy Grammar of Geography for Schools and Young Persons (Longman, Hunt, Rees, Orme and Brown, 1813), p. 35.

66.   'Editorial', The British Colonial Empire, vol.2, no.1 (1892), p. 5.

67.   Sturgeon, 'Teaching of Elementary Geography, p. 91.

68.   Review of Geography for Children: Near Home, or the Countries of Europe Described in SBC, 18 February 1871, pp. 25-6.

69.   Review in SBC, 8 February 1873, p. 364.

70.   Review in SBC, 24 May 1873, p. 358.

71.   Keltie Report, p. 90. It is easy, however, to exaggerate the opposition of the headmasters on these grounds. The general tone of their comments was of conditional support, a major condition being that geography needed to be an examination subject and part of the university curriculum.

72.   Freshfield, 'Place of Geography', p. 706.

73.   Keltie Report, pp. 116-20.

74.   T. Wyse, Educational Reform, or the Necessity of a National System of Education, Vol.1 (1836), p. 140.

75.   Minutes of the Committee of Council on Education, Vol.1 (1845), pp. 234-5.

76.   J. Symons, School Economy (1852; Woburn Press reprint, 1971), pp. 98-9.

77.   J.G. Fitch, Lectures on Teaching (Cambridge University Press, 1884), p. 346.

78.   A. Bain, Education as a Science (Kegan Paul, Trench and Co., 1885), p. 273.

79.   S.S. Laurie, Occasional Addresses on Educational Subjects (Cambridge University Press, 1888), p. 96.

80.   See N. Ball, 'Richard Dawes and the Teaching of Common Things', Educational Review, vol.17, no.1 (1964), pp. 62-4; also D. Layton, Science for the People (Allen and Unwin, 1973), pp. 35-54.

81.   For a good example of the approach, see A. Geikie, Physical Geography, Science Primer (Macmillan, 1873), pp. 2-3, as quoted in W.E. Marsden, 'Sir Archibald Geikie (1835-1924) as Geographical Educationist' in Marsden (ed.), Historical Perspectives, pp. 54-65 (p. 57).

82.   T.H. Huxley, Physiography: An Introduction to the Study of Nature (Macmillan, 1877; 1905 ed.), Preface.

83.   Fitch, Lectures on Teaching, pp. 362-5.

84. See Keltie Report, p. 115.
85. Stoddart, '"That Victorian Science"', p. 25.
86. Freshfield, 'Place of Geography', p. 710.
87. Herbertson, 'Recent Discussions', p. 425.
88. J.S. Keltie, 'Geographical Education', Scottish Geographical Magazine, vol.1, no.10 (1885), pp. 497-505 (pp. 497-9).
89. Ibid., p. 499.
90. Herbertson, 'On the Importance of Geography in Secondary Education', p. 86.
91. Markham, 'The Fifty Years' Work of the RGS', p. 109.
92. RGS Committee Minute Book 1865-1872, 7 February and 3 April 1868.
93. Mill, Royal Geographical Society, pp. 247-8.
94. In discussion following Freshfield's address to the Geographical Section of the British Association's Birmingham meeting, 1886: Freshfield, 'Place of Geography', pp. 714-8.
95. RGS Correspondence Block 1881-1910, Letter from Rev. Edwin Hale to Freshfield dated 7 February 1884.
96. Keltie Report, p. 82.
97. See, for example, a private memorandum by Freshfield: 'Proposals in Substitution for the Public School Prizes', RGS Additional Papers 95 (1884).
98. Keltie Report, pp. 9-10.
99. Ibid., p. 36.
100. Ibid., pp. 79-343.
101. RGS Committee Minute Book 1883-1890, Minutes of Geographical Report Committee, 11 January 1886.
102. Ibid., 26 March 1886.
103. Ibid., 11 February 1887.
104. 'Report of the Education Committee of the Manchester Geographical Society, on the Subject of Geographical Education, to the Council of the Society', Journal of the Manchester Geographical Society, vol.1 (1885), pp. 310-42; see also T.W. Freeman, 'The Manchester Geographical Society 1884-1984', The Manchester Geographer, new series, vol.5 (1984), pp. 2-19.
105. 'Notes on the Educational Policy of the Royal Geographical Society' (1895), RGS Additional Papers 95.
106. Mill, Report of the Sixth International Geographical Congress, pp. 8 and 83-7.
107. Mill, Royal Geographical Society, pp. 135-6.
108. RGS Special Collections, No.47, C.R. Markham, MS.
109. 'Memorandum by the President', May 1895, RGS Additional Papers 95.

110. 'Memorandum by the President', 20 October 1895, RGS Additional Papers 95.

111. See L.J. Jay, Geography Teaching with a Little Latitude (Allen and Unwin, 1981), p. 87.

112. RGS Archives, Memorandum from Freshfield to Council 'On the Conduct of Affairs by the Council of RGS During the Past Two Sessions 1892-4', April 1894.

113. H.J. Fleure, 'Sixty Years of Geography and Education', Geography, vol.38, pt 4 (1953), pp. 231-64 (pp. 236-8).

114. T.C. Warrington, 'The Beginnings of the Geographical Association', Geography, vol.38, pt 4 (1953), pp. 221-30 (p. 229).

115. Discussion following Keltie's Presidential Address to the Geographical Association in 1914: Keltie, 'Thirty Years' Progress', p. 225.

116. Freeman, Hundred Years of Geography, p. 70.

117. D.W. Freshfield, 'Introduction', Geographical Teacher, vol.1, no.1 (1901-2), pp. 1-3.

118. Fleure, 'Sixty Years of Geography', p. 241.

119. A.J. Herbertson, J.F. Unstead and E. MacMunn, Guide to Geographical Books and Appliances (Philip and Son, Liverpool, 1910).

120. See RGS Correspondence Block 1881-1910, Letters from Herbertson to Keltie dated 9 November and 3 December 1901, and 10 January 1902.

121. 'The RGS Syllabus of Instruction in Geography', Geographical Journal, vol.22, no.5 (1903), pp. 573-4.

122. 'Geographical Education at the British Association', (1903), pp. 549-53 (pp. 549-51).

123. Mackinder, 'On the Scope and Methods', p. 174.

124. Freeman, Hundred Years of Geography, pp. 141-3.

125. See S.R. Eyre, 'Determinism and the Ecological Approach to Geography', Geography, vol.49, pt 4 (1964), pp. 369-76 (pp. 370-1); also Jay, 'A.J. Herbertson', p. 358.

126. See W.E. Marsden, 'The Language of the Geography Textbook: An Historical Appraisal', Westminster Studies in Education, vol.2 (1979), pp. 53-66 (pp. 60-3).

127. A.J. Herbertson, 'Recent Regulations and Syllabuses in Geography Affecting Schools', Geographical Journal, vol.27, no.3 (1906), pp. 279-88 (p. 281).

128. Herbertson, 'Recent Discussions', pp. 425-6.

129. A.J. Cooper, 'Regional Teaching of Geography', Geographical Teacher, vol.3, no.13 (1905-6),

pp. 113-16.

130. For fuller discussion, see Marsden, 'Language of the Geography Textbook', pp. 53-65.

131. Keltie, 'Thirty Years' Progress', pp. 215-27.

132. Mill, <u>Royal Geographical Society</u>, p. 251.

133. Keltie, 'Thirty Years' Progress', pp. 225-6.

Chapter Eight

FROM A TEST OF MEMORY TO A TRAINING FOR LIFE:
THE TEACHING OF HISTORY

GORDON BATHO

HISTORY THE CHARACTERISTIC ACTIVITY OF THE NINETEENTH CENTURY?

Professor H.L. Withers of Manchester told a Cambridge University Extension Meeting in August 1900 that 'History in its widest sense is perhaps the most characteristic form of intellectual activity in the nineteenth century.'(1) It is easy to see why Withers said this. Although Regius Professorships in History were established at Oxford and Cambridge as early as 1724, they had no tangible result in original research or in influence upon university studies until well into the nineteenth century. Equally, history was rarely taught as a separate subject in the public schools around 1800 - an exception is Rugby in the headmastership of the underrated Dr James (1778 to 1794) who devoted the first lesson of the week with the fifth and sixth forms, at 7 a.m. on Monday, to Scripture History varied with Goldsmith's Roman History and The History of England.(2) In elementary schools, when history was taught at all, the catechetical approach was used and produced such gems of misinformation as this from a little book which went into many editions in the eighteenth century: Englishwomen 'are very beautiful; they enjoy more rights and greater privileges than those of other countries, especially the married women.'(3) The nineteenth century saw greater changes in history teaching and laid the foundations for the twentieth-century development of the subject to a far greater extent than is commonly recognised.
    The changes were, however, extraordinarily slow in coming. At the universities, although written examinations were introduced at Oxford in 1800 and honours classes in 1807, a separate School of History was not created until 1872 and at Cambridge a

separate Historical Tripos did not appear until 1875
and was not divided into Part I and Part II until
1899.(4) The modern study of history in English universities may fairly be said to have started only
with the appointments of William Stubbs (of Select
Charters fame) to the Oxford chair in 1866 and of
J.R. Seeley (whose The Expansion of England, 1883,
was to earn him a knighthood) to the Cambridge chair
in 1869. Many historians who made their names house-
hold words among the burgeoning middle class readership of the Victorian period - men like Macaulay,
Carlyle and Green - either had no university connection at all or acquired one after their reputation
was secure. Macaulay's first two volumes of the History of England sold 6,000 copies in two months on
its publication in 1848; Carlyle's Letters and
Speeches of Oliver Cromwell (1845) was reprinted
eleven times in the nineteenth century; and Green's
A Short History of the English People (1874) was
selling vigorously for decades. What such works
lacked in scholarship they compensated by the verve
of the writing and the masterly nature of the
authors' command of the sweep of the subject. History came into its own with the public in the mid-
nineteenth century essentially without the universities' input.

It is generally accepted that Thomas Arnold,
Headmaster of Rugby from 1828 to 1841, introduced
the systematic teaching of history in the public
schools. His charismatic personality had an extraordinary influence throughout the century and he saw
history as contributing to the understanding of all
life, to the making of Christian gentlemen by an enrichment of the classical curriculum which had held
unchallenged sway for so long. He favoured a coordi-
nation of geography and history, he made much use of
the blackboard, he drew parallels between ancient
and modern history, he devised a cycle of historical
lessons which he embodied in the school's curriculum. And he was blessed with a devoted pupil in the
articulate Arthur Stanley who recorded:

> No direct instruction could leave on their
> minds a livelier image of Dr Arnold's disgust
> at moral evil, than the black cloud of indig-
> nation which passed over his face when speaking
> of the crimes of Napoleon, or of Caesar, and
> the dead pause which followed as if the acts
> had just been committed in his very presence.(5)

It took a long time for history to become a fully

accepted subject in the curriculum of the public
schools nonetheless. It is reported that history at
St Peter's, York, between 1828 and 1837 consisted
of the reading of Goldsmith's History of England for
one hour in class 'and that was all. The boys did
not know that Europe had a history.'(6) Sir Walter
Scott in Waverley (1829) complains that in schools
'the history of England is now reduced to a game at
cards'.(7) The Report of the Clarendon Commission on
the nine 'great schools' assessed the situation in
1864 in these terms:

> The importance of some attention to history or
> geography is recognised more or less at all the
> schools though in general there is little sys-
> tematic teaching of either. In the lower forms
> it is common to give lessons in the outlines of
> history and in geography but as a boy advances
> in the school it appeared to be generally con-
> sidered that all which can be done for him in
> this particular is to set him a portion of his-
> tory to get up by himself and to examine him in
> it. It appears that the proper degree and meth-
> od of teaching history or of requiring history
> to be learnt at school are matters not settled
> by general practice and upon which indeed Eng-
> lish schoolmasters seem to have arrived at no
> very definite conclusion.(8)

John (later Lord) Morley told the Commissioners that
he learnt no history at Eton 'either in pupil-room
or school-room'.(9)
    The situation was evidently no better in the
private schools and in the endowed grammar schools
in the early and middle years of the century. The
Assistant Commissioner for Yorkshire for the Schools
Inquiry (Taunton) Commission reported in 1868 that
in the best girls' schools he found 'the higher
classes reading Macaulay or Hume with much intelligence and relish and making very clever abstracts or
paraphrases of the most notable passages'.(10) Generally, however, standards of history teaching were
poor and James (later Lord) Bryce, who was Assistant
Commissioner in Lancashire, reported that 'In most
cases, the boys while showing a tolerable, though
often confused, knowledge of the surface facts, have
no comprehension of their meaning and bearing.'(11)
Bryce was to tell the annual meeting of the Historical Association in 1907 that at this time:

> In secondary schools the common thing was to

> set boys to read Goldsmith's History of England
> ... which had the charm of all Goldsmith's
> writings, being composed in a singularly fluent
> and agreeable style, but which did not profess
> ... to be the work of a specially competent
> historian ... But the state of things in girls'
> schools was even worse ... They learnt history
> through a little book called Mangnall's Ques-
> tions ... it was then the regular manual of
> English historical instruction. The facts it
> contained were scrappy, and were not stimu-
> lating to the learner.(12)

Richmal Mangnall (1769-1820), Headmistress of
Crofton Old Hall, had written an extremely popular
schoolroom encyclopedia which was first published
in 1808 and was still being reprinted as late as
1892, but her heirs gained nothing by it for she had
sold the copyright to Longmans for one hundred
guineas.(13) Joshua (later Sir Joshua) Fitch, the
HMI who, unusually for the time, had once been an
elementary schoolmaster, told the Taunton Commission
that in many private schools history, geography and
grammar were all learnt by heart and declared no
form of lesson so barren of intellectual result. He
went on:

> I know few things which have so great a tenden-
> cy to lower the character of the teacher's work
> and to render it mechanical and inanimate as
> the practice of using books in which there are
> printed questions and answers.(14)

The schools inspected by HMI tended to be the better
schools but the accounts given in their reports in
the period 1839 to 1870 do not suggest that history
was taught intelligibly in the majority of English
schools. The Reverend Richard Dawes's school at
King's Somborne, Dorset, was held up as an exception
to the rule. Dawes pursued local studies and impressed Henry (later Canon) Moseley, one of the most
influential HMIs of the time, in the 1840s, by
'dealing with reason rather than facts and with
things rather than words'.(15) HMI frequently drew
attention to the lack of relevance to life of the
teaching that was taking place. For example, Seymour
Tremenheere, inspecting the girls' school of the
British Institution in London in 1842, found a class
'striving to fix in their memories half a page of
small summary, containing within that space, the record of a century':

names that have disappeared from all maps that
children in this condition of life are likely
to have access to; dates that refer to nothing
that is of the slightest moment to remember;
facts that have no bearing on what followed,
and have no connection of importance with what
went before, relationships from which no historical consequences flowed, and which have
long since been consigned to the genealogist.(16)

The blight was not, of course, universal. J. Gill's
Introductory Textbook to Method and School Management, which was widely used, advocated teaching history by the collective lesson, taking three aspects
in depth - social, political and religious - and
dealing with the present day first so as to bring
out comparisons and contrasts. 'This method', Gill
wrote, 'has a value in quickening children's observations as to the things by which they are sur-
rounded and leading them to see some importance in
the matters of everyday life.'(17) Again, the Taunton Commissioners noted that history had always been
a strong subject at King Edward VI's Grammar School,
Grantham, and that it received special attention at
the Somersetshire School, Bath.(18)

The Revised Code of 1862 was the outcome of the
deliberations of the Newcastle Commission, appointed
in 1858 to advise on measures to extend elementary
instruction to all classes. The Code laid down that
the bulk of the governmental grant to inspected
schools should be dependent on the success with
which the three Rs, and plain needlework for girls,
were taught as measured by an annual examination of
each child, the system known as 'payment by results'.
As the Board of Education Report for 1910 to 1911
pointed out:

It was not intended that schools should limit
their curricula to the three 'rudimentary' subjects ... the purpose of the framers of the
Code was to strengthen the lower parts of the
existing schools without narrowing or lowering
the standards of attainment reached in the
higher. But in practice this limitation was
undoubtedly produced in the majority of cases.
The annual Report of the Committee of Council
on Education for 1865 ... admits that 'it has
tended, at least temporarily, to discourage attention to the higher branches of elementary
instruction, Geography, Grammar and History'.(19)

Nancy Ball has suggested that the effects have been exaggerated but there is no doubt that history suffered a severe setback in public elementary schools, which was only marginally alleviated by the Minute of 1867 offering an increased grant to schools which taught at least one specific subject, such as geography, grammar or history, in addition to compulsory subjects as fixed in 1862.

THE PROFESSIONALISATION OF HISTORY TEACHING, 1870-1914

Bryce had commented to the Taunton Commission in 1868:

> History stands almost alone among the common branches of instruction, in that it is not a thing which any good teacher can teach by dint of a little previous study ... to teach History one must have made History a study, and must know something about things which are not to be found in any school-book, perhaps not even in Lingard and Hallam. To make the past intelligible and interesting, even to boys, a man must have learnt in some measure to throw himself back into the past, and realize it in detail as well as in outline; and this nothing but independent study will enable him to do.(20)

It was not a view which was universally accepted in 1868 - witness the Clarendon Report which in 1864 had held that history required 'some sustained but not very laborious efforts of memory'(21) - but by 1898 A.L. Smith could write:

> The days of History as an 'extra' are over, the days when it was left either to any one Master who had some time to fill up, or to each Master to manage as best he could in his own spare time. No school can now be regarded as fully equipped which has not at least one teacher who has been through a regular historical course.(22)

What factors brought about so radical a change?
First, the development of increasingly specialised history courses at the universities raised the status of the subject. Research in history was promoted to the point that Oxford established its BLitt in 1895 and the subject began to compete aggressively for university resources. Young graduate history

specialists were being produced to staff the schools and they carried with them a vision of the subject as a discipline in its own right rather than as an adjunct to literature. From 1868 the Royal Historical Society existed, bringing together professional historians within and without the universities who took a lively interest in the teaching of the subject in school - the Conference on Historical Teaching in Schools at which Mandell Creighton, Professor of History at Cambridge and first Editor of the English Historical Review, presided in 1887, was organised by Oscar Browning, chairman of the council of the Society, and was reported as the largest meeting ever got together for the discussion of an educational question.(23)

Secondly, as C.H.K. Marten remarked in 1938, 'it is difficult to exaggerate the importance of the influence of the Joint Board or of the other School Examining Bodies ... upon the teaching of History in Schools.'(24) The Oxford and Cambridge Schools Examination Board was established in 1873 and its Higher Certificate examination exerted a remarkable influence on the public schools. The Joint Board put paid to an annalistic treatment of history by asking questions which demanded analysis and thought by the candidate. By 1903, a hundred schools were taking the Board's Higher Certificate in history and they were presenting 1,268 candidates - all history specialists in the sixth form and potential aspirants for the history scholarships available at the universities from the 1870s.

Thirdly, the regulations affecting history in the elementary schools were steadily ameliorated. In 1875 the Code included history as one of two class subjects which, if they were taught, had to be taught throughout the school above Standard I. It was a small enough concession and history did poorly yet - in 1890 out of 22,516 departments for older children English was taught in 20,304, geography in 12,367, history in 414 and elementary science in 32. The Cross Commission in 1888 called for more flexibility of choice and the repeal of the requirement that English must be one of the choices.(25) By 1895 history was being taught in 3,597 departments, by 1899 in 5,780 and in 1900 history was at last included in the subjects commonly taught in primary schools.(26) In the words of the Board of Education Report for 1910 to 1911:

> Until 1890 it cannot be said that the subject
> was encouraged by the Code, and in many schools

no attempt was made to teach it at all. Where
such teaching was given it often amounted to
very little beyond reading aloud by the children from a textbook, supplemented by incidental questions and explanations from the teacher.(27)

The history scheme often consisted, where it existed
at all, of stories chosen for their vividness and
simplicity in the classes immediately above the In-
fants, and above this level, of periods, commonly
the Tudors in Standard V, the Stuarts in Standard VI
and the Hanoverians in Standard VII. For preparation, the teacher had in many instances nothing more
to rely upon than his own reading; only a small percentage had the advantage, if advantage it was, of
such college training as is described by J. Runciman
in his Schools and Scholars (1887) which recounts
how the student 'was expected to learn his country's
story from a fivepenny book, which contained strings
of dates and names in horrifying sequence'.(28) By
the time that the Code was abolished in 1895, as
Edmond Holmes put it, for 33 years teachers 'had
been treated as machines, and they were suddenly
asked to act as intelligent beings'.(29) It was
going to take time for new methods to be evolved and
practised to meet the changing circumstances.
    Even at secondary level, a Committee (The Com-
mittee of Seven) appointed by the American Historical Association to investigate the teaching of history in schools reported that in England 'the most
noticeable features are a lack of historical instruction, a common failure to recognise the value
of History, and a certain incoherence and general
confusion.'(30) The Board of Education Report for
1923 confirmed this as a correct evaluation of the
situation around 1900, recording that 'The usual
method pursued was that the pupils were given two or
three pages to learn and were then examined on it by
a series of questions which could be answered in
monosyllables.'(31) Many schools had no libraries,
maps were little used, there was little encouragement to further reading and the examinations for
Senior Locals were often purely a test of memory.
Where progress as we should view it had been made,
not everyone agreed that it was an improvement.
Professor Withers deplored the idea that knowledge
could be 'cut into slices like a melon', which he
declared during the nineteenth century to have de-
stroyed the idea of a liberal education.(32) C.R.L.
Fletcher, Fellow of Magdalen, wrote in 1904:

The substitution of Modern History and other
'modern subjects' in our great schools for
Greek and Latin I regard as nothing short of
an irretrievable calamity.(33)

John Stuart Mill had commented in his Inaugural Lecture at St Andrews in 1867 that he regarded it as 'a
great absurdity that History and Geography should be
taught in Schools - who ever learnt History and Geography except by private reading?'(34) Mill's remark is a salutary reminder to us of the value of
private reading in supplementing formal schooling
for those nineteenth-century pupils whose intellectual curiosity had been aroused and who were in a
position to satisfy it, as well as of the persis-
tence of attitudes founded in circumstances which
had changed out of all recognition in the course of
a century which had seen England become an industri-
alised nation. Even the most sensitive of pupils
would have benefited from more systematised teaching,
however. Sir Charles Webster, the distinguished diplomatic historian, reminisced that at school around
the turn of the century he had been compelled to
study the Tudors three times over and the journeys
of Paul twice with no knowledge of what happened
between save what he picked up from casual reading!
From about 1900 history as a subject enjoyed
enhanced popularity and resources. The specialist
history teachers produced by the university departments of history and the day training colleges established in 1890 at seven of the universities were
entering the schools and training their pupils in
hitherto unknown dimensions of the subject. The
Board of Education Report on History, 1923, draws
attention to the extent to which many of them continued their studies while teaching, often taking a
higher degree by research part-time and sometimes
enjoying a 'grace term' for study or for foreign
travel - school authorities in London were especially generous in this regard. As the Report has it:
'The teacher who has ceased to read History should
cease to teach it.'(35) The Historical Association
was founded in 1906 and this did much to promote
both historical research and historical teaching,
though its unique achievement was to be the successful combination of lay and professional people in
the study and teaching of history among its membership. Conferences were quickly to become one of the
hallmarks of the Association and James Bryce defined
the purpose of history teaching for the members at
the first annual general meeting:

> The great object of teaching History is to en-
> able people to realise that men were very dif-
> ferent formerly from what they are now ... the
> true qualification of the historian consists
> in this - to be able to see the past as if it
> was the past ... to see the past as it appeared
> to the people who then lived ... to know what
> the Germans call their Weltanschauung, their
> idea of the world.(36)

Reports on the teaching of history were prepared for
local education authorities, teachers' groups were
organised to discuss history teaching, the subject
was given a firm place in Board of Education handbooks and memoranda, and publishers brought out a
great many textbooks aimed to satisfy current suggestions on the content and method of history teaching. Professor L.C. Miall, FRS, had been Professor
of Biology in the Yorkshire College, Leeds, but in
his Thirty Years of Teaching (1897) he made the sa-
lient point that the first requirements for improved
history teaching were more time in class and more
time for preparation than schools ordinarily allowed:

> If the time in class is limited to two hours a
> week, and if the teacher has to give five les-
> sons a day on various subjects, there is per-
> haps nothing better than to stick to the his-
> torical glue. But if you can get English His-
> tory taught in the school by men and women who
> know their subject decently, and if they are
> not compelled to pace their rounds like horses
> in a mill, there is a better way open to them.(37)

Miall's colleague in Education at Leeds, James
Welton, in his Principles and Methods of Teaching,
attempted to define the qualities needed by a history teacher. Encyclopedic knowledge was not required
but a grasp of great movements in sufficient detail
to make them real was; sanity and impartiality of
judgement were essential; the power of raising interest and enthusiasm by striking and vivid narrative and skilful questioning was to be expected; and
finally the teacher should have a knowledge of books
of such an order as to allow the training of pupils
in their use.(38)
What were the objects of teaching history in
school in the years immediately prior to the First
World War? Teachers were not short of advice. Welton
held that it was 'to help the individual to

understand the human world in which he lives so far
as it is organised into states and smaller, but in
some respects similar, corporations' and through
that to understand himself more fully.(39) H.L.
Withers argued in 1901 that the inclusion of history in the elementary school course ought to be regarded not as the addition of a new subject but
'rather to mean an explanation of the essential
facts and forces in the condition of mankind as it
is now, and as it has been in the past'.(40) J.W.
Willis Bund, chairman of Worcestershire Education
Committee, in an address on teaching history in
1908, had a more moralistic approach, wanting teachers to bring before the children the lives and work
of English people who 'served God in Church and
State', to show that they did this by courage, en-
durance and self-sacrifice, that as a result the
British Empire was founded and extended and that it
behoved every child to emulate them.(41) There was a
strong school of support for history to be valued
for its promotion of patriotism. As Lady Callcott
had put it in the preface to her phenomenally popular Little Arthur's History of England (1859): 'To
teach the love of our country is almost a religious
duty.'(42) Indeed, some went further. As Edmond
Holmes complained in 1911:

> There are faddists who advocate the teaching of
> patriotism in our elementary schools. There are
> Local Education Committees which insist on
> citizenship being taught in the schools under
> their control. By teaching patriotism and citi-
> zenship is meant treating them as 'subjects',
> finding places for them on the 'time-table',
> and giving formal lessons on them. Where this
> is done, the time of the teachers and the chil-
> dren is wasted. The teaching of patriotism and
> citizenship, if it is to produce any effect,
> must be entirely informal and indirect.(43)

There was a widespread confidence, shared even by
Holmes in all probability, that the study of English
history would have this effect. As Lord Avebury put
it: 'If ever there was a country for which a man
might work with pride, surely it is our own.'(44)
For his part, James Welton preferred to align himself with Messrs Langlois and Seignobos and ask from
history 'truth and nothing more'.(45) On the other
hand, Professor Withers held history to be able to
claim 'an honoured place on the time-table of our
Primary Schools' precisely because 'of its bearing

on the future of our civic and national life, even
more than on account of its value to the imagination
and the understanding'.(46)

In the universities, attention was being given
to what was called the scientific basis of the subject and J.B. Bury's inaugural lecture at Cambridge,
entitled 'The Science of History' and delivered on
26 January 1903, far from being revolutionary as has
sometimes been imagined, fairly reflected a general
movement towards a research base and methodology.(47)
Professor J.W. Allen published his monograph, The
Place of History in Education, in 1909, which called
for the training of schoolchildren in scientific
history, that is in logical and analytical habits.
As he saw it, impartiality was the supreme virtue.(48)
Allen's book contained few practical suggestions,
but the next year the Reader in Education at Oxford,
M.W. Keatinge, produced a book which was aimed specifically at teachers, Studies in the Teaching of
History. This argued that 'the sound method of
teaching any subject in schools must always stand in
close relations with the scientific development of
that subject' and that history 'must be reduced to
problem form and our pupils must be confronted with
documents and forced to exercise their minds upon
them'.(49) As a reviewer of Keatinge's book commented:

> If Professor J.W. Allen's recent work was an
> appeal for the teaching of scientific history,
> Mr. Keatinge's is a counter appeal for the sci-
> entific teaching of history.(50)

There was nothing new in the use of sources in
teaching history. Joshua Fitch advocated the illustrative use of sources in his Lectures on Teaching
at Cambridge in 1880 and George C. Williamson made
the point colourfully in 1891:

> The broadside, the early newspaper, the early
> printed book by Caxton or Wynkyn de Worde, the
> map, the illustrations of sports, costumes, and
> manners, Strutt's Book of Sports, the Missal
> and Prayer Books, are all to be obtained in
> facsimile reproductions, and there are the
> nails of the history ready to hand.(51)

The source method was widely used in the late nineteenth century, and indeed long after, in the United
States of America, and Henry Bourne in a book often
quoted in this country, which first appeared in

1902, warned against its excessive use:

> The ardent advocates of the source method occa-
> sionally forget how much can be accomplished by
> a capable teacher with nothing but a text-book
> to work with, and sometimes without even this
> ... The over-emphasis of the source method
> also leads to the neglect of other ways of cul-
> tivating an interest in history and of training
> the pupil to think soundly upon historical sub-
> jects.(52)

Bourne was probably reacting against the Report of
the Committee of Seven (1899) which stated:

> We believe in the proper use of sources for
> proper pupils, with proper guarantees that
> there shall also be secured a clear outline of
> the whole subject studied, but we find our-
> selves unable to approve a model of teaching
> ... in which pupils have in their hands little
> more than a series of extracts, for the most
> part brief and not very closely related.(53)

What Keatinge objected to was the classification of
history in many schools under 'English Subjects' and
methods of teaching it which he held were 'probably
as casual as the classification'.(54)
    The outcome of the new interest in the use of
original sources was a florescence of source-books.
Publishers responded to other methods of broadening
the approach to history with equal enthusiasm –
Nelson's Highroads of History in its Royal School
Series, for example, specifically refers to the
Board of Education's Suggestions for the Consideration of Teachers (1905) and its advocacy of the use
in the first two years of schooling of 'picturesque
and dramatic stories from history, illustrated by
bright pictures' and of 'visits under skilful guidance ... to the actual places associated with the
great men and deeds of the past'; Books I and II
contained stories, Books III and IV lessons based on
visits. Sir Charles Harding Firth, who had written
the first Historical Association pamphlet, on
Sources, published English History in English Poetry
from the French Revolution to the Death of Queen
Victoria in 1911 both to establish the place of poetry in history reading and to counteract the neglect of nineteenth-century history in English
schools. Things had greatly changed since J.R. Green
had written in the preface to his A Short Geography

of the British Islands in 1880 that 'No drearier
task can be set for the worst of criminals than that
of studying a set of text-books such as the children
in our schools are doomed to use.'(55)

Even so, the oral lesson followed by dictated
notes was still the staple procedure in teaching
history in English schools and remained so for at
least another half a century, despite all the efforts of reformers. As Holmes reported in 1911,
teachers do not change old habits lightly and as a
result of the restrictions imposed between 1862 and
1895 especially, 'there are many schools in which
the teacher now does everything during the oral lesson, while the child does as nearly as possible
nothing'.(56) Welton, on the other hand, while advocating the use of a great variety of aids including
poetry and pictures, properly prepared visits and
lively stories, contends that in the lower forms of
secondary school: 'The real teaching is by means of
oral lessons, and to that all else is subsidiary.'(57)

But what history did people advocate should be
taught in English schools in the 1900s? There was,
and is, a great problem over selection. Gabriel
Compayré had commented in the 1880s on what he
called the English teachers' 'whimsical scheme' of
beginning the study of history in some primary
schools with the contemporary period to give the
child grounding in the ideas of his own time.(58)
Concern for the overloading of the syllabus in the
elementary school, coupled with the knowledge that
some children never reached the upper standards, had
led to the introduction of concentric schemes of
history teaching in place of the periodic scheme
generally adopted above Standard II. But as the
Board of Education Report for 1910 to 1911 has it:

> If the 'periodic' system taught too many de-
> tails, the 'concentric' ... teaches too few;
> its scale is so large that little effect is
> produced upon the children's minds beyond vague
> and confused impressions.(59)

This had led to a compromise and many primary
schools just before the First World War used stories
and biographies in the lowest classes, periodic
studies in the middle school and a review of the
whole course of English history in the higher class,
for example the growth of ideas of government and
the expansion of the Empire. Few had had the courage
to heed Welton's clarion call:

There is a traditional mass of matter grouped
under the successive sovereigns of England
which nearly every school seems to feel itself
called upon to teach ... let us determine that
names of battles, marches, and counter-marches
of armies are frequently of profound historical insignificance.(60)

European, let alone world, history was rarely
taught in the elementary school but Professor
Pollard's Report on the Teaching of History in London Elementary Schools (1911) held that a boy leaving school should have some notion of world history
and Professor Withers had urged in 1901 the study of
representative heroes and heroines of European history in Standard V. Welton was even more opposed to
the neglect of foreign history in the primary
school:

We do not think of abstaining from teaching the
geography of countries other than our own, and
yet that outside geography is not so essential
to the understanding of the geography of England as is the history of other nations to the
understanding of the history of England.(61)

One original suggestion for securing an appropriate
selection of historical material for history teaching was made by Father Edward Rockliff in a little
book which appeared in 1912, An Experiment in History Teaching. He dispensed with the textbook in
the first presentation of a period and used instead
a complex coloured chart employing representative
signs and simple, direct language to show the relationship of facts the one to the other. He believed
that his method engaged the active interest of the
pupil and taught him to discriminate between the
lasting and the ephemeral in European as well as in
English history.(62)
Experimentation was not confined to the elementary school. In the new secondary schools slowly
being developed as a result of the 1902 Education
Act, graduate history masters were using textbooks
specially prepared for the market and often written
by university dons together with supplementary materials like W.H.D. Rouse's Blackie's English School
Texts which first for 8d, then for 6d (such was the
success of the series) put into their hands a
plethora of extracts from English literature, particularly accounts of travel and adventure. Much of
the teaching was 'talk and chalk' and the syllabus

was often almost entirely confined to British history but it included discussion and the encouragement
of personal reading and an often lengthy composition - sound preparation, it may be thought, in a
literary subject. In these years, however, as E.L.
Hasluck was to comment caustically in 1920, a school
of teachers 'mostly of the rising generation' appeared which wanted to increase the interest of
pupils:

> The excursion to the abbey or the picture gal-
> lery, the cinematograph film, and the reading
> from the historical novel will no doubt be
> vastly appreciated by the pupils, but when the
> end of term comes ... the class may be found
> pitiably ignorant of the period it has been
> 'studying'.(63)

Miss Winifred Mercier of Manchester Girls' High
School described An Experiment in the Teaching of
History in Leaflet No. 17 of the Historical Association in 1910 which was essentially the production of
reading plans for groups of girls on set topics. She
explained that she was moved to this by observing
that under conventional methods of teaching many
girls of good intelligence were at eighteen 'instructed rather than educated, drilled rather than
developed ... and possessed of a fatal likeness to
one another'.(64) She wanted to create interest not
just in lessons but in the subject: 'we feed too as-
siduously with the potted-meats of knowledge to allow this Divine discontent to grow'.(65) Her message
could apply to later times than her own.

THE COMING OF AGE OF HISTORY TEACHING, 1914-40

The outbreak of the World War in 1914 had a traumatic and almost an hysterical effect upon some historians. C.R.L. Fletcher had finished his Making of
Western Europe in the spring but left the text unchanged when it was published in the autumn 'as a
penance ... for the hard things I have written in it
about the Slavonic nations'.(66) Professor (Sir)
Richard Lodge wrote an introductory note to Elizabeth Levett's Europe Since Napoleon 1815-1910, a
book which was firmly aimed at the new sixth form
market, and commented that the taunt most frequently
levelled at historians was the impractical nature of
their work:

> Recent events ... show how little real founda-
> tion there is for this taunt. It has suddenly
> become obvious that the teaching of History,
> systematically fostered and directed, may exer-
> cise a decisive influence upon public opinion,
> and through this influence may determine the
> policy of a great state and the fate of a con-
> tinent.(67)

The former Professor of History at Berlin, Heinrich
von Treitschke, was held to be as responsible as
anyone for the War. 'It has been a weakness of our
educational system that we have neglected the history of all countries but our own, and that our instructed historical survey has generally ended with
the Battle of Waterloo.'(68) Between the World Wars
the history teaching profession did ensure that attention was paid at least to European as well as to
British history and that the period studied stretch-
ed to 1890 or even to 1914, but a consideration of
anything beyond the assassination of Archduke Ferdi-
nand was quite exceptional.

The problem of time remained; in secondary
schools, history was usually allocated two periods a
week, sometimes three for the fifth form, and any
teacher who tried to include local history, the development of civilisation and literature, and European history up to contemporary times was clearly
under very real constraints of time. The Headmaster
of Middlesbrough High School appreciated this and as
a consequence the profession was saddled with the
burden of Edwards's Notes on British History from
1909. 'These notes', he wrote in his preface, 'have
been compiled in order to supplement the information
given in the textbook and lessen the amount of time
devoted in school to the mere giving of notes.'(69)
Rivingtons, his publishers, and he enjoyed fantastic
sales but it may be questioned whether, factually
sound as they were, the notes really furthered the
study of history as an intellectual exercise.

They were certainly contrary to the spirit of
the change in the idea of the nature of history
which the source method symbolised. As the editors
of the Oxford Supplementary Histories put it in
their preface in 1915:

> Every boy - even in an elementary school -
> should have a chance of reading at first hand
> at least a few documents upon which history
> books are based ... in this way only will he
> learn the lesson, valuable to him throughout

life, that there are generally two sides to a
question, and that the discovery of a truth
requires the exercise of thought and judgement.(70)

The London Teachers' Association noted that the
Board of Education in its revised Suggestions recognised the importance in history of illustration,
both pictorial and verbal, but failed to explain to
teachers where they could find such materials. The
publishers were quick to advertise that Black's
History Pictures, English History Illustrated from
Original Sources and Documents of British History
met the demands expressed by the London teachers:

The 'History Picture' Series contain nearly 500
illustrations, which vary from photographs of
medals to reproductions of paintings in our
public galleries, while the Original Sources
and Documents include nearly the same number of
extracts, and supply 'intimate detail' from
writings which range from the Anglo-Saxon
Chronicles to articles from The Times.(71)

The great change in secondary history teaching
was the introduction in 1917 of a new, simplified
system of examinations at 16+ and 18+, the School
Certificate and the Higher School Certificate. The
syllabuses encouraged the teaching in depth of more
European and more contemporary history to the examination forms. A usual pattern in 'Advanced Courses'
for sixth forms was to take three papers - one in a
period of English history, one in a similar period
of European history and one on a special subject
within one of the periods studied in outline. Thus,
a typical course which might be taken by candidates
for the University of Durham's Higher Certificate
examination in the 1930s was Modern History with a
three-hour paper on British and Foreign History
(European and Empire) between 1815 and 1871 and another on European History 1789-1890 with a third
paper on The First and Second Empire in France. Candidates were required to answer five questions on
the special period but in the first two papers they
had a choice of answering either five or four questions. If they chose to answer four questions, the
first had to be answered in greater detail than the
other three and an asterisk prefixed to it. The
first two papers were sectionalised to ensure that
candidates did not concentrate too heavily on an
even more limited period. The Higher School

Certificate gave every opportunity, therefore, for
the development of discipleship between the sixth
form history teacher and the usually small cadre of
candidates in studying a defined period of history
in depth. Too rarely, the Board of Education Report
on History (1923) bemoaned, was a period of American
history selected, though the opportunity was provided. The Report was also concerned to call for the
exposure of science specialists in the sixth forms
to historical studies:

> Many of them, finding their chief interest in
> Chemistry or Physics, would have another side
> of their intellectual life awakened if they
> knew that Priestley, who played so great a part
> in building up their own Science, was also in-
> terested in the Revolutionary movement of the
> eighteenth century, and that Galileo, the
> founder of modern Physics, was visited in his
> blind old age by the English Poet of Puritan-
> ism, the Latin Secretary of Oliver Cromwell.(72)

The Board of Education offered schools grants
for the teaching of 'Advanced Courses' in an attempt
to secure organic unity in sixth form teaching between 1917 and 1935. At first, history was included
in Modern (Humanistic) Studies along with two foreign languages; the other groupings were Science and
Mathematics, and Classics. From 1921, however, a
fourth group was agreed - History, English and
Latin. History was to be well supported as a Higher
School Certificate subject in the maintained grammar
schools as well as in the independent sector in the
1920s and 1930s.
The Board of Education Report also offered advice on an acceptable general plan for the history
syllabus for the lower forms of secondary schools
and its advice was widely adopted in its essentials.
Just as the chronological approach to teaching history was advocated in the nineteenth century on the
grounds that it matched the psychological laws of
the child's development, so now the Board of Education suggested that some early lessons of a simple
kind be given on the Ancient World, followed by a
course in English history 'with its concurrent
stream of European' down to modern times but then in
the senior classes a series of special lessons or
lectures on World History might be arranged 'three
or four a term, not for examination'.(73) 'Our first
concern will be with those conditions which immediately surround us' but 'we must extend our view both

to what went before and what accompanies them in the larger world.'(74) As E.L. Hasluck had written in 1920 - passionately as always:

> We are Britons and Europeans, we may be Kent-ishmen or Cornishmen or Londoners or Liver-pudlians, we all share in a common World Histo-ry, but we are not Frenchmen or 'Western Euro-peans' or 'Severn Valleymen'.(75)

Hasluck opposed the teaching of survey courses in the lower secondary school, arguing that twelve to fourteen-year-olds were not ready for a continuous narrative of the history of the English State. 'When we ask our pupils of twelve and thirteen to learn the continuous narrative from the days of the Ancient Britons to the reign of George V we are asking too much from them!'(76) Social and biographical history he held to be more appropriate. After fourteen he favoured a chronological rather than a concentric approach suggesting that English history (with relevant references to European) might be taught in the fourth year to 1509, in the fifth to 1815 and in the sixth beyond 1815. Hasluck contended fiercely that the question of the appropriate selection of material within the course had not been squarely faced 'as a rapid perusal of the numerous text-books published during the last fifteen years will show'.(77) He referred scornfully to the appearance of Ranulf Flambard in many of the textbooks and declared himself unable to recognise him as a character of first-rate importance in national history!

Hasluck was also against the attention being paid by many of his contemporaries to particular aspects of history such as social science, source-work and European history. 'History teaching', he wrote, 'has suffered recently from the excessive wave of reaction against the grinding methods of our fathers.'(78) He reminded his readers that teachers were not meant to amuse or to interest except in as far as it helped the acquisition of a good and lasting knowledge of the outlines of history. He wanted teachers to select well-written, up-to-date, textbooks and to get the pupils to use them - read them aloud in class or silently, answer questions on their reading orally and in writing, learn to use the index:

> It has been somewhat cynically remarked that whereas in the old-fashioned school the pupil

> learnt the lesson and the teacher heard it, in
> the modern school the teacher learns the lesson
> and the pupil hears it.(79)

Hasluck wanted the teacher to give the pupil nothing
which could be discovered in the textbook and to
punctuate oral teaching by the dictation of notes.
On the other hand, he castigated any 'excessive devotion to the "find-out" method':

> A little exercise in primitive enquiry and in
> the methods of the advanced student is useful
> at some time or other in nearly all school
> courses, but to make empirical research the
> main feature of a school training in any sub-
> ject is, with its unavoidable sacrifice of
> time, to throw away the birthright of the
> rising generation.(80)

Despite all the efforts which were made in the
immediate aftermath of the First World War to improve the teaching of history in secondary schools,
the Incorporated Association of Assistant Masters in
its Memorandum on the Teaching of History in 1925
recorded that although history was popular with lower secondary classes very often 'School Certificate
candidates have lost their liking for it'.(81) Perhaps as Helen Madeley commented in her History as a
School of Citizenship (1920):

> History's factors are too complex, too diffi-
> cult of isolation and abstraction, to make it
> the best medium for cultivating independence of
> observation or of judgement, and it demands too
> much initial grind to be a facile starting
> place for originality in imagination and ex-
> pression.(82)

Certainly the later 1920s saw much soul-
searching among history teachers. The Historical Association's journal, History, contains a lot of debate on how the value of the study could be better
demonstrated at school level and C.H.K. Marten was
moved to contemplate the abandonment of all history
examinations to save the subject. F.C. Happold was
beginning to fly his personal kite of the English
subjects synthesis and a new form of history examination (the 'Salisbury experiment') involving the
use of extracts from primary and secondary sources -
an examination which a critic held would allow a ca-
pable pupil to 'gain high marks on intelligence

alone'. Happold declared in a Historical Association pamphlet that Keatinge's use of sources had
failed because 'neither method nor material were
suitable for their purpose'.(83) G. Talbot Griffith
considered the dichotomy between school and university teaching in History in 1929 and concluded that,
where university teachers asked for 'training in
critical method and a scholarly mental outlook',
schoolteachers stressed the merits of exact historical knowledge.(84) It was a very cognate thought to
Happold's point in the preface to his Approach to
History (1928) when he called for 'the substitution
of historical training for the new teaching of History in schools'.(85) J.H. Badley, the founder of
Bedales, the co-educational progressive public
school, wrote a preface to a book by a former colleague - H. Ann Drummond's History in School - in
1929 and declared history to have a high educational
value of two kinds - 'as a means of general culture,
a widening of the mental horizon' and 'as giving a
particular kind of training ... which is not to be
obtained so well in other branches of school work'.(86)
    One issue throughout the period was the train-
ing in citizenship which some held history to offer.
Ann Drummond recognised that there existed little
desire for such a course but advocated the organisation of schools to allow children responsibilities
for the conduct of their own affairs, the inculca-
tion of the right attitude to current affairs and to
work, incidental reference to relevant matter in all
subjects and definite instruction in history, even a
course on civics as such:

> A training in citizenship ... should be part of
> the work of every school, through conscious and
> unconscious moulding of the character of the
> children, and also through a carefully planned
> history course embracing the present as well as
> the past.(87)

Professor (Sir Fred) Clarke took the argument a
stage further in his Foundations of History-
Teaching: A Critique for Teachers (1929), contending that 'a changed conception of history and of the
purpose of studying History has become powerful in
the world at large, while the teaching of History in
the schools remains largely unadjusted to the new
situation'.(88) Men were demanding social change and
expected history to respond not with sentimental-
ities but with solid explanation of past developments, and to provide the justification for change

in modern society. Of that change the League of Nations was held to have the potential to be the supreme instrument. The Board of Education's Handbook
of Suggestions contained a 23-page appendix on the
League and indicated that it hoped that a discussion
of its purpose would arise out of a history course
for 'senior classes' which would emphasise British
and Imperial History in a wider context.(89) Ann
Drummond argued that definite training was needed
rather than the occasional lecture or the formation
of a school branch of the League of Nations Union.
'The child at school ... should be brought to real-
ize the solidarity of mankind and to have a feeling
of community, indifferent to class or nation or
race.'(90) To achieve this, she advocated the teaching of world history and especially European history, drawing attention to H.G. Wells's suggestion in
his The New Teaching of History (1921) that the
broad facts of history should be taught in practically the same terms throughout Europe.(91) F.S.
Marvin and G.T. Hankin, HMI, were active in encouraging the study of contemporary and of international
history in the schools and the influential historian
G.P. Gooch wrote in 1930 that history offered 'precisely the synthesis of intellectual enlightenment
and moral stimulus which citizenship requires and
demands'.(92)
    The Hadow reorganisation with its sentence of
death for all-age elementary schools and its conception of a new system of 'modern' schools for children over eleven who failed to gain a place at a
selective school had its impact on history teaching
in a liberalisation of the curriculum. Coupled with
the development of a range of teaching aids, notably
broadcasting and the film, and the appointment to
the schools, including the secondary modern schools,
of graduates trained in the developing university
departments of education and in the expanding number
of local authority as well as diocesan training colleges, the standard of history teaching across the
country was greatly improved. The university departments of history, in spite of public acclaim afford-
ed the few dons who wrote literary tours de force
like Professor G.M. Trevelyan of Cambridge and Professor J.E. Neale of University College, London, remained ultra-conservative in their outlook and dominated by an Oxford-style concentration on charters
and political history. The number of students in
British universities in the 1930s remained static
around 50,000 after an expansion from 20,000 in 1900
but the majority were intending teachers, and women

were admitted to degrees at Oxford in 1920 and to 'titular' degrees at Cambridge in 1921.(93)

The Spens Committee held that the School Certificate examinations had raised the level of standards in secondary schools. The effect of the changes in the period in history is epitomised by the contrast between the approach of two standard books for examination classes produced by the same publisher at an interval of twenty years - A.J. Grant's History of Europe (1918) and D. Richards's An Illustrated History of Modern Europe, 1789-1938 with its more appealing style and its Punch cartoons. The same publisher had launched a series of Britain in World History in 1932 by E.H. Dance, the Senior History Master at Wolverhampton Grammar School who was to acquire an international reputation for his services to history teaching, especially world history teaching. In the primary school the change was even greater. The training colleges inculcated a belief that the interests of the child must come before the interests of the subject and their products brought to the primary schools a plethora of new methods of teaching history. These are symbolised by some of the books used in the period like the ubiquitous Piers Plowman Histories with their emphasis on how life used to be; the evocative stories of the Power sisters, Rhoda and Eileen Power, Boys and Girls of History; H.W.C. Davis's series History Through Biography; Philip's Junior Historical Atlas; and H.W. Whitbread's Plays of Myth and History - to name but a few.(94)

The problems of selection and of securing the interest of pupils remained. As the Second World War approached despite the attention which had been given to internationalism, two books appeared which were to be of consequence in the continuing discussions on history teaching. F.R. Worts, Headmaster of the City of Leeds School, had the courage to argue that precedence should be given to ethical over intellectual values:

> ... that History in schools ought not primarily to be regarded as inducing a certain habit of mind or as an agent of mental discipline, but should be appreciated and used as a subject richer than all others in releasing powers of a general educative nature by which the growing personality of the pupil can be strengthened.(95)

It required courage to throw down a gauntlet of that order to the advocates of academic history in

schools. M.V.C. Jeffreys, shortly to be appointed
Professor of Education at Durham, sought to solve
the problem of selection by choosing relevant themes
such as the home, medicine, transport or, it should
be remembered, religion, and tracing their development through the ages. He did not intend that the
themes should always centre on material changes or
should be studied in isolation from one another but
was concerned to link them through teachers' presen-
tations. Lines of development in the event were used
as much in primary schools as in secondary and
rather in secondary modern schools than in grammar
schools and, like all reformers, Jeffreys suffered
from the misinterpretations and misapplications of
his followers. His essential message, however, sums
up the essence of the thinking between the wars:
'children should learn less and do more with what
they learn'.(96)

NOTES AND REFERENCES

1. H.L. Withers, 'The Teaching of History in
England in the Nineteenth Century', a lecture delivered at the Cambridge University Extension Summer
Meeting, August 1900, in J.H. Fowler (ed.), The
Teaching of History and Other Papers by H.L. Withers
(Manchester University Press, 1904), pp. 142-3.
2. Withers, 'The Teaching of History', p. 148.
3. J. Lockman, A New History of England by
Question and Answer (1730 (?); C. and J. Rivington,
1794), p. 20.
4. J. Kenyon, The History Men: The Historical
Profession in England since the Renaissance (Weidenfeld and Nicolson, 1983), p. 145.
5. A.P. Stanley, The Life and Correspondence
of Thomas Arnold (B. Fellowes, 1845), pp. 84-5.
6. See C.H.K. Marten, On the Teaching of History and Other Addresses (Basil Blackwell, Oxford,
1938), pp. 17-22.
7. For Scott's ideas on how to instil a love
of history see J.G. Lockhart, Memoirs of Sir Walter
Scott, Vol.6 (A. and C. Black, 1869), p. 324.
8. Report of Her Majesty's Commissioners Appointed to Inquire into the Revenues and Management
of Certain Colleges and Schools, and the Studies
Pursued and Instruction Given Therein (Clarendon
Report), (HMSO, 1864), quoted in Marten, On the
Teaching of History, p. 21; see especially Vol.4,
pt 2, Evidence.
9. Clarendon Report, Vol.3, p. 256, Q. 7731-3.

10. Schools Inquiry Commission, (Taunton Report) Vol.9 (HMSO, 1868), p. 291.
11. Taunton Report, Vol.9, p. 613.
12. J. Bryce, On the Teaching of History in Schools, address at the first annual meeting of the Historical Association at University College, London, 8 February 1907; Historical Association Leaflet No. 4 (1907).
13. Marten, On the Teaching of History, p. 26.
14. Taunton Report, Vol.9, pp. 274-5.
15. Minutes of the Committee of Council on Education 1847-48, Vol.1 (HMSO, 1848), p. 7.
16. Minutes of the Committee of Council on Education 1842-43 (HMSO, 1844), p. 493.
17. J. Gill, Introductory Textbook to Method and School Management (Cheltenham, 1857; Longmans, 8th ed., 1862), p. 148.
18. Quoted in Marten, On the Teaching of History, p. 23.
19. Board of Education, Report of the Board of Education for the Year 1910-1911 (HMSO, 1912), pp. 7-8.
20. Quoted in Marten, On the Teaching of History, pp. 24-5. Lingard refers to J. Lingard, A History of England, 8 vols. (1819-30; editions to 1915 at least); Hallam to H. Hallam, The Constitutional History of England, 2 vols. (1827, later John Murray; editions to 1912 at least).
21. Quoted in Marten, On the Teaching of History, p. 21.
22. A.L. Smith, 'The Teaching of Modern History' in C. Cookson (ed.), Essays on Secondary Education (1898).
23. R.A. Humphreys, The Royal Historical Society 1868-1968 (Royal Historical Society, 1969), pp. 21-22.
24. Marten, On the Teaching of History, p. 36.
25. Board of Education, Report 1910-1911, p. 15.
26. H.L. Withers, 'Memorandum on the Teaching of History in the Schools of the London School Board (1901)' in J.H. Fowler (ed.), The Teaching of History and Other Papers by H.L. Withers (Manchester University Press, 1904), p. 168.
27. Board of Education, Report 1910-1911, p. 33.
28. J. Runciman, Schools and Scholars (Chatto and Windus, 1887), p. 142. See G.R. Batho 'Sources for the History of History Teaching in Elementary Schools, 1835-1914' in T.G. Cook (ed.) Local Studies and the History of Education (Methuen, 1972),

The Teaching of History

pp. 137-52.
29. E. Holmes, What Is and What Might Be: A Study of Education in General and Elementary Education in Particular (Constable, 1911), p. 111.
30. Report of the Committee of Seven: The Study of History in Schools (American Historical Association, New York, 1899) quoted in J. Welton, Principles and Methods of Teaching (University Tutorial Press, 1906; 3rd ed., 1924), p. 221.
31. Board of Education, The Teaching of History, Educational Pamphlet No. 37 (HMSO, 1923), p. 7.
32. Withers, 'The Teaching of History', p. 161.
33. C.R.L. Fletcher, An Introductory History of England, 4 vols. (John Murray, 1904), Vol.1, p. vii. See G.R. Batho, 'History Text-books, 1870 - 1914: A Note on the Historical Association Collection at Durham', History of Education Society Bulletin, no. 33, Spring (1984) and supplement: A Catalogue of the Historical Association Collection of Outdated History Text-books First Published before 1915.
34. Quoted in Marten, On the Teaching of History, p. 27.
35. Board of Education, The Teaching of History, pp. 9-10.
36. Bryce, Teaching of History in Schools, pp. 4-5.
37. L.C. Miall, Thirty Years of Teaching (Macmillan, 1897), pp. 11-12.
38. Welton, Principles, p. 222.
39. Ibid., p. 225.
40. Withers, 'Memorandum', p. 173.
41. J.W. Willis Bund, The Teaching of History in Elementary Schools, an address on 3 April 1908 (Worcestershire Education Committee, 1908).
42. Maria (Graham), Lady Callcott, Little Arthur's History of England (John Murray, 1835; ed. 1859), p. iv. Editions were published for over a century.
43. Holmes, What Is and What Might Be, pp. 292-3
44. J. Lubbock, Lord Avebury, The Use of Life (Macmillan, 1894), ch. 10. Compare the sentiment of Compayré (who was much read by the later Victorians) 'history is an admirable school of patriotism. By means of it one's country ceases to be a cold abstraction': Gabriel Compayré, Lectures on Pedagogy: Theoretical and Practical, trans. W.H. Payne (D.C. Heath, Boston, 1889), pp. 343-4.
45. Welton, Principles, p. 232, quoting C.V. Langlois and C. Seignobos, Introduction to the Study of History, trans. G.G. Berry, preface by F.Y.

240

Powell (Duckworth, 1898).
    46.   Withers, 'Memorandum', p. 200.
    47.   Kenyon, The History Men, pp. 174-5.
    48.   J.W. Allen, The Place of History in Education (W. Blackwood and Sons, 1909).
    49.   M.W. Keatinge, Studies in the Teaching of History (A. and C. Black, 1910), pp. 23 and 38.
    50.   Journal of Education, June 1910, p. 411.
    51.   Transactions of the Royal Historical Society, new series, vol.5 (1891), pp. 245-6.
    52.   H.E. Bourne, The Teaching of History and Civics in the Elementary and in the Secondary School (Longmans, Green and Co., New York, 1902; revised ed., 1910), p. 184.
    53.   Report of the Committee of Seven.
    54.   Keatinge, Studies, p. 19.
    55.   J.R. Green, A Short Geography of the British Islands (Macmillan, 1880), preface.
    56.   Holmes, What Is and What Might Be, pp. 135-6.
    57.   Welton, Principles, p. 237.
    58.   Compayré, Lectures, p. 350.
    59.   Board of Education, Report 1910-1911, p. 34.
    60.   Welton, Principles, p. 239.
    61.   Ibid., pp. 238-9.
    62.   E. Rockliff, An Experiment in History Teaching (Longmans, 1912).
    63.   E.L. Hasluck, The Teaching of History (Cambridge University Press, 1920), p. 31.
    64.   W. Mercier, An Experiment in the Teaching of History, Historical Association Leaflet No. 17 (1910), p. 1.
    65.   Ibid., p. 2; see Marten, On the Teaching of History, p. 63, for an account of Warner's methods at Harrow, 1891-1916. See also J. Roach, 'History Teaching and Examining in Secondary Schools, 1850-1900', History of Education, vol.5, no.2 (1976), pp. 127-40.
    66.   C.R.L. Fletcher, Making of Modern Europe, Vol.2 (John Murray, 1914), p. vii.
    67.   R. Lodge in foreword to E. Levett, Europe since Napoleon 1815-1910 (Blackie, 1913; 2nd ed. 1914), p. ix.
    68.   Ibid., p. xi.
    69.   W. Edwards, Notes on British History (Rivingtons, 1909), preface.
    70.   Men and Scenes of Tudor Times, Oxford Supplementary Histories (Oxford University Press and Hodder and Stoughton, 1915), preface, p. 4.
    71.   Advertisement on back cover of G.H. Reed, Black's History Pictures: Stuart Period 1603-1714 (A. and C. Black, 1915). See also G.T. Warner (ed.),

English History Illustrated from Original Sources (A. and C. Black, 1901 onwards) and M.W. Keatinge and N.L. Frazer, Documents of British History (A. and C. Black, 1912 onwards).
72.   Board of Education, The Teaching of History, p. 21.
73.   Ibid., p. 18.
74.   Ibid., p. 17.
75.   Hasluck, The Teaching of History, p. 5.
76.   Ibid., p. 9.
77.   Ibid., p. 16.
78.   Ibid., p. 31.
79.   Ibid., p. 37.
80.   Ibid., p. 36.
81.   Incorporated Association of Assistant Masters in Secondary Schools, Memorandum on the Teaching of History (Cambridge University Press, 1925), p. 53.
82.   H.M. Madeley, History as a School of Citizenship (Oxford University Press, 1920), p. 66. See also P.B. Showan, Citizenship and the School (Cambridge University Press, 1923).
83.   F.C. Happold, The Study of History in Schools, Historical Association Pamphlet No. 69 (1927), p. 5. See also his The Study of History in Schools, as a Training in the Art of Thought (Bell, 1927).
84.   G.T. Griffith, 'The Correlation of School and University Teaching', History (Journal of the Historical Association), vol. 14 (1929), pp. 33-42.
85.   F.C. Happold, An Approach to History (Christophers, 1928), preface. See also his Citizens in the Making (Christophers, 1935).
86.   H.A. Drummond, History in School: A Study of Some of Its Problems (Harrap, 1929), p. 7.
87.   Ibid., p. 77. See also S. King-Hall and K.C. Boswell, Tracing History Backwards, 2 vols. (Evans Brothers, 1934).
88.   F. Clarke, The Foundations of History - Teaching: A Critique for Teachers (Oxford University Press, 1929), pp. 162 ff.
89.   Board of Education, Handbook of Suggestions for the Consideration of Teachers and Others Concerned in the Work of Public Elementary Schools (HMSO, 1927), pp. 125-6 and 428-50.
90.   Drummond, History in School, p. 81.
91.   Ibid., p. 82.
92.   G.P. Gooch, 'History as a Training for Citizenship', New Era, April 1930.
93.   On broadcasting, see B.J. Elliott, 'The Development of History Teaching in England, 1918 to

1939', unpublished PhD thesis, University of Sheffield, 1975, ch. 7. On film, see F. Consitt, Report
on the Value of Films in History Teaching (Bell for
the Historical Association, 1931). For statistics of
teachers, see J. Lawson and H. Silver, A Social History of Education in England (Methuen, 1973), p. 403.
   94. See J.S. Thompson, Handlist of History
Books for Schools, First Published between 1915 and
1939, Held in the University of Durham and the
introduction by G.R. Batho (University of Durham
School of Education, 1985).
   95. F.R. Worts, The Teaching of History in
Schools: A New Approach (William Heinemann, 1935),
p. 3.
   96. M.V.C. Jeffreys, History in Schools: The
Study of Development (Pitman, 1939), p. 9. See also
M.V.C. Jeffreys, 'The Subject-Matter of History in
Schools', History, vol. 20 (1935), pp. 233-42 and
'The Teaching of History by Means of "Lines of Development"', History, vol. 21 (1936), pp. 230-8.

Chapter Nine

CONCLUSION

MICHAEL PRICE

The richness, variety and complexity of school subject history in the context of English secondary
education in the period 1870-1940, and particularly
during the three decades from 1890 to 1920, have
been amply demonstrated in the previous chapters.
The various contributors have in relation to their
own particular subjects and major curricular themes
drawn attention in various ways to a number of common features and concerns in school subject history.
Firstly, there are the developments in the form and
nature of the debates and conflicts concerning the
place and shape of a particular subject in the secondary school curriculum, related questions of pedagogy, and relationships with other subjects and
phases of education, particularly university study
and research. We are here much concerned with the
rhetoric in curriculum history. Secondly, and in
relationship to the rhetoric of ideals and pedagogical principles, there is the reality of the changing
content and methods in a subject as found in schools
for boys and girls, insofar as this can be determined from primary and other historical sources. Thirdly, there are some distinguishable 'instruments'
involved in the growing professionalisation and curricular initiatives associated with a particular
subject. These include notable individuals and associations of various kinds, and particularly the
subject associations; government departments, com-
missions and committees, and particularly the Board
of Education; the universities and school examining
bodies; publishers, authors, educational suppliers
and their output; and the teaching force, its supply, education and specific training for school
work. In these terms, curricular activity with varying degrees of strength across subjects and sub-
periods has been a notable feature of English

244

secondary education for over a century. What the
subject studies of this book clearly reveal is that
reference to the 'academic' secondary curriculum
conceals a rich complex of historical developments
from the late nineteenth century. In particular,
'curriculum development' as a phenomenon in English
education predates the 1960s by many decades.

Given the school subject orientation and general contextual uniformity adopted for this book, it
is appropriate in this conclusion to provide an
overview of the previous chapters, drawing attention
both to some common features, patterns and relationships among the subject studies as well as to some
contrasts and anomalies which appear particularly
striking. However, a cautious attitude will be
adopted in relation to the possibility of major gen-
eralisation in school subject history, and general
theoretical models for school subject development
will neither be exploited nor generated from these
studies. In the period under consideration each of
the seven subject contributors has emphasised distinctive patterns of development regarding both a
subject's status and form in the curriculum. For example, the developments in classics, geography and
mathematics are sharply differentiated. In the case
of classics, the principal concern is with the defence of the subject's status, and wider issues of
power and control in the curriculum, as well as with
the question of pupils' varying access to classics
in some form. By contrast, the focus on geography
brings to prominence a subject 'on the attack' merely to establish itself in some form for all secondary pupils. In the case of mathematics, subject status was unimportant for the Perry movement. Rather,
the struggle is principally a major internal one
concerning alternative paradigms for secondary
school mathematics and associated questions of purpose and pedagogy. In many ways what is striking
about mathematics is the uniqueness of its development in this period. Nevertheless, both in relation
to external relationships among subjects and their
internal development there are certain striking general 'curricular tensions' which permeate these subject studies.

The tension between classical and 'modern' em-
phases in the secondary curriculum from the late
nineteenth century is well known and has been well
documented in the general history of education.
Typically, emphasis has been placed on the development of new schools, alternative 'sides' within
schools, science schools and classes earning grants

from the Department of Science and Art for teaching
scientific and technical subjects, and the mounting
concerns for the 'warping' of the secondary curriculum and for its definition in relation to technical
education. All this culminated in the work of the
Bryce Commission and the establishment of the Board
of Education with separate branches for elementary,
technical and secondary education, and with new
regulations for grant-aided secondary schools from
1904. Much attention has been paid in the historical
literature to these Secondary Regulations with their
list of prescribed subjects and minimum hours,
though detailed timetable engineering was in fact
abandoned from 1907. As Stray and Rowlinson demonstrate, the Regulations were significant in relation
to the overall status of classical and modern languages in the curriculum at this time. But it has
been argued that these Regulations per se have tended to be accorded an exaggerated curricular importance in the general history of secondary education:
data concerning examination entries, actual timetables and the existing and persisting strength of
the various school subject interests attest to this.
(1) In any case, as regards the shape of a particular subject they are of little interest to the curriculum historian. Nevertheless, curricular tensions
associated with the classical/modern dichotomy were
real and important, and penetrated particular school
subjects and their interrelationships.

   As Stray clearly shows, the paradigm of classical education became associated with two distinct
ideologies: high culture, and mental and moral discipline. Uniquely, within classics there was a fundamental tension between these two ideologies, which
were associated with Greek and Latin respectively.
More general and cross-curricular however, was the
tension between the classical and modern paradigms,
the latter becoming associated with an ideology of
utility and practicality, particularly in relation
to scientific, technical and commercial subjects.
These tensions were also closely related to the
question of curricular differentiation on the basis
of social class and the problematic categorisation
of 'secondary' education itself, as opposed to 'elementary' and 'technical' education in the late
nineteenth century.

   Curiously, in the case of the nineteenth-
century emergence of school science, as Jenkins
shows, the notion of 'scientific method' became
prominent and this became aligned with the ideology
of discipline as opposed to utility, as this

Conclusion

provided a parallel rationale to that associated
with the well-established classics, and also mathematics. Secondary school mathematics was in the
period 1870-1900 closely aligned with the classics
and its disciplinary ideology. However, as we have
seen, within mathematics a fundamental tension
emerged between the older paradigm of 'academic
mathematics' and the newer paradigm of 'practical
mathematics' with its utilitarian ideology, which
was central to the Perry movement. This tension produced a major shift in the character of secondary
school mathematics: exceptionally, a 'revolution'
within one secondary school subject. Other subjects
too felt the effects of major curricular tensions.

In relation both to problems of status and
questions of pedagogy modern languages became linked
with the classics, and particularly Latin for its
disciplinary values. The alternative paradigm of
'language as communication' was associated with an
ideology based on utility. This paradigm was inferior in terms of social status and made little general headway in public and grammar schools, as
Rowlinson shows. English too came to exploit important links with classics, again in the interests of
the subject's status and its pedagogy. As Wright
points out, the rhetoric concerning English in secondary education was far removed from the basic
ideologies of utility and discipline, and boldly embraced a new cultural and creative ideology with
moral and emotional as well as intellectual values.
However, despite the distinctive grounds for English
as opposed to classics, in practice the subject became predominantly 'classics in the vernacular' and
its pedagogy largely followed the disciplinary paradigm of Latin.

Renewed cross-curricular concern, again centred
on science, developed during the years of the First
World War, with the protagonists of science opposed
by the literary and humanistic establishment.
Furthermore, in the period 1916-21 four major subject committees, for classics, modern languages,
English and science, were active and produced major
reports. The level of general curricular activity at
this time is notable and warrants further investigation. The four reports are valuable sources for the
curriculum historian and strong in rhetorical terms
but their practical curricular effects appear to
have been of little consequence. They did however
bring to prominence the congested nature of the secondary curriculum and this prompted the Board of
Education to issue a circular on the matter.(2)

Conclusion

Turning to the internal development of school subjects, various chapters bring to prominence a number of common themes and concerns. Subject content, internal demarcations and differentiation in terms of access to a subject are significant variables in a number of the present studies. 'What type of history?' is a question which features prominently in Batho's study as does the parallel question in Marsden's chapter on geography. The importance of the Latin/Greek demarcation in classics has already been emphasised. In modern languages, French was dominant throughout the period though German and Spanish were alternative School Certificate subjects. The focus on school science is necessarily complicated by its subdivision into physics, chemistry and biology, in various forms, and also by the emergence of general science as an alternative paradigm with concomitant problems of status. Mathematics comprised the basic three branches of arithmetic, algebra and geometry with the possibility also of extending the curriculum to include other more 'advanced' branches. Practical or 'general' mathematics cut across these traditional demarcations and in relation to status there are interesting parallels with general science.

Although public and grammar schools have been the major focus throughout this book, it is not without interest that in relation to the emerging notion of a secondary 'modern' curriculum in the interwar years, some of the newer and more progressive paradigms within certain subjects feature more prominently. This is so in the case of approaches to history teaching as a 'training for life'; in modern languages as a means of communication for girls particularly as well as 'modern' school pupils; in general science and social biology, again with some female bias; and in the re-emergence of 'practical mathematics' as an alternative more accessible form of mathematics for post-primary pupils. By contrast, the conservatism of higher status subject paradigms for the public and grammar schools is striking in the interwar period.

Another major thread running through a number of chapters is the developing professionalisation in relation to specific school subjects. Two major aspects here are organisation and pedagogy. The development of subject associations in the period 1890-1910 was noted in the introductory chapter. Exceptionally, Marsden considers the role in geography of a society whose initial concerns were not educational, but which became so, principally in the

Conclusion

interests of the subject's status and growth. Differentiation then occurred, with the establishment
of the Geographical Association in 1893: the Royal
Geographical Society's educational work was essentially strategic in character; the Geographical Association was from the outset school orientated and
concerned with tactical details and pedagogy. Differentiation is also highlighted in Stray's work on
classics which probes the interests and activities
of the Headmasters' Conference, the Classical Association and the Association for the Reform of Latin
Teaching. The first two associations were involved
with the strategic defence of classics and also with
more general concerns of state intervention in secondary education. By contrast, the ARLT's scope was
much more limited and essentially pedagogical, indeed narrowly so. Significantly, its status was inferior to that of the CA and there was initially a
striking female bias in its membership. In mathematics, it is perhaps surprising that it was not the
Mathematical Association but the British Association
for the Advancement of Science which was centrally
involved in the major upheaval of 1900-1903, with
the Mathematical Association's educational concerns
growing out of the state of subject instability at
this time. In addition, the important role of the
British Association in school science education is
highlighted by Jenkins. The organisational aspect of
professionalisation in school subjects would seem to
be a potentially fruitful area for further investigation.

In parallel with the organisational development
of school subjects, there were major advances in the
rhetoric and pedagogy, and particular developments
and refinements feature prominently in all the chapters. In geography, a general pedagogical shift from
'Capes and Bays' to the 'Higher Units' is emphasised
and the emergence of an alternative heimatskunde approach is also notable. In history, a major theme is
the shift from the discipline of memory training to
a much wider and deeper 'training for life', and
the source method is also a prominent feature. In
science, the major focus is on scientific method,
including Armstrong's heuristic method in particular
and the development of practical work in school laboratories. There are links here with the 'practical'
ideals and pedagogy of the Perry movement which are
analysed in the chapter on mathematics. Turning to
the languages, the direct method is central to the
chapter on modern languages and this method also
features in the chapter on classics, particularly in

Conclusion

the case of Latin teaching. In the English chapter,
new enlightenment in the rhetoric and pedagogical
refinements in principle are discussed in detail,
but a major mismatch between this rhetoric and the
reality of interwar textbooks is also exposed. There
is also some evidence of reaction to 'progressive'
thinking and innovation in the case of some subjects.

In mathematics, major reactions to the 'practical' shift in school mathematics and to practical
mathematics as an alternative paradigm are evident.
In science too, there is evidence of some reaction
to the shift from content to process with a renewed
concern for the importance of scientific knowledge
and ideas as opposed to method. In modern languages,
'the retreat from reform' i.e. from direct method
teaching is the major theme. There is also some evidence of reaction to the source method in the chapter on history teaching.

Finally, although not central to the initial
framework for the subject studies of this book, it
does appear that the gender variable in relation to
curriculum history is another potential area for
collaboration. It is hoped that this book at least
demonstrates the value of a co-ordinated approach to
themes in curriculum history, and the potential of
school subject collaborations in particular. Clearly
there is much scope for further work and refinement
in this developing field of educational study.

NOTES AND REFERENCES

1. On examination entries see B.S. Cane,
'Scientific and Technical Subjects in the Curriculum
of the English Secondary Schools at the Turn of the
Century', British Journal of Educational Studies,
vol.8, no.1 (1959), pp. 52-64. On timetables and the
importance of tradition ('national curricular
style') see M. Smith, 'The Evaluation of Curricular
Priorities in Secondary Schools: Regulations, Opinions and School Practices in England, 1903-4', British Journal of Sociology of Education, vol.1, no.2
(1980), pp. 153-72. In practice, mathematics took up
much of the time devoted to scientific and technical
studies.

2. Board of Education, Curricula of Secondary
Schools in England, Circular 1294 (HMSO, 1922). The
'squeeze of subjects' was also considered by a prewar
circular: Board of Education, Curricula of Secondary
Schools, Circular 826 (HMSO, 1913).

250

CONTRIBUTORS

Gordon R. Batho
    Professor of Education
    University of Durham

Edgar W. Jenkins
    Senior Lecturer in Education
    University of Leeds

William E. Marsden
    Reader in Education
    University of Liverpool

Michael H. Price
    Lecturer in Education
    University of Leicester

William Rowlinson
    Formerly Senior Lecturer in Education
    University of Sheffield

Christopher A. Stray
    Research Student in Sociology
    University College of Swansea

Eleanor M. Wright
    Lecturer in Education
    University of Liverpool

Acton, Lord 168
algebra 105, 106, 108,
    120, 123, 130, 138,
    139, 248
    see also mathematics
Allen, Prof. J.W. 225
American Historical Asso-
    ciation 221
arithmetic 105, 106, 108,
    120, 123, 130, 248
    see also mathematics
Armstrong, H.E. 103-5,
    111, 112, 116, 137,
    140, 164-9, 171, 175
Arnold, M. 79
Arnold, T. 215
Assistant Masters' Asso-
    ciation (AMA) 24,
    30-1, 56, 58-60, 68,
    234
Association for the Re-
    form of Latin Teach-
    ing (ARLT) 31-4, 39-
    40, 249
Association of Assistant
    Mistresses in Second-
    ary Schools 50, 71
Association of Public
    School Science Masters
    (APSSM) 170-2
    see also Science Mas-
    ters' Association
    (SMA)
Avebury, Lord 224
Ayrton, William 104-5,
    124

Badley, J.H. 235
Bain, A. 196
Ballard, P.B. 127
Barrow, R.H. 41
Bate, R.S. 58-9, 60-1
Beagle, HMS 184
Bedales School 235
Bell, Alexander Graham
    81
Bell, Alexander Melville
    81
Bell, G.M. 127
Bentham, J. 156
Berkhamsted School 165
biology 159-60, 163-4,
    173-5, 176, 248
    see also science
Black, A. and C. (pub-
    lishers) 231
Blackie, J.S. 28, 81
Board of Education 4,
    244, 246, 247
    and classics 19-20,
    25-7, 30, 33-6, 40-1
    and English 50
    and history 218, 220-
    3, 226-7, 231-3, 236
    and mathematics 116,
    123, 127, 131, 141-2
    and modern languages
    84-7, 89-90
    and science 163, 166,
    172, 173-6
    see also Department
    of Science and Art
Boer War 19, 82, 185

Index

Borchardt, W.G. and
   Perrott, A.D. 139
botany see biology
Bourne, Henry 225-6
Bradford Grammar School
   163
Branford, B. 133
Brenkmann, C. 93
Breul, Karl 82
Bridges, Robert 30
British Association for
   the Advancement of
   Science 112, 116, 118,
   120-1, 128-9, 131-2,
   140, 156-60, 165, 168-
   70, 172-3, 188-9, 249
British Empire 23, 77,
   174, 185, 186, 187,
   193, 224, 227, 231,
   236
British Institution 217-
   18
British Science Guild 168
Brock, W.H. 162
Browning, Oscar 220
Bruce, W.N. 35
Bryan, G.H. 112, 136, 143
Bryce Commission 4, 5-6,
   18-19, 80, 246
   see also Bryce, J.
Bryce, J. 27, 35, 198,
   216-17, 219, 222-3
   see also Bryce Commis-
   sion
Bryce Report see Bryce
   Commission
Burney, Fanny 62
Bury, J.B. 168, 225
Butcher, S.H. 27, 32

Cajori, Florian 142
calculus 105-6, 120, 139-
   40
Callcott, Lady 224
Cambridge Locals 122,
   157, 160-1, 170
   see also Cambridge
   Previous, Cambridge
   University, Joint
   Board, Oxford Locals,
   Oxford Responsions,

Oxford University
Cambridge Previous 22,
   37, 122-3
   see also Cambridge
   Locals, Cambridge Uni-
   versity, Joint Board,
   Oxford Locals, Oxford
   Responsions, Oxford
   University
Cambridge University
   and classics 17, 32,
   34-5
   and English 53-4
   and history 214-15, 237
   and mathematics 106,
   108, 118, 135
   and modern languages
   78, 88, 91
   see also Cambridge
   Locals, Cambridge
   Previous, Joint Board,
   Oxford Locals, Oxford
   Responsions and Oxford
   University
Carson, G.E.StL. 140-1
Charterhouse School 21,
   162
Chaucer, G. 64
Chelmsford Committee 174
chemistry 160, 162, 163,
   165-6, 173, 176, 232,
   248
   see also science
Christ's Hospital School
   163
City and Guilds of Lon-
   don Institute 91
City of Leeds School 237
Civil Service Commission
   121-2, 132-3, 170,
   172, 184-5, 203
Clarendon Commission 14,
   16, 18, 88, 156, 158,
   216, 219
Clarendon Report see
   Clarendon Commission
Clarke, Prof. Sir
   Frederick 235
Classical Association
   (CA) 5, 11, 19, 20-36,
   38-41, 249

253

'classical' versus 'modern' 29-30, 34-5,
112-14, 190-1, 203,
221-2, 232, 245-6
classics 4, 6, 7, 10-48,
245-7, 249-50
and English 51-2, 54,
55, 56, 59, 67-9, 70-2
and history 215, 221-2
and mathematics 112-
13, 134
and modern languages
84-5, 88-9, 91-2
and science 156, 158,
170
see also Greek, Latin
Clifford, W.K. 167
Clifton College 104, 127,
163, 165
College of Preceptors
110, 113, 157
Collins, H.F. 93
Collins, Sir Richard 21-2
Combe, George 156
Comenius, J.A. 92
Compayré, Gabriel 227
Conference on Historical
Teaching in Schools
220
Conjoint Board of Scientific Societies 35
Cook, H. Caldwell 30, 52,
57-8, 63
Cooper, A.J. 202
Council for Humanistic
Studies 35
Cowper, William 62
Creighton, Mandell 220
Cromer, Lord 27
Cross Commission 220
Cruse, A. 62
Curzon, Lord 27

Dance, E.H. 237
Darwin, Charles 14
Davis, H.W.C. 237
Dawes, Richard 196, 217
Department of Science and
Art (DSA) 245-6
and classics 18, 26
and geography 188, 196

and mathematics 105-8,
112, 114, 121-2, 130
and science 161-4
see also Board of Education, Department of
Science and Art Examinations
Department of Science and
Art Examinations 161,
196, 198
see also Department
of Science and Art
Devonshire Commission
158-9, 183-4
direct method (in classics and modern languages) 21, 28-9, 39,
66, 81-4, 86-7, 88,
92, 93, 94-5
see also methodology,
Rouse
discipline 246-7
in classics 12-13,
16, 22-4, 28, 41-2
in geography 188, 190
in history 220, 237
in mathematics 113,
136
in modern languages
78, 80, 91
in science 157-8
see also moral discipline
Drinkwater, John 64
Drummond, H. Ann 235-6
Duff, Grant 200
Dulwich College 197
Durham University 91,
231-2, 238

Education Act (1902) 4,
20, 108, 228
Educational Times (journal) 115
Edwards, W. 230
Eggar, W.D. 111, 118,
120, 127
Einstein, A. 168
Endowed Schools Act 17-18
Engineer (journal) 113,
135

Engineering (journal)
114-15, 123
engineering 104-5, 114-
15, 116, 128-9, 135,
136
see also technical
education
English 5, 6, 7, 49-76,
85, 90, 247, 250
English Association 5,
49, 51, 53, 64
Eton College 16, 17, 88,
111, 118, 162, 163,
164, 197, 216
Euclid 104-5, 106, 113,
117-18, 119-20, 121-2,
125-6, 141-2
see also geometry
examinations see Cam-
bridge Locals, Cam-
bridge Previous, Civ-
il Service Commission,
Department of Science
and Art Examinations,
Joint Board, London
Matriculation, Oxford
Locals, Oxford Respon-
sions, Royal Society
of Arts Examinations,
School Certificate Ex-
aminations

Farrar, Reverend F.W.
159-60
Fawdry, R.C. 127-8, 138
Federated Associations of
London Non-Primary
Teachers 130-1
Finch, R. 51
Findlay, J.J. 110, 111,
115, 127, 129
Finsbury Technical Col-
lege 105, 109, 137
First World War 31, 38,
77, 94, 169-70, 171,
229-30, 247
Firth, Sir Charles
Harding 226
Fisher, Herbert 36-8
Fitch, J.G. 195-6, 217,
225

Fitzroy, Captain Robert
184
Fletcher, C.R.L. 221-2,
229
Forsyth, A.R. 117, 118,
120-1, 135, 136
Fowler, J.H. 69
Fowles, G. 162
Franco-Prussian War 184,
185
French 5, 13, 59, 77-102
passim
see also modern lan-
guages
Freshfield, Douglas 186,
187, 189, 190-1, 195,
196, 199-200, 204
see also Geographical
Association
Froebel, F. 109

Galton, Francis 188, 199-
200, 205
see also Galton's Geo-
graphical Prizes
Scheme
Galton's Geographical
Prizes Scheme 188, 197
see also Galton,
Francis
Gardner, Percy 28, 33
see also Page, Times
Geikie, Sir Archibald
188, 189-90, 196, 203
gender differentiation
248, 250
in classics 22-3, 40
in English 53
in geography 201
in history 216-17
in mathematics 108,
129
in modern languages
79, 90, 99n5
in science 173, 176-7
Geographical Association
5, 200-1, 203, 204,
249
see also Freshfield,
Geographical Teacher
Geographical Journal 201

geographical societies
182
    Manchester Geographical Society 193-4,
    198-9
    Scottish Geographical Society 198
    see also Royal Geographical Society
Geographical Teacher
    (journal) 201
geography 1, 5-7, 182-
    213, 245, 248-9
    and classics 14
    and history 215-20,
    222, 228
    and modern languages
    84-5
geology 162
geometry 104-5, 106, 108,
    110, 111, 116, 120-1,
    122, 123, 125-6, 129,
    130, 133-4, 138, 248
    see also Euclid,
    mathematics
German 5, 13, 33, 80, 86-
    9, 93, 248
    see also modern languages
Gill, J. 218
Godfrey, Charles 119-20,
    122, 125, 126, 127,
    133-4, 138, 139, 142
Goldsmith, Reverend J.
    193
Goldsmith's History of
    England 214, 216, 217
Gooch, G.P. 236
Goodson, Ivor 1, 3
Gordon, P. and Lawton, D.
    1
Gouin, François 81
Grant, A.J. 237
graphs 104-6, 120, 123,
    124-5
Greek 5, 10-48 passim,
    68, 246
    see also classics,
    Latin
Green, J.R. 215, 226-7
Greening Lamborn, E.A.

51, 52, 63, 67
Gregory, Richard 171, 175
Gresham's School 165-6
Griffith, G. Talbot 235

Hadow Report (1926) 90,
    92, 95-6, 98, 236
Hall, H.S. 124-5
Hamilton, W.R. 183, 187
Hammond, C.E.L. 59, 70
Hankins, G.T. 236
Happold, F.C. 234-5
Harrow School 88, 127,
    134, 159, 162, 163,
    165
Hartog, P.J. 52, 69-70
Hasluck, E.L. 229, 233-4
Headlam, J.W. 22-3, 26-7,
    36
Headmasters' Conference
    (HMC) 15, 17, 27, 30,
    32-4, 249
health education 174
Henrici, O. 121
Herbertson, A.J. 185,
    191, 196, 197, 199,
    201-2, 204
Her/His Majesty's Inspectorate (HMI) 4, 37,
    41, 93-4, 96
heurism 111-14, 164-9,
    175-7
    see also Armstrong,
    methodology
Higher School Certificate
    90-2
Historical Association 5,
    216-17, 222-3, 226,
    229, 234-5
history 5-6, 214-43,
    248-50
    and classics 14
    and English 54
    and geography 188
    and modern languages
    85, 90, 95
    and science 168
History (journal) 234-5
History of Education Society 1, 2
Hobson, E.W. 134, 135

Holmes, Edmond 221, 224, 227
Horn, P. 82
Howson, A.G. 141-2
Hughes, William 188, 205
humanities 14, 26, 35, 38, 190, 202, 204-5
Huxley, T.H. 14, 156, 164, 166-7, 188, 189, 192, 196, 202

Incorporated Association of Assistant Masters see Assistant Masters' Association
industrial revolution 13-14
Institute of Electrical Engineers 115
International Commission on the Teaching of Mathematics 138, 139-40
see also International Congress of Mathematicians
International Congress of Mathematicians 136, 138
see also International Commission on the Teaching of Mathematics
International Geographical Congress 199
International Phonetic Association 81

James, Dr 15-16, 214
see also Rugby School
Jeffreys, M.V.C. 238
Jespersen, Otto 52, 81, 83-4
Joint Board (Oxford and Cambridge) 118, 162, 171-2, 220
Joint Committee on Grammatical Terminology 58
Jones, Francis 161
Journal of Education 115

Kandel, I.L. 97
Keatinge, M.W. 225-6, 235
Keltie, J. Scott 184, 189, 195, 197, 198, 203-4
see also Keltie Report
Keltie Report 189, 197, 198, 199, 200
see also Keltie, J. Scott
Kennedy's Public School Latin Primer 25
Kenny, E.J. 58, 64, 66
Kenyon, Sir Frederic 35, 38
Kidd, Benjamin 167-8
kindergarten methods 108, 109-10
see also Froebel
King Edward VI School, Birmingham 162
King Edward VI's School, Grantham 218
Kingsley, Charles 166
Kuhn, T.S. 159

laboratory work see heurism
Lankester, Ray 20, 35
Latin 5, 10-48 passim, 68, 90, 246-7, 249-50
see also classics, Greek
Laurie, S.S. 196
Lawson, J. and Silver, H. 5
Lawton, D. see Gordon and Lawton
League of Nations 236
Leathes Report see Leathes, Stanley
Leathes, Stanley 87-90
Leavis, F.R. 53-4
Leeds University 40
Levett, Elizabeth 229
Lewis, R.T. 63
Liverpool College 197
Liverpool University 40
Livingstone, David 184
Livingstone, R.W. 38, 42
Local Taxation (Customs

and Excise) Act 163
Lodge, Prof. Sir Richard
    229-30
London Matriculation 91,
    122
London Teachers' Associa-
    tion 231
London University 108,
    118, 122-4, 161, 199
    Geographical Institute
    200
    see also London Ma-
    triculation
Longmans (publishers)
    161, 217
Love, A.E.H. 118, 129
Lyell, Sir Charles 84

Macaulay, T. 62, 215
MacGowan, W.S. 82
Mackail, J.W. 11-12, 19-
    20, 24, 26-7, 34, 35-6
MacKay, Reverend
    Alexander 194
Mackinder, Sir Halford
    186-7, 189, 190-1,
    200-2, 204
Macmillan (publishers)
    115, 118-19, 161, 189
    see also School World
MacMunn, E. 201
Macnaughton, D.A. 41
Macpherson, A.S. 93
Madeley, Helen 234
Mair, D. 121
Mais, S.P.B. 64
Manchester Geographical
    Society see geo-
    graphical societies
Manchester Girls' High
    School 90, 229
Manchester Grammar School
    161, 163
Manchester University 40,
    199
Mangnall, Richmal 217
Markham, Sir Clements
    189, 199-200, 203
Marsden, W.E. 1
Marten, C.H.K. 220, 234
Marvin, F.S. 236

Marwick, A. 2
Mathematical Association
    5, 119-20, 130-1, 134,
    135, 137, 139, 142,
    143, 249
Mathematical Gazette 119,
    127, 132, 134, 141
mathematics 1, 6-7, 103-
    55, 245, 247, 249-50
    and English 53-4
    and modern languages
    85, 90, 95
    see also algebra,
    arithmetic, calculus,
    geometry, mechanics,
    trigonometry
Mathieson, M. 50, 52, 55
Mayo, C.H.P. 134
mechanics 105-6, 127,
    162, 176
mental discipline see
    discipline
Mercier, Winifred 229
methodology 249-50
    in classics 28-32
    in English 51, 54-5,
    56-67, 69
    in geography 191-6
    in history 216-18,
    221-2, 225-9, 233-5
    in mathematics 106,
    110-12, 128, 131-3,
    138, 140-1
    in modern languages
    79-80, 81-4, 86-7, 88-
    9, 92, 94-6
    in science 162-9
    see also Armstrong,
    direct method, heurism
Miall, Prof. L.C. 223
Middlesbrough High
    School 230
Mill, H.R. 201
Mill, J.S. 167, 222
Milner, Reverend T. 192
Milton, J. 64
Model School, Belfast 104
modern languages 4-6, 77-
    102, 246-7, 249-50
    and classics 28-9
    and English 53

see also French,
German, Spanish
Modern Languages Associa-
tion 5, 82
Modern Languages Commit-
tee see Leathes,
Stanley
Moore, E.H. 106
moral discipline 246
in English 57
in history 224
in Latin 19
see also discipline
Morant, Sir Robert 26,
30, 83-4
see also Secondary
Regulations
Morley, John 216
Moseley, Henry 195, 197,
217
Moseley, H.N. 198
Murchison, Sir Roderick
189, 199
Murray, Gilbert 20-1, 27,
28, 36-7, 38, 42

Nature (journal) 115,
119, 121-2, 122-3,
134-5, 136, 137
Neale, J.E. 236
Nelson (publishers) 226
Nesfield, J.C. 67
Newbolt Report (English
teaching) 49-50, 67-9,
71
Newcastle Commission 218
Newcastle University 40
Newton, I. 168
Nicolson, Harold 42
Northcote-Trevelyan Re-
port (1853) 15
Norwood, Cyril 38
numerical tables 120,
123, 129-30

O'Grady, H. 51
Oliphant, L. 60, 66-7
open scholarships (Oxford
and Cambridge) 78
Oundle School 127
Oxford Delegacy for the

Training of Secondary
Teachers 202
Oxford Locals 122-4, 157,
160-1, 170
see also Cambridge Lo-
cals, Cambridge Pre-
vious, Cambridge Uni-
versity, Joint Board,
Oxford Responsions,
Oxford University
Oxford Responsions 22,
37, 122-4
see also Cambridge Lo-
cals, Cambridge Pre-
vious, Cambridge Uni-
versity, Joint Board,
Oxford Locals, Oxford
University
Oxford Supplementary His-
tories 230-1
Oxford University
and classics 17, 32,
34-5
and English 53
and geography 189,
190, 197-9
and history 214-15,
219-20, 236-7
and mathematics 108,
118
and modern languages
78, 88, 91
and science 157, 160-1,
170
see also Cambridge Lo-
cals, Cambridge Pre-
vious, Cambridge Uni-
versity, Joint Board,
Oxford Locals, Oxford
Responsions
Oxford University Commis-
sion 84

Page, T.E. 21, 33
see also Gardner,
Times
Palmer, Harold 94-5
payment by results 5,
108, 218-19
Pearson, Karl 167
pedagogy see methodology

Percival, Dr 104
  see also Clifton
  College
Percy, Lord Eustace 42
Perrott, A.D. see
  Borchardt and Perrott
Perry, John 103-55 passim
  163, 245, 247, 249
Perse School, Cambridge
  29-30
  see also Rouse
Pestalozzi see Froebel
physics 160, 163, 173,
  176, 232, 248
  see also science
Piaggio, H.T.H. 137
Pillans, Prof. J. 192-3
Pollard, Prof. 228
Postgate, J.P. 20, 32
Power, Eileen and Rhoda
  237
Prime Minister's Commit-
  tee on Classics 37-8
Prior, Oliver 78
Pritchard, F.H. 64-5, 66

Queen's College, Belfast
  104
Quick, Reverend R.H. 84

Ravenstein, E.G. 185, 198
Ravetz, J.R. 169
Regulations for Secondary
  Schools see Second-
  ary Regulations
religion 5, 184, 192-3,
  218, 238
Report of the Committee
  of Seven (1899) 221,
  226
Report of the Consulta-
  tive Committee on Ex-
  aminations in Second-
  ary Schools (1911) 91
Report of the Royal Com-
  mission on Secondary
  Education (1895) see
  Bryce Commission
Report on Modern Lan-
  guages (1918) see
  Leathes, Stanley

Revised Code (1862) 218-
  19
Richards, D. 237
Ritchie Committee's Re-
  port (1928) 92
Rockliff, Father Edward
  228
Rosebery, Lord 185-6
Rossall School 163
Rouse, W.H.D. 28-32, 39,
  228
  see also Association
  for the Reform of
  Latin Teaching, direct
  method
Royal College of Science
  (South Kensington) 105
Royal Commission on Sec-
  ondary Education see
  Bryce Commission
Royal Geographical Soci-
  ety (RGS) 7, 182-213
  passim, 248-9
Royal Historical Society
  220
Royal Society 159
Royal Society of Arts Ex-
  aminations 91, 160-1
Rugby School 15-16, 17,
  29, 162, 214, 215
Runciman, J. 221
Russell, Bertrand 119-20,
  134

Saint Peter's School,
  York 216
Sampson, George 30, 51-2,
  69-71
Sandhurst Military Acad-
  emy 170
Sauveur, Lambert 92
Saxelby, E. 93
School Board Chronicle
  194
School Boards 192, 194
  see also School Board
  Chronicle
School Certificate Ex-
  aminations 4, 6, 248
  in classics 40-1
  in English 50

in history 231-2, 237
in mathematics 140
in modern languages
78, 87, 90-2, 94
in science 171-3, 176
School World (journal)
115, 119, 122-3, 128,
133, 136
see also Macmillan
science 1, 4-6, 156-81,
246-9
and classics 14, 18-
19, 26, 28-9, 35
and English 53-4
and geography 182-4,
187-8
and history 220, 223
and mathematics 110-
14, 126-7, 129-30
and modern languages
85, 90
see also biology,
chemistry, 'classical'
versus 'modern', me-
chanics, physics
science and art grants
see Department of Sci-
ence and Art
Science Masters' Associa-
tion (SMA) 5, 172, 173
see also Association
of Public School Sci-
ence Masters
Scotch Education Depart-
ment 88
Scott, Walter 216
Scottish Geographical So-
ciety see geographi-
cal societies
Secondary Regulations 80,
84-5, 246
see also Morant
Second World War 77, 97-8
Selby-Bigge, L.A. 37
Shakespeare, W. 64
Shaw, Napier 169
Shayer, D. 50, 51, 72
Sheffield University 40
Sherington, G.E. 36-7
Sidgewick, Prof. Henry 82
Silver, H. see Lawson

and Silver
Smith, A.L. 219
Smith, D.E. 118, 138
Smith, J.C. 64
Smithells, Arthur 169,
171
Société nationale des
professeurs de
français en
Angleterre 80
Society for the Promo-
tion of Hellenic Stud-
ies 28
Society for the Promo-
tion of Roman Studies
28
Somersetshire School,
Bath 218
Somerville, Mary 187-8
Sonnenschein, E.A. 58
South Kensington Depart-
ment see Department of
Science and Art
Spanish 99n2, 248
see also modern lan-
guages
Spencer, Herbert 156,
166-7
Spens Report (1938) 90,
92, 96-8, 237
Spenser, E. 64
Stanley, Arthur 215
Stephen, Lesley 167
Stoddart, D.R. 188
Strachan, J. 132
Stubbs, William 215
Sturgeon, Miss 193-4
Sweet, Henry 81, 82-3
Symons, Jelinger 195

Taunton Commission 14,
15, 17-18, 41-2, 79,
80, 82, 96, 156, 216,
217, 218, 219
Taunton Report see
Taunton Commission
Taylor, J.E. 194
teaching materials
in English 50, 56-67
in geography 198-9
in mathematics 124-30,

138
in modern languages
93, 95-6
in science 163-5
see also textbooks
teaching methods see
methodology
Teaching of English in
England, The see
Newbolt Report
technical education 19,
104-5, 107-8, 112,
114-15, 116-17, 134-7,
141-2
see also engineering
Technical Instruction
Act (1889) 112
Test Act (1871) 15
textbooks
in classics 25
in English 7, 55-63,
68-9
in geography 189, 191-
4, 196, 201-3
in history 226-8, 231,
233-4, 237
in mathematics 124-8
in modern languages
92-3
in science 161-4
see also teaching ma-
terials
Thomson Committee 170,
171, 173
Thomson Report (1918)
see Thomson Committee
Times, The 23, 28, 33,
35, 115
Times Educational Sup-
plement 23
Tomkinson, W.S. 51
Treble, H.A. and Vallins,
G.R. 59, 67
Treitschke, Heinrich von
230
Tremenheere, Seymour 217-
18
Trevelyan, G.M. 236
trigonometry 106, 120,
138-9
Turner, H.H. 125, 171

Unstead, J.F. 201

Vallins, G.R. see Treble
and Vallins
Vassall, Archer 170
Viëtor, W. 81, 82

Walmsley, A.M. 67
Webster, Sir Charles 222
Wellington College 163
Wells, H.G. 20, 35, 236
Welton, James 223-4, 227-
8
Whitbread, H.W. 237
Whitbread, N. 1-2
White, Sir William 136
Widgery, W.H. 82
Williamson, George C. 225
Willis Bund, J.W. 224
Wilson, J.M. 160
Winchester College 119,
127
Withers, H.L. 214, 221,
224-5
Wolff, G. 117
Wollstonecraft, Mary 156
Wormell, Richard 109-10,
111
Worthington, A.M. 111-12,
163
Worts, F.R. 237-8
Wyse, T. 195

Yoxall, J.H. 185